Deadly Innocence

Feminist theology and the mythology of sin

ANGELA WEST

Cassell
Wellington House
125 Strand
London
WC2R 0BB

215 Park Avenue South
New York
NY 10003

First published 1995

British Library Cataloguing-in-Publication Data
A catalogue record for this book is available from the
British Library.

ISBN Hardback (Cassell) edition 0–304–33734–X
ISBN Paperback (Mowbray) edition 0–264–67341–7
Mowbray is an imprint of Cassell, London

Typeset by Chapter One (London)
Printed and bound in Great Britain by Biddles Ltd, Guildford and King's Lynn

To Heloise
in sympathy with the dolours of daughterhood

To my mother
who first caused me to wonder about
Exodus 20. 5–6

To Roger
my friend and partner
who knows me

Contents

Acknowledgements

Thanks are due first to my publisher Judith Longman, who has pursued the idea of this book with me over the last twelve years — long before it was officially conceived as a project. She has consistently shown faith in its possibility even when its uneven progress was interrupted by other conceptions and their outcome. It is in large measure due to her support and encouragement that it has at last seen the light of day.

Much gratitude also to Sue Dowell who also showed her faith in the project from its outset, and sustained me along the way in sisterly dialogue, with comments and criticism, and by drawing my attention to other writings relevant to my concerns. As an author herself, she also helped to initiate me into the various stages of writing a book and to ensure, with a bit of gentle bullying, that I didn't get terminally bogged down.

Grateful thanks are due to Janet Soskice who provided a reader's report on my first draft, going far beyond the call of duty in giving me extensive commentary and advice. These were invaluable in enabling me to re-write the book, trying this time to avoid the trap which she had so tactfully exposed in my first attempt, i.e. taking the sisters to task for a certain high moral tone which I had not managed to avoid myself.

My thanks also to Sara Maitland, who like Sue and Janet, has reminded me of the blessings and benefits of Christian feminist sisterhood: and in particular for her help and advice in the matter of negotiating the contract with the publisher.

As Jean Bethke Elshtain so rightly comments in the acknowledgements to her book *Women and War* 'No author is the sole creator of his/her work. This book is a collaborative effort.' With this in mind, I acknowledge all those sisters (and some brothers too) who over the past two decades, have helped me by their friendship, insights and sharing of experience in various ways to arrive at my present understanding of the matters I have explored in this book. In particular, I must thank my friends in the Oxford Christian Women's Network, in the Catholic Women's Network in Bristol, and those with whom I shared the keeping of the Greenham Vigil between 1984 and 1987.

Among all these sisters in spirit, I would also like to spare a word for my sister after the flesh, who helped me to cope with my troubled back in its worse moments by giving me the benefits of both her professional advice as an osteopath as well as her sisterly concern.

In acknowledging those who have helped us by their friendship, I think it is appropriate to remember also those who are among the dead: in particular, Kathy Keay, another member of the Christian feminist sisterhood, who by happy chance, came to live in our street in the summer of 1993 together with her partner and baby daughter. As we both struggled with our respective writing projects, we had some richly memorable conversations. During this time, Kathy faced a painful new twist in her own life course, as she coped with the bitter consequences of breast cancer, and faced these with an unforgettable vitality that was so characteristic of her. On 18 December 1994 we met, according to the custom we had evolved, on a Sunday afternoon to light the Advent candles with our children. But Advent for her that year was to be the coming of life eternal, which she entered into a week later. She has left me with a vivid image of how a Christian sister dresses herself for life — and how the garment of the faith we profess must fit us also for our death.

Among the dead who have helped me in other ways is my grandfather Michael West, who wrote textbooks for teaching English to school-children in India. Many of these have survived in use into the post-colonial world, thus allowing him to contribute posthumously to my own writing by the income from his work. My great aunt and god-mother, Joan Mary West, an Edwardian lady with many artistic talents, left me half of her estate in the 1970s, when I had just become a single parent. Without her generosity, I think I never would have got beyond the struggle to put a roof over the heads of myself and my daughter. My own father has been more than generous in continuing and supplementing the help I received from these benefactors.

Back among the living, I suppose I should extend some thanks to my son Sean, without whose birth in 1988 the whole project would have been completed a good deal sooner (but would no doubt have been an entirely different book). And this leads me to my last acknowledgement — to my partner Roger, who as father of Sean, contributed to the major interruption of my work in 1988, but has since made up for this some-what in a number of ways: by being an active and full-time father to our son and also to my daughter Heloise; by reading, commenting and helping to edit my text in its various drafts; by supplementing my inadequate word processing skills at every stage; by arguing with me on many matters both helpful and unhelpful; by putting up with my not infrequent bouts of ill-health and ill-temper; and last but not least by preparing nearly all our meals in the last six years, he has provided me with the necessary 'food for thought' without which the writing of *Deadly Innocence* could not have been sustained.

Introduction

Sometime in the mid 1970s in Britain, women were declared innocent. All charges against them were to be dropped. Women were not guilty and never had been.

But what exactly was the charge? Perhaps a little background to the case is necessary — the case of the feminists v. the patriarchs. The feminists took it as their task to reverse the verdict of patriarchal religion and society which for so long had held women responsible for most of the ills of our mortal state. They exposed this verdict as a miscarriage of justice, and speaking from the dock, as it were, they endeavoured to overturn this verdict and reverse it. They took the finger that was pointed accusingly at women and pointed it back at the accusers. It is men, they declared, and not women, who are responsible for all the mortal ills of our society. They have had the power (including the share of power they stole from women) and they have abused it; right through history they have abused it for their own ends and for the sake of maintaining the exclusion and exploitation of women. It is they who stand condemned — women are innocent.

Feminist theology was at the forefront of this exposé of patriarchal religion, and as it began to make its appearance on the scene in Britain, its American pioneers, Rosemary Ruether, Mary Daly *et al.*, revealed to us how men had made God in their own image; how they had tried to lay upon women the burden of guilt for human weakness and evil that they could not cope with in themselves. Woman had been framed in the person of Eve — that creature made from Adam's rib on the only occasion when a woman was 'born' from a man. On her was now foisted the full responsibility for the downfall of the human race. And then there comes the male saviour who is not only male but divine, and woman is allowed only a subordinate role in this salvation drama as the mother of the saviour — a submissive virgin who knows her place, and the circumstances of whose childbearing (as virgin mother) are so peculiar that no

woman could imitate them even if she wanted to. The model of Mary's
submissive purity and the image of Eve's wayward sinfulness are both,
as the feminist theologians explained to us, a patriarchal trap which
women in future must strive to avoid. If women were guilty of anything,
it was of the failure to actualize themselves — the sin of too much self-
sacrifice on the altar of the patriarchal gods. From now on we were to be
our own women, no longer to be taken in by the claims to magisterial
authority and universality made by the male theologians. These were
exposed for what they were — the self-interested perspective of the male
élite. It was part and parcel of that fundamental mind–body dualism of
patriarchal thought which was now brought to light by these critics.

Those of us who received the message did so wide-eyed at the nature of
the revelation. For the first time we were seeing them — the masters of
theology — for what they were. And in this vision, we began to recognize
who *we* were — women, the underside of the tradition, silenced yet feared.
We, together with all subjected peoples, were the repressed bodily half of
the self-divinizing male order. In those days, the meaning of liberation
seemed very clear to us. The task was to expose this ancient cover-up, to
name the injustice that was being done to us. We had discovered the real
meaning of the gospel for ourselves. Fired by this feminist faith, we began
to spread the good news that henceforth women could go in peace, and be
free from the crippling guilt caused by dualist male theology which had
limited our autonomy and held us in check for centuries. Now at last we
could be free to celebrate our female bodiliness, and forswear theology
done on the basis of abstract male premises. We would create a theology
instead that embodied the reality of women's experience .

As I write about it, I remember once again the excitement of it all;
the atmosphere of the small non-hierarchical groups, who aspired to
raise women's consciousness, to create an embodied theology based on
women's spiritual qualities, and fashion a politics where women were no
longer powerless but exercised their free choice to promote peace, life,
non-violence and respect for the earth.

So what happened to this lovely dream? How come that when I hear
the familiar rhetoric — of holistic spirituality and wholesome politics —
these days I no longer experience the stimulating wind of the spirit, but
sense rather the stifling air of the ghetto? When the text extols the
women/nature connection, I drop it in favour of a good novel. When the
speaker stresses special female fitness for bringing peace on earth, I stifle
a yawn. When I'm told about how women eschew male power games
and hierarchies, and naturally prefer mutually empowering relationships, a glazed look appears in my eyes. There seem to be some signs
here of a serious loss of faith.

Is it time then to ask myself: what exactly was the nature of the faith
we shared in the heyday of the seventies and eighties? Though this

feminist faith was always held by a minority of women, in these decades they were, it seems, a confident and fervent minority. Yet the reality now seems somewhat different. A recent enquiry into sexual politics on the campus[1] found that women's groups on campus these days were unlikely to be preaching radical politics and separatism, and were under pressure to justify their existence. Though women's groups now, as in the past, were concerned about equality, the style had altered considerably: 'In the 70s they sang and made banners, in the 80s they shaved their heads and screamed, and now in the caring, sharing 90s, some hold aromatherapy sessions, and invite men to their meetings.' These days gender studies are beginning to replace women's studies, and sisterhood has become a rather dated word. 'Screeching lefties' was how one student described women's groups, and her opinion was echoed by many other young women.

Such attitudes would shock and sadden many of us who were active in feminist politics of the seventies and eighties, and those who have come up in that tradition. Yet it seems that if we want to 'keep faith' with those days, if we think that there is something worth passing on, we will need to be concerned with my question: what exactly was the nature of the faith we shared in those days? Could there be some connection between my loss of faith and the lack of faith among many young women? Or are we prepared to put it down to the cynicism of middle age and the ignorance and prejudice of youth? Or can we, with the wisdom of hindsight, now see what is worth preserving among the things which we held dear in those days and what we can afford to let pass away with those times? Since feminism, like all traditions worthy of the name, is a self-questioning tradition, it is surely appropriate that we undertake this examination. If we cannot interrogate our own faith, whether buoyant or failing, what hope do we have of communicating it to women who do not share it?

Since I have spoken of a loss of faith, one might ask whether or in what sense I remain a feminist. I have no doubts that much of women's experience over the centuries has been oppressive, and continues to be so. I believe that feminist theology did an important job in exposing how religion has colluded with and upheld this oppression. And I also believe that such critique — of the idolatry of oppressive religion — is the perennial task of faith. But at the same time, I have become aware of how our own brand of theology tended to contain a new version of some of the errors that were exposed by the original critique. Some of our radical critiques no longer seem as radical as we once thought they were. The picture of the Trial I sketched at the beginning, of the Wrongful Conviction of Women under Patriarchy, and of the Reversal of the Verdict by Feminism, seems to me to be a kind of foundational image for quite a large proportion of feminist theology. And as I have contemplated this picture over the years, I have gradually become aware that something was missing. I have been irked by this missing bit, and, as with an unfinished jigsaw, my attention was engaged by the part that was absent. I began to suspect that perhaps the case of feminists v. the patriarchs was not quite as open and shut as it had once appeared.

Feminist theory has not, of course, stood still since those days, and many aspects of the theory which presented difficulties for me have already been the subject of critique by other feminist theorists and theologians, some of whose conclusions I have used. But I have not proceeded entirely by the straight route of examining and comparing feminist theory and theology and analysing its development. This is not from a lack of respect for theory. On the contrary, I am persuaded that it is our theory (mode of seeing) that to a large extent determines how we experience. Yet at the same time, it is clear to me that our experience sends us back to the theory with questions. It is this process that I wanted to observe in detail, and for this purpose my own experience has been one of the most accessible and convenient locations for observing it. The feminism that I encountered in the 1980s was particularly insistent on the value of women's personal experience as a basis for doing theology. Yet, in my own case, I have found that it is through the evaluation of this same personal experience that I have become acutely aware of the dangers of the tendency to falsely universalize our own experience. This, it seems to me, is one of the most characteristic delusions that we have been prone to in the movement. For despite our enduring obsessions about language and its power to shape and distort, it is startling to realize how much we have also underestimated this most central of human practices, particularly as it concerns the springs of our own thought.

My aim therefore has been to examine the use of personal experience in theological exploration while at the same time demonstrating its limitations. The particular experience in which I have grounded this enquiry is the politics that I was most familiar with in the 1980s, namely the politics which centred on the phenomenon of the Women's Peace Camp at Greenham Common. In many ways this expressed most powerfully the dominant form of feminism of the eighties, shaped as it was both by the preceding struggle of the Women's Liberation Movement in the seventies, and by the radical feminism that reached us on the 'second wave' coming from the USA. It was a strong affirmation of the frame-up theory, which protested women's innocence of the murderous violence that threatens the human race, and claimed that our best hope was to put trust in women, and in their female instincts to protect and preserve the earth and her children rather than the mad obsession of men with their military machines in the service of the nation state.

But the course of events at Greenham forced me to confront certain fundamental questions. As I began to examine the political context of the peace camp, I soon realized that it was not only feminists who employed the language of freedom inherited from the Enlightenment. Women whose politics were of a very different kind from ours also made use of this language of freedom — a rather different use of it from us. I realized that the very existence of women actively engaged in twentieth-century politics that were not feminist was in a sense disturbing. For if women's experience, actively reflected on, was supposed to lead to feminism, why had they not come to the same conclusions as us?

These doubts became more urgent as major conflict overtook the peace camp and shattered its internal peace, dividing the peace women into two hostile camps exchanging bitter recriminations. These events obliged me to re-consider the nature of the claim about women's experience, which we had predicated as the basis and source for feminist theology — the claim that women were somehow innocent of history and its violence. I needed to know; were there some aspects of women's experience which we had conspicuously ignored? Could it be that the radical feminist solution posed the questions in such a way that it covered up the particular problem which I was trying to identify?

Thus it came about that the questions I was forced to confront at Greenham became for me the point of departure for a sustained reflection about the nature of faith — not only the particular faith that we, as peace-minded feminists, held in the eighties but also, eventually, the faith that I hold as a member of the Christian church. For those whose sympathies lie with only one of these sides, the connection with the other may seem of dubious relevance. But for me, the connection has been an important and fruitful one. For each side has raised questions to the other in such a way as to take forward my reflection on faith and deepen my understanding of what it is about.

My experience of the events at Greenham led me to doubt that women can be held to be 'innocent' of history. Yet the presumption of female innocence was implicit in much feminist theology of the time. It was this same theology that directed me to personal experience as an essential resource for feminist theological exploration. And ironically it was this personal experience that now in turn enabled me to formulate that question which the assumptions of feminist theology had not allowed me to articulate. And the question, which has a wider relevance for all sorts of theologizing, was this: in what sense are we born 'innocent' of all that happened before we were born? Are we not born into a community of language through which we inherit the sins of the mothers — and yes, of the fathers too? I began to suspect that in the very act of affirming our innocence we appropriate the structures of our particular community of language — of Western post-Enlightenment culture — and thus also our inheritance in its characteristic structures of violence and repression. The act of affirming our innocence had seemed to us like a radical act, a new departure. But could it be that in doing so we were in fact merely following the prescription of the culture that had formed us, a prescription designed to obscure the roots of that self-same violence that we sought to condemn?

I became aware that feminist theology's pursuit of liberation from guilt through the maintenance of a claim to innocence is part of a very ancient pattern — but one that nevertheless has a multitude of specific modern manifestations. Basically it is a pattern that can be found in both pre-Christian and Christian forms, as well as non-Christian and post-Christian versions. What marks them all is the hunger for purity or innocence, and its inevitable outcome in the election of the scapegoat. This is the one or ones who are charged with the role of carrying away everything that spoils the picture that we have re-drawn of ourselves. And so the inevitable cycle of violence is once more set on its course.

Thus, our picture of the Trial (or the Re-trial) is, for all its insight, in some sense flawed. The radical feminist version of (women's) innocence turns out to be not all that innocent and not all that radical. But the image is an archetypal one, and the drama that is enacted here represents not merely the condition of female humanity but that of humanity itself. Feminist theology has had much to say about the 'silencing' of women's voices by male misappropriation of theology. I suggest that we have in our turn appropriated some of the misappropriations — and by this means performed a new silencing of that aspect of Christian tradition which might actually be able to help us with our quest for innocence. For this quest, despite its seeming impossibility, is a stubborn and ineradicable part of the human condition. My own researches have led me to the conclusion that if we are serious about the pursuit of innocence as the non-doing of harm rather than the election of the scapegoat, the route to it must proceed along the path of our prior acknowledgement — and discovery — of our sins. I realized that the Christian gospel is the story of how this is possible, and that, as such, it is the true form of that good news of liberation from guilt which feminists have been labouring to discover and proclaim. The implication of this, as I understand it, is that there are one or two stones from the theological edifice which we have been seeking to demolish that are vital to the re-construction in which we have placed our hope. It is therefore very necessary that we understand which these are and how they can be used. I hope that this book will help towards that task.

Note

1 Gina Todd, 'The body politic', *Guardian*, 8 March 1994.

1 Feminists redefine the doing of theology

The origins of modern feminist theology, according to a current consensus,[1] begin with an article by Valerie Saiving, 'The human situation: a feminine view',[2] in which she called for a review of the categories of sin and redemption in the light of women's experience. In this article, published in 1960, she focused on the work of Anders Nygren and Reinhold Niebuhr, and proposed that what they represented as the universal human sins of pride in the form of self-assertion are really the particular sins of certain male experiences of the world. The female temptation to sin, however, was not so much that of pride or self-assertion but rather the *lack* of self-assertion — the under-development or negation of the self. In Niebuhr's terms, it would be akin to the traditional sin of sloth.

In 1980, Judith Plaskow took up and developed Saiving's thesis in her book *Sex, Sin and Grace: Women's Experience and the Theologies of Reinhold Niebuhr and Paul Tillich.*[3] Her point was that in much of Christian theo-logy, women's experience had been regarded as secondary, and the Christian message used to reinforce this. Thus, what had been repre-sented as inclusively human experience was in fact merely male experi-ence. The result had been an impoverishment of theology and had given rise to the problem that Saiving had identified — the failure of women to take responsibility for their self-actualization.

A space of twenty years intervened between these two pieces of work, and in this period the 'second wave' of feminism had its origin in the US somewhere between 1969 and 1970. At this time, the whole question of the nature of women's experience came strongly into the foreground. The history of feminist theology is not entirely separable from the history of this 'second wave' of feminism. They are, I suggest, both aspects of the same faith. The dominant form of the new wave was that of radical feminism, which had its roots in the liberal precepts of the civil rights movement and the more Marxist-inspired politics of the new left.

Characteristic of this new feminism was the conviction that women's oppression was the archetype of all oppression[4] and its beginning was signalled by the publication of three books: *The Female Eunuch* by Germaine Greer, *The Church and the Second Sex* by Mary Daly, and *Sexual Politics* by Kate Millett.[5] It was Millett's work that laid the basis for the new feminist analysis, with her re-interpretation of the sociological category of 'patriarchy' to mean the whole ideological basis of Western culture, whose effect was the subordination of women. According to Millett, the conflict between the rulers and the ruled, that is between men and women, is such that these have come to inhabit different cultures: that of women is a vulnerable, alternative culture that must be developed, through liberating praxis, into a lifestyle capable of resisting the whole military industrial complex of Western patriarchal hegemony.[6]

The response to this analysis was a decade of consciousness-raising (CR) groups — by which women were to be formed in the new understanding of their identity, and through which, it was thought, women could escape the bondage of patriarchal naming of reality, and re-conceive their experience from within the liberating bonds of sisterhood.

Millett concentrated on the androcentric nature of Freudian analysis and the limiting constraints of the ideology of romantic love, while other feminist analysts approached the question of the sexual slavery of women from a slightly different angle. Authors such as Susan Griffin and Susan Brownmiller proposed physical violence against women (with its cultural manifestation in pornography) as the basis of gender conditioning.[7]

The early part of the debate had presupposed the classic liberal assumption that men and women had fundamentally the same nature, and that their differences were the result of nurture and culture, of the different workings of law and production. But by the mid 1970s, there were growing doubts about this political androgyny, and a shift began to develop towards 'woman-centred analysis'.[8] Women were seen as carriers for society of certain aspects of total human experience. It was a time when anger about women's dismal history was to be channelled into creative research into women's experience and culture. Women's studies came into vogue, and the exploration of women's history was on the agenda. The CR groups were to serve not just as the provision of mutual support and conscientization, but as an exploration of women's cultural and spiritual tradition.

It was in this soil, so to speak, that feminist theology had its roots. Unlike in Europe where the feminist tradition was more rooted in secular enlightenment, US feminism had always had a critique of Christianity high on its agenda. This was often a critique from within, a tradition that went back to the eighteenth and nineteenth centuries, and to sects such as Christian Science and Shakers. In its latest manifestation, the feminist critique of Christian tradition identified the double standard in the cultural values of Western tradition as being derived from the myth of the Fall. The story of Eve's role in this was seen to underpin the belief in the innate inferiority and moral weakness of women — the belief that woman as suffering wife and mother was the divinely ordained punishment for female sin.[9] Both radical feminists and feminist theologians saw it as their task to reverse this judgement on the female sex. They identified the cardinal sin of patriarchy as being dualism — fear and hatred of the flesh, and the projection of this hatred onto women and their bodies. So the new theology took as central to its task the affirmation and celebration of women's bodies and bodiliness.

The new wave broke against the English shores in the mid 1970s, and I remember reading *The Female Eunuch*[10] as I was pregnant with my first child. A few months later I had become a member of a CR group of Christian women, which over the next few years soaked up the good news about women that was reaching us from across the Atlantic. Fired with enthusiasm for our new faith, we addressed ourselves to the task of creating an embodied theology. Bodiliness was Good News for us in those days, and this idea featured in the title of an article I wrote in 1983, which described the efforts of our Christian women's group to communicate with and challenge the bishops (Catholic in this case). Their lack of response was predictable, but we were undeterred. My conclusion was:

Even if the bishops had not listened to us, we had learned to listen to each other and believe in the value of what we said. In a society where women are not generally encouraged to listen to and learn from each other's experiences — except where these are mediated through male-dominated meanings — this represented a real stage in liberation. It gave us a great sense of exhilaration — even of power. For we had, as it were, tasted for ourselves the Good News — that in the freedom of Jesus is the freedom of all women, and for all of humiliated humankind. And we had begun to disbelieve the bad news that had been hammered into us for so long — that women's concerns were just 'women's issues' whereas men's concerns were the issues of the whole Church.[11]

But the church in England, more particularly the Church of England, soon demonstrated its disinclination to hear the good news from women. In 1978, the General Synod rejected a motion for women's ordination (though this was already a reality in the US). The decision produced a great sense of let-down among many women in the church who had had high hopes for change on this front. Two of them, Susan Dowell and Linda Hurcombe, got together to write a book which expressed not just the disillusion but also the sense of exuberant hope and optimism that the new faith in feminism had engendered in women, despite the failure of the patriarchal church to take them seriously. *Dispossessed Daughters of Eve* was one of the first books to herald the arrival of feminist theology on the British scene.[12] It calls the church to account for its failure to give women their rightful place — a sexist, clericalist church that is marked by a complacency and indifference towards the frustrated hopes and wasted talents of its women members. But despite these strictures, *Dispossessed Daughters* is a very forgiving piece of work compared to later expressions of the genre. It still assumes that the church is a place where women can and should be.[13] Though they accuse the church of corrupting its ideals into tools of female repression, they can still envisage that the church as an institution may be forgiven for this failure and entrusted with its mission of healing and redemption. Despite the recognition of the misogyny and myopia that are endemic in the Christian tradition, there is still the sense of shared bonds — theological, cultural and even literary — in the common ground of faith. The dispossessed daughters are nevertheless still joint heirs to a common inheritance, and the book is written from within a very intimate association with the ancient body of the church: both the authors were married to clergymen and had young children at the time. Their vision of the church was of an institution, like marriage, not simply to be upheld, but to be redeemed from patterns of subservience and domination.[14] It was a vision that had a strong sense of the constraints that a shared bodiliness imposes.

But this sense was increasingly rejected or lacking in the work of other feminist authors, for all their enthusiasm for the concept of embodied theology. One of these was Mary Daly, whose work took feminist theology in a very different direction. She too was originally a devout member of her church, a Catholic this time. But after the publication of her doctoral thesis as *The Church and the Second Sex*[15] with some 'modest proposals' that the church should listen to the suggestions of Christian feminists, she underwent a reverse conversion and rejected the church as irredeemably sexist. The magisterium had not responded to her invitation to partnership. So she refuted her previous book with a new 'post-Christian' introduction and went on to write — in *Beyond God the Father* — a new mythological framework for women's religious experience which was to replace 'Godfather, Son and Co' with the dream of a communion of sisterhood.[16]

Thus, with Daly the possibility of the redemption of the church was denied. And even for those feminist theologians who remained within the boundaries of the tradition, a radical 'hermeneutic of suspicion' was introduced into all theological enterprise and towards the biblical foundations of faith. This meant roughly that women were to check out the credibility of all theological claims by examining them in the light of their own experience. As Elisabeth Schüssler Fiorenza declared:

Intellectual neutrality is not possible in a historical world of exploitation and oppression. If this is the case, then theology cannot talk about human existence in general, or about biblical theology in particular, without identifying whose human existence is meant, and whose God is found in biblical symbols and texts.[17]

This hermeneutic of suspicion, the invention of the Latin American liberation theology from which feminist theology was partly descended, ceased to be an academic tool for many feminists and came to mean just simply suspicion of all patriarchal religion. There was a rejection of the idea of a unique revelation of God in the canonical scriptures. Instead, radical feminists claimed that authoritative revelation for women was to be found within the 'emancipatory praxis' of the Women's Liberation Movement, and in particular the CR groups. And the revelatory texts were no longer those to be found in canonical scripture, but in those sources for Western female sub-culture (letters, novels, Gnostic Christian texts, etc.) which were deemed to facilitate this 'emancipatory praxis' — the new basis for 'doing theology'.

I remember how suddenly the boundaries of what constituted doing theology for a feminist widened dramatically to include just about anything she wished to include: even having thoughts about God in the bath could be counted as 'doing theology'. (Of course, there were a few things that would probably have been frowned upon; reading and studying the works of the Fathers, for instance, was not included.) But the inclusiveness of feminist theology was part of its proud boast, and was paralleled in the secular realm by a similarly inclusive definition of what constituted doing political theory. As Julia Hopkins concludes, in summarizing her response to the work of Dale Spender on feminist theory:

In practice, any woman who thinks about her experience politically, is a political theorist, even if her account takes the form of fiction, art, drama, cooking, or choosing to give birth in the squatting position.[18]

Thus, since I have often thought about God in the bath, and once chose (unsuccessfully) to give birth in the squatting position, I can no doubt claim to represent myself as both feminist theologian and a feminist political theorist. Nothing to it really. And yet even as I present my credentials, I have to confess that these very credentials eventually came to form the basis for my doubts — my doubts, in particular, about the way we used the concept of 'women's experience' as the foundation for our theology.

As I reflect on all this a decade later, I am struck by the heady quality of our faith in this new mystical body of sisterhood of all women. Heady in two senses — heady because of the evident sense of exhilaration and self-confidence it gave us; but heady in another sense too. Despite the strong emphasis on the bodily, nevertheless this new kinship with all women which we proclaimed was something very much in the head, i.e. the bonds with all womanhood were not quite the same as the bonds we had with family, or friends or people with whom we had grown up, which are inherently local or particular. The kinship with women was far more ambitious in its scope, extending in both time and space. We saw ourselves as sisters of all oppressed women in other societies and in other ages too. We believed that we, who had newly found our voice, could speak on behalf of the many millions who were still silenced — especially the toiling millions of the Third World. The fact that we were well-fed and they were hungry, that we were the products of a Western education and they could not read and write, was ultimately less significant, so we thought, than the fact that we were all women, and had a common history of oppression.

It is clear that our faith and confidence in bodiliness had something to do with the fact that our own bodies were relatively reliable and strong in those days. Many of us were in our twenties and had not yet given birth, or had newly done so. Those who were older and had rather more ambiguous feelings about bodiliness were no doubt encouraged to have their experience given serious theological significance, rather than reacted to with the fear, contempt or exploitation that is so often the lot of women's bodies in this society.

But in retrospect, it is easier to see that the reality of our much proclaimed experience of sisterhood was in fact those little non-hierarchical groups of mainly middle-class women, disenchanted in various degrees with their experience of church, society and the medical profession. To say this is not to imply that their experience was insignificant — only that its significance was different and rather more complex than the one we attributed to it. Much as we enjoyed our newly discovered experience of being 'universal' people, the fact is that in reality we remained rather particular people, people of a particular class, and race, and religious or non-religious background. Our entry into the mystical body of sisterhood, though it may have changed the way we viewed these facts, did not abolish them; and our claim to speak for and represent the experience of women of other races and ages remained at best untested.

'Sisterhood is powerful' we proudly declared in those days, and in our mind's eye, great battalions of oppressed women marched under this banner from all corners of the globe and back from out of the mists of history. Meanwhile, we had coffee and biscuits in each other's sitting rooms and hatched plots to needle the bishops or confound the Ministry of Defence.

But sisterhood, as we began to discover, though it is full of power and exhilaration in the abstract, has a way of being difficult at the level of the particular. Bodiliness was good news, yes, but why was it that there was always someBody in a group of sisters who had problems with some-Body else? These sisterly differences were not really quite accounted for in the theory. Nor was it a matter of simply our little 'differences' — it was rather more a problem of the similarity of our desires and aspirations. It was precisely the similarity of these, in some cases, that led to the 'differences'.

A decade and many woman-experiences later, I have come to feel that the question of differences between women on the matter of their experience is a significant one. Is it the case that a woman's bodily experience rightly interpreted must lead her to the truth of a feminist self-understanding? And if it does not, how does the theory account for this?

Notes

1 See Ann Loades (ed.), *Feminist Theology: A Reader* (London: SPCK, 1990), p. 81. Also Susan Brooks Thistlethwaite, *Sex, Race, and God: Christian Feminism in Black and White* (London: Geoffrey Chapman, 1990), p. 77.

2 Valerie Saiving, 'The human situation: a feminine view', *Journal of Religion*, vol. 40 (1960), pp. 100-12

3 Judith Plaskow, *Sex, Sin and Grace: Women's Experience and the Theologies of Reinhold Niebuhr and Paul Tillich* (Washington: University Press of America, 1980).

4 Alison Jagger, *Feminist Politics and Human Nature* (Sussex: Harvester Press, 1983), pp. 5ff.

5 Quoted by Julia M. Hopkins, 'The understanding of history in English speaking Western Christian feminist theology', Doctoral thesis no. A2724, Bristol University Library (1988), p. 45.

6 Hopkins, p. 45.

7 Susan Griffin, 'Rape: the all-American crime', *Ramparts*, vol. 10 (1971), pp. 26–35 and Susan Brownmiller *Against Our Will: Men, Women and Rape* (Harmondsworth: Penguin, 1977). See Hopkins, p. 47.

8 See Jean Baker Miller (ed.), *Psychoanalysis and Women* (Harmondsworth: Penguin, 1973).

9 See Hopkins, p. 53.

10 Germaine Greer, *The Female Eunuch* (London: MacGibbon and Kee, 1971).

11 Angela West, 'Bodiliness and the Good News', *New Blackfriars* (Oxford) vol. 64, no 755 (May 1983), p. 209.

12 Susan Dowell and Linda Hurcombe, *Dispossessed Daughters of Eve: Faith and Feminism* (London: SCM Press, 1981).

13 Dowell and Hurcombe, p. 46.

14 Dowell and Hurcombe, p. 88.

15 Mary Daly, *The Church and the Second Sex* (Boston: Beacon, 1985).

16 Mary Daly, *Beyond God the Father* (Boston: Beacon, 1973). See Hopkins, p. 56.

17 E. Schüssler Fiorenza, *Bread Not Stone: The Challenge of Feminist Biblical Interpretation* (Edinburgh: T & T Clark, 1990), p. 45.

18 Hopkins, p. 56.

2 Accounting for our differences

Perhaps I can illustrate an aspect of the problem of women's differences as I have experienced it, by saying something about my relationship with my doctor. My doctor is a youngish woman at the outset of her medical and childbearing career. It is, of course, no accident that as a feminist I have a female doctor — for as any feminist will tell you, a female doctor is much more likely to empathize with the situation of a female patient, because as a woman herself she has access to female bodily experience. A male doctor, on the other hand, has no such access, but is the product of a dualistic medical tradition which seeks to control the body, and the female body in particular.

According to the theory then, a visit to my doctor should be an affirming sort of experience. I have to confess that it has not been that sort of experience. I would come away from my doctor with a deep sense of humiliation — of failure. I had failed to be medically interesting. The disease I seemed to be suffering from (though she was too polite to put it that way) is that of being female and ageing — it is chronic, incurable and very common. In my worst flights of paranoid fantasy, I would begin to believe that it was also highly contagious (to women). I suspected that if I didn't remove myself from my doctor's consulting room fairly fast, she might just catch it. So to spare her and me more pain, I have done just that. I have taken refuge (so to speak) with another doctor in the practice — also youngish, this time male. I have no dramatic improvement in my state of health to report. However, I am relieved to be made to feel this time that I am merely a member of the human race who has the misfortune to be suffering from backache — and a few other small problems, mainly the result of belated childbirth, which may or may not go away with time.

My troubled relation with my doctor cannot be said to be an objective case-study. It is highly subjective. But feminist theology, you may recall, has tended to rejoice in the subjective nature of women's experience, so let us explore it for what it is worth. What has happened to the theory in this case? Has my female doctor completely failed to empathize with me? Has she, as some feminists would want to say, been so conditioned by the language and mores of a male-dominated profession, that she has entirely suppressed her female capacity to empathize with female patients? And is this state of affairs the product of a world where, according to Dale Spender, the separate world of women's experience has been suppressed by male hierarchical thinking and women are left with the reality of their bodily experiences which they are unable to decode?[1]

Or perhaps one should look at it from a slightly different angle and say: perhaps my doctor is not at all unable to empathize with me, but can do so all too well. And that is precisely the problem. For if she were to empathize with every middle-aged female patient who came into the surgery, would she ever get home to spend time with her little ones before they went to bed? And if she did so, would she after a while begin to reflect on the nature of female experience in such a way as to cause her to regard her own female body as a potential traitor that could easily undermine her professional identity if too much scope were given to its claims?

When the concept of women's experience seemed to falter in its function as the royal road to feminist theological self-understanding, the concept of female conditioning was sometimes brought in to make good the damage. Thus, a feminist could be seen as one who has managed to break out of the mental straightjacket of patriarchal thought, and, through the vehicle of a heightened consciousness, has made a heroic escape from the mill of patriarchal thought processing.

But gradually I began to find the conditioning theory a little unsatisfactory. It reminded me of the sort of doctor who knows exactly what's wrong with you without taking the trouble to listen to what you actually have to say about your ailments. Despite my difficulties with her, I am reluctant to let my doctor be written off as a species of conditioned woman, one of the benighted ones who must wait upon us bringing her the Good News of the feminist gospel. For all I know, she may already be a feminist. I am reluctant because, for one thing, it lets us off the hook — the hook of a certain discipline of self-knowledge, of self-recognition. It seems to me that there is a very important question here — one that we often paid lip service to, but did not seriously confront. The question is about us — the women who make the judgement. Are we not particular people, having a particular historical and social background, speaking a particular language? Surely the feminism through which we make our judgements is one such particular language, complete with its own particular history, that conditions us to conceive in some ways and not others.

My doctor, whether or not she is a feminist, probably represents those women who, in achieving a level of educational and professional equality with men in our society, are the fulfilment of the dream of liberal feminism. The dream had its origins with Mary Wollstonecraft, the founder mother of feminism who first advocated that women should be given moral, rational and educational equality with men. Women would emulate the virtues of man, she believed, once they came to share his rights.[2] Yet those who suspect that my doctor may be fatally conditioned by male thinking also stand within that same tradition. How can these contraries be reconciled?

The language of rights, though it was reconceived by radical feminism, remained fundamental to this feminist enterprise and to the feminist theology that grew out of it. The new political theory, 'the personal is political', was linked to the assumption that there is in each woman an experience of being female that can be the basis for a new language about the female condition — which is feminism. But could it be that we got the thing the wrong way round? There is in feminist thought these days a much greater acknowledgement of the possibility that language shapes the nature of experience rather than experience providing the language. Since human rights in our day has become a generic concept, shorn of its historical determinants, feminism has in the past had a tendency to adopt this 'universal' language uncritically as the only way to talk about freedom. Yet the historical conditions in which women came to define their freedom in terms of rights and equality is significant for the way in which that freedom is understood.

The language of equality and human rights first came fully on to the political stage with the French Revolution, notably in the Declaration of the Rights of Man, and in the rhetoric surrounding the making of a new constitution in France. Here it meant equality before the law and the destruction of privilege based on birth, principally that of the aristocracy. Men were to be individually all the same in their enjoyment of certain rights — freedom from tyranny, from arbitrary arrest, and the enjoyment of property. But the Rights of Man from a feminist point of view was just that — the rights of men. Suffrage was for taxpayers, and did not include women or servants: 'In political terms, equality was the perquisite of the moderately comfortable male. Social equality was far from the thoughts of the men of '89'.[3]

The architects of the Declaration were also those who subscribed to a belief in the sovereignty of the market economy. And from the beginning the rights of the few rested, as they had done in the previous social formation, on the poverty, dependence, and labour of the many. Women remained dependent on their husbands and fathers, and were regarded as less than fully rational. Their function was to breed sons for the Republic of Virtue, whose philosophical architect was Rousseau. Mary

Wollstonecraft, while subscribing enthusiastically to his basic ideas about freedom and the rights of citizenship, was also a strong critic of Rousseau, believing that he had misidentified civic virtue as a male preserve. Her contention was that through education, women could become men's equal in virtue, and be full citizens with them.[4] But for Rousseau, virtue was inextricably bound up with the Latin sense of its derivation — virtue was manliness and could not be divorced from the bearing of arms in defence of the republic. Women's virtue, according to him, was in the bearing of sons for the bearers of arms.

As Wollstonecraft was the one who first shaped the political discourse which we have inherited, she is a key figure for us in understanding our identity as feminists. As Jean Bethke Elshtain has pointed out in her brilliant study, *Women and War*, by taking on the language of rights, even with her reservations, Mary Wollstonecraft unwittingly endorsed the new body politic of the emergent nation state[5] — the centralized state in which natural man had been defined as civic man, and whose very identity came to require the conscription of a standing army — and in our own day, the maintenance of ever more elaborate military technology, by whose production the economy is fundamentally shaped.

Thus, by assuming the language of rights, feminists have sometimes failed to notice that it was historically the claim of the newest occupants of privilege. Without our realizing it, the assumptions of our language committed us to an inbuilt agenda, which centres on the question: are women citizens of the nation state? And if so, on what terms? It is this agenda which has in many respects defined the nature of our experience. And there is a sense in which both women's politics and theology since the eighteenth century can be read as a fascinating and complex enactment of it. As Denise Riley says, there is something in the nature of women's childbearing role that consistently puts a brake on their 'flight into the universal'.[6] Thus, on the political level, this leads to the existence of two poles of feminist discourse and struggle which Riley has expressed as 'the perennial impasse' of women's situation. Thus, on the one hand women must address the problem of how they can ascend into personhood, and achieve full citizen status symbolized by voting rights, given their systematic exclusion in the past from the normatively human. And on the other hand, once enfranchised, women face the question of how they can make a claim for their 'special needs' stemming from their reproductive role without losing the ground of their generality. She identifies a pattern of 'spasmodic oscillation' between the politics of equality and the politics of difference. This, I suppose you might say, is the basis of the undiagnosed problem between me and my female doctor — with her representing the 'equality' pole, and me standing in for 'women's special needs'. It may also be a clue, as I want to suggest, to a problem in our theology which we did not fully diagnose. When speaking of women's experience as the basis for our theology, we were apt to ignore the particularity of our own female condition. Its particularity lies in the fact that our conditioning as women has taken place in the context of a given society, one which holds the hegemonic power in world society. It is in the values and assumptions of this society that we have been educated, and despite our critical stance towards these, we were largely unaware of how they conditioned the very root of our thinking. We did not see how philosophically we were daughters and descendants of the Enlightenment, and technologically of the era of relatively safe and effective contraception and childbirth. The freedom which we affirmed was to a large extent predicated on these conditions; we were, in a sense, its products. Because we had received the first instalment of this freedom, we assumed its universal availability, and demanded our right to further instalments. We were aware that the majority of women in the world did not in the past have access to this freedom and still do not: but implicitly we cast ourselves as the 'type' of freedom for them; we were what they might hope to become. The possibility that our freedom was a limited edition seems to be one that we never fully considered.

Thus, there was something a little problematical when we invoked women's experience in our doing of theology, as if we had privileged access to it; whereas in fact what is most typical of women's experiences historically and world-wide — the lack of education on equal terms with men, the subjection to childbearing and its unmitigated effects — was, in many respects, what was least typical of our situation as feminists. And to the extent that we had become the makers of ethical judgements, and not merely the recipients of them, we had crossed over into territory which made our experience quite as different from the experience of most women as it was from that of men.

But I am moving on too fast, as is so easy to do in the fast-track world of general ideas. I had started to indicate how doubts crept into my new-found faith in the feminist ideal of sisterhood, and in a theology that embodied this ideal through the route of woman's bodily experience, supposed as a universal. I had begun to discover that, at the level of individual bodily experience, the theory was beginning to leak a little — to give rise to reflections that no longer seemed to lead in the prescribed direction.

Notes

1   Dale Spender, *Man Made Language* (London: Routledge, 1980), p. 75 and p. 183.
2   Mary Wollstonecraft, *A Vindication of the Rights of Woman* (New York: W. W. Norton, 1967), p. 75.
3   Olwen Hufton, 'Historians talking: a living legacy — equality', in *The French Revolution* (London, Channel Four TV, 1989), p. 21.
4   Jean Bethke Elshtain, *Women and War* (Sussex: Harvester Press, 1987), p. 72.
5   Elshtain, pp. 71–2.
6   Denise Riley, *Am I That Name? Feminism and the Category of 'Women' in History* (London: Macmillan, 1988), pp. 68–9.

3 *Being right and radical at Greenham*

The feminist theology that reached us in the seventies and eighties took as the basis of its hope the revaluation of women's experience, their desire to become historical agents and achieve transcendence through participation in a liberating praxis. In the interpretation of social change as the practical meaning of theological hope, this theology displayed its origins in the empirical and humanist philosophies of the Enlightenment, which saw human history in the here and now as the arena of human transcendence.[1] This replaced the ancient Christian eschatology which looked forward to a consummation at the end of world history in which divine judgement would set to rights the misery and injustice of the world. Liberation theology, one of the ancestors of feminist theology, had pioneered new modes of inductive theology, based not on biblical or dogmatic first principles of traditional theology but on a praxis in which the oppressed reflected on their experience and out of this developed new goals of personal transcendence and communal liberation.

Thus, the hallmark of this theology was the belief not in redemption effected by God in Christ, but in the agency of human groups to set and work towards their own salvific goals. Feminist theology took over this scheme of redemption via revolution and understood its own politics to be the latest and most radical flowering of it. Rosemary Radford Ruether, one of the earliest in the field, called upon women to reject the silencing and pacification they had endured from the church, and to seriously revise the kind of eschatological thinking that had kept them in their place and rendered them unequipped to struggle against their lot.[2] The identification of a particular class or race with the oppressed was, in feminist eyes, inadequate because it ignored the fundamental and universal oppression of all women by men. Only women, because of their heritage as the bearers of the exigencies of history, had the potential for a truly radical history and theology, for they were the sex who, 'through war, famine, revolution and class struggle sought to retain a commitment to life holistically'.[3]

Thus, in order to explore feminist theology fully we need to understand not only its principles, but its practice, the radical politics it endorsed because, as we have seen, this was central to its understanding of salvation. And in line with this self-understanding, I shall take as the starting point for my investigations my own experience of the radical feminist politics of the late seventies and eighties and its political context in Britain.

Lynne Segal in her book *Is the Future Female?* analyses forms of feminist politics in the last two decades. Feminism, she suggests, was in many ways the most radical force to emerge from and outlive the Western protest movement of the sixties. It burst on to the political arena in the seventies with energy and confidence, and was able to get issues of childcare and equal pay, sexual harassment and abortion on to the national agenda at all levels from trade unions to parliament, and as far as the European Assembly.[4] In this early phase of the new wave, the classic liberal concerns with civil rights were most evident as well as the new left's concern with class structures of injustice. Yet despite some notable victories (Equal Pay and Sex Discrimination Acts) and a generally increased social acceptance of feminist goals, the progress of this feminist impetus encountered a barrier which caused the mood and modes of feminism in the eighties to take a rather different turn. The 'oscillation' became visible, as the emphasis on equality or parity with men began to shift towards a greater stress on women's difference, their special nature and needs.

It was at this turning point between the more optimistic times of the seventies and the darker feminist political mood of the eighties that the politics of radical feminism emerged. And it was here that the history of the Women's Peace Camp at Greenham Common had its beginning and was in many ways its most characteristic and influential expression. Since this period and its politics was most formative for my own feminism, I want to examine it in some detail. It is important to explain at this point that I was not one of those women who lived in fragile benders beside the perimeter fence and braved the mud, the bailiffs, and the bitter cold through several winters. Rather I was one of that larger pool of camp followers who visited and supported the camp on many occasions and in many ways, and for whom its existence was central to our political and feminist consciousness at the time.

From the late seventies, men's violence towards women had become a prevailing theme, together with the rejection of political alliances with them. Pessimism over men's violence and greed formed the basis of a global political analysis that imaged the multiple catastrophe of nuclear and ecological holocaust and Third World exploitation and starvation.

Feminism at this point, as Segal observes, sounded an apocalyptic note, as it portrayed a Manichean struggle between female virtue and male vice, with ensuing catastrophe unless 'female' morality prevailed.[5] It was a time of euphoric feminist utopianism when women celebrated the superior virtue and spirituality of women in opposition to the violence and technology of men. There was an emphasis on 'refuges' of various sorts for women who were in flight from this male sphere of violence — refuges for battered women, women's therapy centres, women's peace camps.[6]

This then was the context in which Greenham Women's Peace Camp came into being. It began when a group of women, children and men left Cardiff on 27 August 1981, to march 125 miles to the USAF/RAF base at Greenham Common near Newbury, in protest at NATO's decision to site American cruise missiles there in December 1983. When the group arrived there ten days later, they asked for a televised debate on this issue. This request was refused so the peace camp was set up in protest at this lack of response and in order to gain publicity for the issue.

The original march from Cardiff to Greenham was organized by a group of women called Women for Life on Earth. In the early months of the peace camp there were some men living there, but most of the women felt that the way they wanted to run the camp would be jeopardized if men continued to live there. So after February 1983, and much debate, the camp became a women-only space. The feeling behind this decision was expressed in March 1982 by Katrina Howse, who later became one of the camp's most permanent residents:

I want to say very strongly that having women's actions, in my view, has got nothing to do with excluding men. It's got to do with — for once, just once — giving women a chance, *including* women. It's so women — who have been kept out of politics and all walks of life for so long, who've been pushed back into the home and told they can function in one small closed-in area to do with children and nurturing — can come out of those areas and take part in politics, and can actually begin to affect and change the world. Women have been isolated as individuals for so long. They've had to struggle to join together and work on issues. This way women can join together. Hundreds of women can join together and find their strength, and it's essential at this point in our history that women's strength is utilised and seen and works, and is regarded as important.[7]

On 12 December 1982, 30,000 women from all over Britain, as well as groups from Sweden, Holland, West Germany and Ireland, arrived at Greenham Common to 'embrace the base'. The Women's Peace Camp had been there now for sixteen months, maintaining its vigil at the perimeter fence in all weathers. Now, at last it became national news, and the public debate was started which the women had called for previously.[8]

To pause over this snapshot of ourselves embracing the base is for many women no doubt to open the floodgates of nostalgia for the early days. Here we are as we like to remember ourselves — thousands of women publicly taking strong 'womanly' action for peace; women creating their own space and at the same time reclaiming the common space that had been misappropriated by the men with their military machine. It was a time of wonderful imagery and disarming tactics as women pioneered new forms of non-violent direct action like embracing the base of male power, besieging it with women's bodies, rocking their fences until they collapsed, snipping holes in the chain mail of male armour (the perimeter fence), hanging out the nappies on their defences, keeping watch on those appointed to be our protectors. It was a time when women gladly went to court and to prison to defend their belief that nuclear weapons as a form of national defence was a fundamental obscenity as well as a suicidal absurdity.

As the peace camp established itself, it came to represent that current understanding of feminism which was also fundamental to the project of feminist theology — namely, that women were possessors of the true spiritual qualities, those qualities that were necessary for peace, the preservation of the race, and proper care of the earth and its resources. Women's 'essential and unchanging nature' embodied the values of procreation, warmth and security, solidarity, nurturance and creativity. And this essential female nature was seen as a challenge and a contradiction to everything that comprised patriarchal society and its military bastion at Greenham. It was a kind of theological challenge: for femaleness — and its spiritual attributes — was next to godliness.

The camp continued to survive and endure in gruelling conditions, against all expectations, and to attract support from a wide spectrum of women. But as time went on, it also began to change. The new mode of women's sexuality and freedom that had marked its early days lost something of the playful quality it had possessed even amid the utter seriousness of the women's intention to defend the planet against the imminent threat of its destruction. Contact with men that was not confrontational became seriously polluting, and a fierce new puritanism began to undermine the relations of women who lived in or supported the camps. Women's space now became territory that had to be defended — even eventually from other women, those who did not measure up to the ideal of gender purity that Greenham had come to stand for. What began as a movement of women loving women and making space for each other ended up with women tearing each other apart in the name of sisterhood. By a sad and telling irony, the latter days of the camp at Greenham Common became a spectacle of peace women split into two hostile camps and locked in bitter strife with each other.

Meanwhile, the cruise missiles that had arrived in 1983 miraculously departed again a few years later in 1991. Had the women won their battle to get rid of them? Undoubtedly the men had been forced to retreat a little by the relentless wire snippings and porridge-and-paint assaults on the cruise missile launchers on their supposedly secret forays. They had lost face even if they had managed to keep their military equipment intact. But if the women didn't quite manage to end the cold war single-handed, this objective was nevertheless achieved a few years later by an abrupt shift in world politics. But sadly, by this time, the women were deeply engaged in their own little cold war. The appearance of the Enemy within their own number may have distracted their attention somewhat from the amazing spectacle of the old cold war enemy suddenly crumbling, thus making the whole apparatus of Western nuclear defence look silly and ridiculous — just what the women at Greenham had been doing for years in fact. The world could now see what the women had been trying to tell them for years — that the emperor was wearing no clothes; or rather that those who were armed to the teeth with the nuclear shield were distinctly over-dressed.

The need for the enemy was, you might say, a problem that was felt on both sides of the wire at Greenham. Our rulers, both national and trans-atlantic, were deeply embarrassed at the turn of events which rendered them bereft of a suitable foe. It was almost as if — to shift the metaphor somewhat — they had been caught in a posture of indecent exposure. They rushed to cover-up, and in the nick of time a new enemy was found in the Gulf to everyone's relief. And even better, this new enemy necessitated the bringing back — to cheers — of the good old type of war, where real fighting took place, and Real Men could go into action to defend Real Women, who stayed in their proper place — at home, watching it all happen on TV. And the Real Women — who were a majority of the female population — showed their gratitude by lining up their political loyalties behind 'our boys' and welcoming them home with bunting and tears for their bravery. And so, Greenham was no longer the frontier of peace, but the site of an old battle, where women still gathered nostalgically from time to time to recall their brief moments of glory. Men, it seems, once again won their war and we lost ours.

What was so appealing to many women in the heyday of Greenham was the wonderful clarity and simplicity of it all — men on one side of the wire representing death, destruction, oppression, etc., and women on the other standing for peace, life, love and solidarity and so on. Why couldn't it last? How come the wretched conflict arose producing two hostile camps which no longer communicated with each other despite the urgent necessity of their common situation? Was it inevitable? Or was there some kind of Trojan horse that somehow smuggled in all those worst aspects of 'male' thinking and behaviour that the women had so boldly challenged when they first besieged the base?

Much could be written about how this sad state of affairs came about, and about who was responsible and how much of the original spirit of Greenham continued despite these troubles: yet the fact remains that it was really the death blow to any simple faith in female solidarity and salvation by sisterhood. For what it had shown us was that even feminists, rooted in a common female experience, and having a like mind in matters of peace, male violence and the preservation of the earth and its peoples could not, in the end, manage to live in peace. Feminists who had extended to each other a full absolution from all guilt on the basis that men's tendency to violence and hierarchical thinking was the root of all evil, now fell to damning and excommunicating each other with a vengeance. Women, it seems, are not only the age-old victims of guilt manipulation, but — as some of them discovered to their cost — are also fairly expert users of the same for their own purposes.

What happened at Greenham is also interesting because of the tension it reveals to be inherent in women's legacy from the Enlightenment. So it may be appropriate to go back and have a second, closer look at the context of Greenham. There may be some aspects of this that we failed to notice the first time around.

Notes

1   Julia M. Hopkins, *The understanding of history in English speaking Western Christian feminist theology*, Doctoral thesis no. A2724, Bristol University Library (1988), p. 89.
2   Rosemary Radford Ruether, *Womanguides: Readings Towards a Feminist Theology* (Barton: Beacon Press, 1985), p. 224. See also Ruether, *To Change the World: Christology and Cultural Criticism* (London: SCM Press, 1981), p. 15; and *Sexism and God Talk: Towards a Feminist Theology* (London: SCM Press, 1983).
3   Hopkins, p. 281.
4   Lynne Segal, *Is the Future Female? Troubled Thoughts on Contemporary Feminism* (London: Virago, 1987), p. x and p. 38.
5   Segal, p. xiii and p. ix; see also p. 12 and p. 36.
6   Hopkins, pp.48–9.
7   Alice Cook and Gwyn Kirk, *Greenham Women Everywhere: Dreams, Ideas and Actions from the Women's Peace Movement* (London: Pluto, 1983), p. 80.
8   Cook and Kirk, p. 32.

4 Being right and radical elsewhere

Many of those women who became active supporters of the Greenham camps had become feminists in the seventies. The new wave had originated in the US in the late sixties, and was carried along on the principle that 'the personal is political'. Its practice was guided by the belief that women formed their feminism for themselves through the activity of consciousness-raising groups and a commitment to direct democracy. In the UK, as we have noted, the seventies was a time of political triumphs for feminism, and by the end of the decade there was a strong alliance between Labour women MPs and the women's movement outside Parliament, which began to have effects on the Labour party as a whole. The 1975 social contract was the first national wages strategy to give any priority to the demands of women, the low-paid and the elderly. The Equal Pay and Sex Discrimination Acts in 1975 represented a limited but significant state intervention in the distribution of incomes between men and women.[1]

These achievements however, were to prove the high water mark of the new wave's influence on public political life. After this the tide turned against further feminist progress in the national arena. The social contract foundered in the midst of the Labour government's financial crises. There was a return to free collective bargaining – the process by which male-dominated trade unions protected their differentials and skills. The skilled working-class males had begun to register and resent the feminist attempt to revise the pattern of male privilege at work, and their reaction was part of the basis for the emergence of the new right.[2]

It was not only men who were threatened by the feminist challenge to the existing order of things. There were many women too who were dismayed by the implications of the new freedoms that feminists claimed and exhibited. For though it may be uncongenial for us to recall it, the fact is that as the politics of radical feminism was blossoming at

Greenham, another blossoming of female politics was taking place on the radical right in Britain.

These women too were also politically active in pursuing their understanding of women's goals. When we speak of the women's movement there is usually the implication that there was only really one serious movement of women active in politics at that time and this comprised feminists and women of the left. But Beatrix Campbell, in her powerful study of women on the right, *The Iron Ladies*, shows that since the end of the nineteenth century, women have been a major force in the modernization of the Tory party and the creation of its popular base; and most recently in the emergence of the new right. The Greenham Peace Camp, representing as it did a new manifestation of active and radical women's politics, took place at the beginning of a decade which saw the ascendancy of a new right with a strong popular base, the result of quite a different tradition of female political activism. Both groups had strong attitudes to the question of women's role, and the role of sexuality in the relations between the sexes.

The sexual revolution of the sixties had seemed to offer women the possibility of sex separated from reproduction, and thus set up the hope, in some women at least, that the bad old history of sexual inequality and the double standard could at last be transcended, and relations between the sexes go forward on a new basis. But for many of the women at the forefront of the sexual revolution of the sixties, these hopes were destined to be rudely shattered. The ideology of the new radicals scorned the family as irredeemably bourgeois, and private life as having nothing to contribute. But since it was largely out of these spheres that women were emerging, this in effect amounted to nullifying and downgrading the skills and perspectives they might bring to the new politics. The anti-bourgeois rhetoric of the new male radicals masked the assertion of an old privilege, by which men expected women to be available for sexual servicing. By the seventies, just as the 'gains' of the sexual revolution were being consolidated at the political level, some women were beginning seriously to question the new sexual freedom as it related to women. What kind of freedom was it for women that they were being allowed to serve tea and sex for the masculine revolution? Their conclusions were in many ways the basis of the sexual separatism that characterized radical feminism and was a dominant feature of feminism at Greenham.

If women on the left were disappointed in the hopes raised by an era of relatively safe contraception, women on the right were deeply dismayed by it for quite other reasons. The student rebellion against the Vietnam war, and industrial insurgency of the unions, filled them with anger and panic born of a sense that the moral order, with its proper divisions between sexes and classes, was breaking down, and chaos was imminent. They could hardly have been surprised by the latest feminist 'discovery' that free male sexuality was wayward and not woman-friendly, for they subscribed to a set of values that had reckoned with this problem long ago and provided a remedy on which most of them had based their lives — a belief that in the context of the family, feminine values would find their fulfilment and act as a civilizing container for the potentially disruptive force of male sexuality.

It is clear however, that the threat — actual and potential — of rampant male sexuality had not gone far from the consciousness of such women. In the 1950s, Tory women had been the backbone of the 'hang 'em and flog 'em brigade' — those who pressed for corporal punishment for adults and juveniles, for crimes which included violent sexual assault on women and children. For them, the role of 'proper' men was to protect women and their offspring from men who were outside the pale of women's civilizing influence, and protection in this instance implied the passing of legislation that abolished 'lenient' sentencing for violent 'louts'. As Beatrix Campbell says:

In the absence of a feminist movement to sustain a critique of patriarchal practices and to monitor physical abuse and sexual exploitation, women's sense of themselves as an endangered sex kept surfacing and searching for safety. In such situations, women's sexual fear becomes a cuckoo; homeless, it nests in another bird's debate.[3]

Yet the presence of an articulate feminist movement did nothing to allay these fears but, on the contrary, added fuel to them. Right-wing women clearly didn't consider feminism a 'proper' nest for their sexual fear. Modern society as they saw it, with its new sexual freedoms, was the source of many social evils; they were disturbed by the new forms of women's political activity, and by feminist disparagement of women's role as they had traditionally defined it. There may also have been an element of resentment against 'upstart girls educated at Polys' from women who had lacked this opportunity to educate themselves.

Tory women had been accustomed to understand their party as the marriage of family, empire and capital. And within that framework they had seen themselves as keepers of 'personal' values and of the party's conscience in these matters. It was not only developments on the left and in society that dismayed them, but also within their own party. With the coming of the Heath government, it seemed that the personal values that they stood for were being set aside in favour of a technocratic and egalitarian future. As the issue of immigration came to prominence in the 1960s, the sexual fear of women of the right gained another element — that of colour. The black mugger replaced the lout as the image of the violent sexual attacker, and galvanized Tory women to action in defence of the values they felt were being ignored.

The new right was able to take up all the fears that emerged around issues of race, sex and class and forge them into a new wave of populism around which the Tory party re-aligned itself. Many of these issues were based on fears articulated by women — but significantly, and most iron-ically, it was a woman, who was anything but fearful, who was able to capitalize on these fears. British feminists, looking around sometimes obsessively for new images of women and women's power, have found this one nearest to home the most difficult to deal with. Thatcher, the Iron Lady, was Britain's only ever female Prime Minister during thirteen years of highly 'successful' Tory rule. Shouldn't this be the ultimate vindication of equal rights, the pledge that Mary Wollstonecraft's dream can come true? The fact that this dream-come-true represented more of a nightmare for most feminists is I think indicative of the fundamental contradiction that lies at the heart of the language of rights and equality that we have inherited and that underpinned our seemingly most radical notions of freedom.

Thus, as the politics of right-wing women were finding a new focus under Thatcher, the politics of left-wing women encountered the resis-tance of reaction to their progress. And from here they also sought an exit from disarray, and eventually found it in the rise of the Women's Peace Camp. The timing of the establishment of the peace camp at Greenham is, I think, highly significant. Segal asks why this less hopeful brand of feminism emerged at this point. Why the prominence at this point of the passionate rhetoric about male violence? She concludes that it had something to do with the frustration of the goals of the Women's Liberation Movement. As she says, in real terms, political and economic equality remained as distant as ever for the vast majority of women and it could be seen as a case of the traditional consolation of the powerless — to take refuge in the claim to superior virtue. Faced with its lack of success for the majority, the Women's Liberation Movement was also beginning to experience fragmentation, and the need for a simple theory of who-was-to-blame, so that feminists could bury their differences and unite behind the pointing finger of accusation.[4]

Yet, I suggest, vistas of failure were only part of the reason. Perhaps another part was what might be called the awful threat of success — the realization that success on an individual basis *was* a possibility within the existing political system for those who, like Mrs Thatcher, could make a deft combination of traditional and modern language about women. For Mrs Thatcher, and the many Tory women political hopefuls that Campbell studies in her book, are by no means simply traditionalist women preserving traditional values by traditional means. They too are post-Enlightenment women speaking and operating the language of rights and equality, women who have a sense of how to get the best out of both worlds. There is a sense in which their politics could be described as radical, i.e. like feminists in the past, they are willing to work with men in a common political arena. And by the same token, one could describe what happened at Greenham as a return to a 'conservative' form of women's politics — that which chooses to operate only from within a 'women's realm'. Thus, it begins to be apparent that the roots of what we think of as our radicalism connect us at another level to that which we see as separate from and opposite to our own political self-understanding. If feminist theology takes women's experience as its starting point, then perhaps we need to ask at some stage how the experience of women that is politically articulated in a different manner to ours fits into our picture. What happens when the personal receives a rather different political embodiment? And what are the implications for our theology? Perhaps those whom we saw ourselves as opposed to are rather more connected to us than we care to realize: and those with whom we believed ourselves to be united are in fact rather more profoundly different from us than we would wish to recognize.

As we have seen, the women at Greenham addressed themselves to a problem that is an issue for women on both sides of the political spectrum — female distrust of male sexuality, and fear of male violence. Women who had participated in the student rebellion of the sixties were fed up with finding themselves relegated to the role of camp followers, and had decided to establish their own camp — a camp from which men were excluded and male sexuality and violence exposed as that which had subordinated women. From now on, the preferred form of sex was to be women with women — which preserved the freedom of non-reproductive sex, and protected women from subordination and violence within the heterosexist family system. Lesbian sexual orientation was the basis of the new model of female 'purity'. Thus by a novel route, Greenham returned to a traditional theme of female politics and re-enshrined women, not as competitors and potential winners in the political system, but as age-old losers, the endangered species in need of protection — albeit this time collective self-protection.

The setting up of an enclosed sphere of female activity and the stress on female purity is a theme which can be instantly recognizable as the age-old pattern of life imposed on nuns by a patriarchal church. But the similarities cannot be taken too far. Within the Greenham Women's Peace Camp, no lip service was paid to the role of the male protector. In fact this role was abolished and mercilessly exposed as a deception and a hypocrisy. Women now reserved to their own gender the role of defending life. They claimed that it was women who had traditionally been concerned with the giving and preserving of life, while men had routinely exposed to slaughter and death the precious products of their labour and love. Henceforth, men could not be trusted to protect women and their children grown or not yet grown. The whole monstrous absurdity of the nuclear 'defence' programme demonstrated this conclusively. And it was women, the new defenders of the nation's peace and freedom, who were determined to bring this vast folly to the attention of the nation and if possible the world.

The answer of the Greenham Peace Camp to the threat of male sexuality and violence was, as we have seen, expressed in terms that were the polar opposite to the way in which this threat was dealt with by those women who followed Mrs Thatcher to victory and whose values and concerns were in many ways responsible for putting her there in the first place. Yet, it is one of the paradoxes of politics of those times that the action of the women at Greenham produced for a brief moment a resonance that seemed to have struck a chord with women on the right. In 1983, the Tories had won the election, and Labour, which had thrown in its lot with disarmament, had lost. With this defeat was lost for the time being feminist hopes for further progress towards women's equality on the political and economic front. It seems there was a popular mandate for deploying cruise missiles in the English countryside. Yet Campbell's analysis of the voting figures shows that in that year, which was also the climax of the Greenham Peace Camp, 67 per cent of women were opposed to the US missiles. By autumn 1986, Libya and Chernobyl extended the women's majority to the population as a whole: 54 per cent were opposed to the US missiles and 65 per cent were opposed to the use of bases in Britain for the Libyan raid.[5]

Campbell's analysis of this paradox leads her to the conclusion that this was one of those rare occasions when women's experience of the events in question led them to articulate a *common* reaction on both sides of the political spectrum:

Women's anti-nuclear kinship crossed party boundaries in a movement of thought and feeling articulated almost entirely at the level of civil society — outside the institutions and processes of state power, outside the traditional discourses of politics. It challenged the distinction between public and private which had marginalised women's politics, keeping them in a separate sphere. Conservative women opposed to nuclear weapons consulted their personal passions to order their political perspective on peace. They relied on feelings usually designated private and therefore outside political discourse. In that sense they adhered, whether consciously or not, to the principle of the 'personal is political'. In any case, that principle already formed some of Conservative women's political glossary — it was a language they understood. The culture of the women's peace movement appropriated a term hijacked by the right, personal responsibility, and transformed it from self-interest to the global interest — to personal responsibility for the protection of the planet.[6]

Feminism of the eighties made many claims for the common basis of women's experience. And indeed, the foregoing suggests that among British women of the most recent period of history there is in some sense a common element of their experience, their lack of power vis-à-vis the male establishment, their fear of aggressive male sexuality. Yet it is also clear that these areas of common experience and concern do not lead women to arrive at the same political conclusions. On the contrary, except on rare and significant occasions, they are very likely to end up in different and opposing camps.

The existence of these two camps is in a very real sense a stumbling block for feminists, if they assume that all women must naturally aspire to equality. There has been a tendency among feminists to underestimate the position of right-wing women on the relations between the sexes; to assume that their reactions emerge from passivity, a lack of thought, and a failure to identify the problem which keeps them trapped in a false consciousness. But for many right-wing women, it is not that they have failed to identify the problem: rather they have come up with a different interpretation and a different solution. As women they aspire to a secure place within patriarchal structures from which they can influence and civilize patriarchal domination, rather than challenge it head-on — a strategy which they might well consider to be doomed to defeat.

Yet quite a few of the women of the new right, as Campbell shows, have aggressively adopted the values of equality and strongly aspire to equality of opportunity in the political sphere with men of their own class and party persuasion. Thus, they demonstrate that it is not at all impossible for women to speak a language of rights and equality, while at the same time upholding a conservative view of society. We are again reminded that the language of rights is not always self-evidently a matter of justice for the oppressed. It can equally well be the language of an articulate group asserting its own claim to privilege.

To look at this question within the context of the feminist movement itself may be painful for us. Thus, when feminism was the preserve of a tiny band of the committed few, who suffered gladly the contempt of the world, the intense solidarity of sisterhood was relatively easy to maintain. But as the movement broadened its appeal and drew in not only the daughters of the men of 1789, but some of the daughters of the servants of the men of 1789 and even the daughters of their slaves, sharp differences of opinion and allegiance began to make themselves felt. Could it be that the feminist 'revolution' shared a family likeness with its grandparent, the bourgeois revolution? Perhaps here also the rights of the few rested, as before, on the poverty, dependence and labour of the many. When the 'universal' language of feminism was extended to those who weren't the inheritors of privilege in the first place, some awkward questions of difference began to appear. Embarrassing as it may be, it rather begins to look as if we are definitely related to our sisters on the right; a different branch of the family, no doubt, but as we shall see with some distinct family likenesses.

From this vantage point, the Women's Peace Camp can be understood as partly a reaction to the difficulties and problems that are involved when women pursue freedom through the language of rights and equality. Thus the ideal of equality in eighties feminism had become either muted or transformed. As a slogan on a lesbian feminist calendar of this period remarked, 'A woman who wants to be equal to a man lacks ambition'. The peace camp in effect set aside the simple goal of equality and replaced it with a different ideal. This was the idea of a women's separate culture based on women's special nature and experience, and enshrining her superior virtue and peaceableness. But the fact that the peace camp ended up as a miniature action re-play of the cold war, with each side treating the other as The Other although both were in fact on the same side, suggests that this idea also is not free from contradiction; a case perhaps of 'out of the frying pan and into the camp fire'.

The Women's Peace Camp claimed to be liberating women from the isolation of their homes and the burden, individually borne, of nurturing children and families. It laid them open to the charge of having abandoned their families, as they gathered into a new unity on the basis of women's special experience in order to undertake a new and exciting form of political work. Yet the question arises here: what was the special nature of women's experience? Was it not precisely in that experience of childbearing, confinement in the home and the nuclear family, etc., that Greenham enabled them to transcend, but which constantly reappeared in the symbols that were used by women at Greenham: the webs made out of knitting wool, the nappies and baby-gros and wedding dresses, the pictures of children and grandchildren on the wire, the endless tea-making ritual of the camp fires? It is difficult to escape the conclusion that that which was identified as the condition of oppression had become the foundation of the new ideal.

Quite a lot of feminist literature of the washing-nappies-makes-you-more-relational variety took this problematical feminist ideal as its premise. But it was becoming clear to me and no doubt to a good few others that washing nappies doesn't normally make you immune to angst, or connect you up in some mystical way with the experience of women through the ages. It's just as likely to make you bad-tempered and give you backache — and ready to greet the invention of disposables with unmitigated enthusiasm. Thus, as Segal and others have suggested, many of women's 'special experiences' are the particular experiences of Western women undergoing motherhood in a modern capitalist society.[7] As such, they are as likely to produce isolation, dependence, trivialization and enslavement to the consumer society as they are to lead to the display of those much-vaunted female spiritual qualities on which we were seeking to base our theological enterprise.

All these reflections led me to some disturbing questions. For if feminism could no longer be seen to be the obvious and reasonable interpretation of women's experience, because the experience as it came to us is already mediated, then what is it founded on? It began to seem that the term 'faith' to describe these convictions was a more appropriate metaphor than we had realized. For whatever its undoubted foundation in an experiential reality of female life, it was becoming clear there must be something else at work in the process that results in some women becoming feminists while others do not.

Since those days, of course, feminist criticism (of the post-structural variety) has moved on from the somewhat naive essentialism of the notion of women's experience that informed our feminism at that time. It has exposed the 'disease of thinking in essences' as a hallmark of the bourgeois mythology,[8] and re-affirmed that the 'natural' is produced by the social. Thus the category of woman and her experience cannot be taken as natural or given, but must be interrogated to see how this difference has been produced. Feminism, according to this understanding, must concern itself with the radicality of difference.[9]

But for the moment, rather than proceed along the fast track of these theorists, I want to take the slow boat of retracing my own experience and reflections thereon. I hope to show that there may be some advantages in this mode of intellectual travel. For although the higher reaches of feminist criticism may have in theory dispelled our illusions about the real nature of women's experience, in practice there are still quite a few at the grassroots of feminist theological faith who preserve some version of it. This hunger for the essence of 'real' experience is not after all unique to feminists. As Diana Fuss comments:

The entire history of metaphysics can be read as an interminable pursuit of the essence of essence, motivated by the anxiety that essence may well be accidental, changing and unknowable.[10]

Perhaps, with an understandable instinct for self-preservation, they are hanging on until a new metaphysical place of safety is perceived. For, as it became increasingly clear to me, it was a risky enterprise for a feminist to examine her history. Maybe a health warning should have been attached: close attention to history can seriously damage your ideological health.

Notes

1 See Beatrix Campbell, *The Iron Ladies: Why Do Women Vote Tory?* (London: Virago, 1987), pp. 103 – 4.
2 Campbell, pp. 105 – 6.
3 Campbell, p. 67.
4 Lynne Segal, *Is the Future Female?: Troubled Thoughts on Contemporary Feminism* (London: Virago, 1987), p. 66.
5 Campbell, p. 124.
6 Campbell, pp. 137– 8.
7 Segal, pp. 4 –10.
8 The 'disease of thinking in essences is at the bottom of every bourgeois mythology': Roland Barthes, *Mythologies*, quoted in Diana Fuss, *Essentially Speaking: Feminism, Nature and Difference* (London: Routledge, 1990), p. xii.
9 Fuss, pp. 3ff.
10 Fuss, p. 20.

5 The problem of herstory and the Third Reich

To come to the conclusion that there is no necessary correlation between women's experience and the logic of feminism; to discover that there is something in common between the politics of radical feminism and women's politics of the new right was somewhat disturbing. Expelled abruptly from the warm womb of feminist certainties, I was forced to look with a sceptical eye at much of what I had come to take for granted.

One of these was the main feminist strategy for dealing with history. In 1975, an American feminist historian, Gerda Lerner, argued that 'the true history of women is the history of their functioning in the male-defined world on their own terms'.[1] She hinted that this would consist of an unresearched alternative history, which when reconstructed could eventually pave the way for a genuine universal history, one that would take due account of the dialectical relations between male and female culture.

This notion of an alternative female culture has in fact presented a number of difficulties for those feminist historians who have tried to work with it. But for feminists on the ground, so to speak, the idea of 'herstory' had a powerful appeal.[2] Herstory holds that women's authentic experience has never been properly told, because it has been suppressed and concealed under the record of men's violent and hierarchical rule. Thus, herstory is a kind of innocent version of history, for women cannot be held responsible for the violent, shameful and cruel deeds of male history, because they are, typically, the victims of this history. The most that can be conceded to the possibility of female culpability is that women have sometimes allowed themselves to lapse into passivity and dependence rather than struggle against it. The herstory idea seems to have as its foundation some version of the Saiving-Plaskow hypothesis.

In my new state of scepticism about some articles of feminist faith, I felt obliged to check the herstory idea against the record, so to speak.

As a student of history during my university career, I had made some study of the Third Reich, that most brutal and destructive of male-dominated regimes in the whole of history, and my obsession with this period and its relevance for citizens of the twentieth century had never quite left me. I needed to know what 'herstory' looked like in this context. Surely this, if anything, would provide a classic case to confirm the theory. And, as luck would have it, I came across an excellent study by Claudia Koonz, *Mothers in the Fatherland*,[3] which examined the pattern of women's experience and participation in these times, making it possible to see to what extent it fits in with the feminist pre-conceptions I was familiar with. How did women, both as individuals and in their organizations, fare in these times?

The results were not altogether reassuring. Certainly, the female sins of passivity, dependence, and — dare we say it? — gullibility can be amply illustrated from the pages of this book. But that is not the whole story. Women, it seems, did not just passively accept the Nazi rise to power in mute recognition of their own lack of power. As Koonz shows, they contributed actively to it in many and varied ways.

Since the end of the nineteenth century, the German women's movement had fought a long struggle for women's suffrage, and with the coming of the Weimar Republic in 1919 this was achieved. Socialist and middle-class women had organized rival organizations, and thus came to their newly won emancipation with different expectations. Middle-class women had formed the Federation of German Women's Associations (BDF) which co-ordinated a broad-based struggle for women's rights without male participation. Socialist women, by contrast, worked closely with their male colleagues, who since the 1890s had incorporated women's equality into their party programme. But it is interesting to note that, despite the differences of these two women's political groupings, they both rested their argument for women's position on the Enlightenment belief in universal and equal human nature.[4] Socialists stressed the economic basis of this equality whereas for liberals it was legal and political. But for both sides, it was essential to their feminist understanding that male and female nature was fundamentally similar; the idea that woman has a 'special nature' was considered anti-feminist.

Under the Weimar Constitution, women had their first taste of participation in public political life, as women delegates were elected to the Reichstag for the first time. Women from all parties deplored the double standard in matters to do with the sexes and expected to use the constitutional guarantee of equality to combat it. But divisions among them appeared as soon as the discussion turned to practical solutions. In this period there were many measures introduced that addressed women's rights — such as protective legislation for the re-employment of unmarried mothers, divorce reform, abortion, education and public morality. Practically none of them became law. Whereas women found it impossible to agree on how to support the measures, men seemed to find no difficulty in combining instinctively to deflect any threat to the status quo. Before 1918, women had felt unified by the very fact of their exclusion from public life. But once they entered this arena, this unity quickly disappeared. Women from all parties experienced apathy or hostility from the men in relation to the reform they sought. Middle-class women had high hopes of arousing a new spirituality in public life, and hoped to trade on their image of virtue and purity. But they quickly discovered that purity had very little exchange value in the normal world of male politics. Socialist women didn't have much faith in spiritual power, but they counted on their men's long-standing commitment to the programme of women's equality. But when it came to the test after 1919, they discovered the shallowness of the support of their male comrades, who soon showed that they preferred their women to devote more time to their families, leaving them (the men) to interpret the best interests of women and children at the level of political reform. Despite the difficulties women delegates faced, they did not resort to forming a much feared 'women's block' across party lines. Rather than a frontal attack they preferred to rely on persuasion. In the event, socialist and middle-class women closed ranks with the men who shared their political views, and avoided appeals to co-operate with women across the political spectrum.[5]

Thus, women's first participation in public life was disillusioning for those who experienced it. And meanwhile outside on the broader area of civil life, the whole basis of their emancipation was coming under threat. Women's victory on the suffrage front became associated in the public mind with the occasion of Germany's defeat in war, i.e. men's defeat on the battlefield. In the aftermath of national economic humiliation, the rumours grew and circulated that the gallant German army had been stabbed in the back by the defeatist collusion of Liberals and Socialists and — some said — by women and Jews.[6]

In this dominant climate of disillusion and disapproval, many women now rejected a 'political' role for themselves, cast aside with contempt Wollstonecraft's dream of equality. Once again the 'oscillation' between the two poles of women's politics was visible. Instead, they sought 'emancipation from emancipation'[7] and actively pursued the more familiar idea of a 'women's sphere' where women would be free to devote themselves to their concerns, such as the welfare and future of the race. And although they cheerfully eschewed male politics — from which they felt excluded anyway — they did not hesitate to use the newly won ballot to give their support to parties which promoted 'women's sphere' politics. One of these was the new movement of National Socialism. Here women organized a women-based politics of small but active local groups, whose task was to campaign among women and instruct them in the new ideology. For many women, despite the emphasis on their domestic role, it was ironically their first real experience of political involvement, and they responded enthusiastically to the chance to move beyond the domestic front and play their part in the building of a national movement.[8]

Reading Koonz' account of women's activities and participation in the run up to the Nazi takeover, I was struck at times by a sense of sinister parallel: how similar it all was in some ways to the activity of consciousness-raising among feminist women in the 1980s! It confronted me with the possibility that I had not hitherto seriously considered — that there is more than one way of 'raising consciousness' among women. Witness the case of the woman who initially rejected Nazi racism but after the patient efforts of the other women in her group, came to see the error of her ways:

[I thought] racial thinking was un-Christian and unjust, especially concerning the Jewish question. I regarded Jewishness as entirely a religious issue. After many endless debates, I realised that this attitude confused religion and race — one of the world's greatest historical errors ... [Finally] I learned to reject the belief that appearance does not matter. Because I believe that a meaningful order pervades all creation, I understand that this order rests on unconditional differences between the races.[9]

The majority of German women in this period were broadly sympathetic to the conservative and nationalist aims of Hitler, but did not identify themselves as Nazis. Most remained within their existing women's organizations, largely church organizations, and worked to preserve their autonomy while being prepared to concede most of what was required by the ruling ideology. Could this be described as 'functioning in the male-defined world on their own terms' (Lerner)? How then would we categorize the minority who became passionately committed Nazis, who nurtured and supported the movement from its earliest days, and provided much of its organizational backbone? It would be rather difficult to describe these women simply as being guilty of a failure to take responsibility for their self-actualization.

The loyalty of Nazi women to their leader was intense and unswerving — and apparently undeterred by his contempt for women. As Hitler rose to power and became Führer, their idolization of him came to be shared by millions of women. The records testify to the quasi-religious feelings of adulation that many women felt for him. Koonz suggests that in describing the attraction they felt for him, they seem to have borrowed from a religious vocabulary they learned as children studying the life of Christ. A teenager begged her Nazi uncle to tell her bedtime stories about Hitler:

He had given me a little picture of him which I kept like a shrine to which I could look up in adoration. I enclosed him in my little heart and was determined not to rest until I had finally grasped the meaning of his idea and battle.[10]

Another early convert wrote: 'At last I found a man willing to die for his faith; a feeling rushed through me like fire.' And another: 'I who had never been able to recognize any authority over me at all … I will follow a life of permanent obedience.' One woman saw him as a Messiah figure: 'From a thousand wounds rose his sweet face, enlivened by a child-like smile of holy self-confidence. Hitler strengthens the spiritual power of the entire volk.'[11] For millions of women, Hitler was a saviour figure who would restore a world where men could be men and women take their rightful place as women.

Yet this 'craving for submission' was not only evident in the recorded language and feelings of women — it was also shared by millions of men. The desire for passivity and dependence, in ways that seem to contradict the real interests of the individual, is not, as the history of Nazism shows, the exclusive prerogative of women. But likewise, as that same history shows, the desire for power and the determination to get it and use it by whatever means and whatever price, is by no means a male prerogative. Hitler envisaged no role at all for women at the top levels of Nazi administration, but he needed women to organize and galvanize other women to support him, particularly in certain areas of policy. Koonz records how many women saw their chance in this situation, and went for it without any inhibition. She shows how ruthlessly they fought for their share of power, how they employed and exploited their different styles and powerbases in the fight for survival and to gain every possible advantage against their rivals, hoping to rest secure at last in Hitler's favour.

Yet in the end, of course, all these women lost out, whatever their starting point, and whatever temporary victories they may have seemed to win on the way. Hitler made use of both the wholehearted and the conditional co-operation of the women's church organizations to carry out his racial hygiene programme, which involved both euthanasia and sterilization of the racially unfit. Yet he did not, as many had hoped and calculated, reward them or their organizations with status and autonomy; instead he liquidated, appropriated or transformed these organizations beyond recognition. And even those women who had thrown in their lot completely with Hitler from the very beginning did not get the rewards they hoped for after Hitler came to power in 1935. Clearly, without the co-operation of women, Hitler would not have got very far; yet this did not in any way dispose him to reward them for their co-operation, hard work and loyalty.

So do we have here a classic case of herstory? Should we speculate as to whether, if women had been allowed to retain control over their own organizations, they would have carried out the work of ridding Germany of the racially unfit more efficiently? Or would it have been better if women had never acquired the vote which they subsequently used to elect Hitler? Would it have made any difference anyway? For women, so herstory goes, are not in control of history. And, as real power was not in the hands of women, they cannot ultimately be held responsible. At one level, this seems to fit the facts. Women's political gains were reversed under Hitler, and they had no share in policy-making of the Third Reich and its genocidal schemes. As Koonz reminds us, women were not the ones who conceived these schemes, nor did they carry out the orders to arrest, deport, brutalize or murder. The chain of command was entirely in men's domain. Women took no part in planning the final solution, and except for a few thousand matrons and camp guards, they didn't participate in murder.[12]

Yet murder on this scale required more than a few men giving orders; it required a whole society to play host to the enterprise. It was not simply blood on the hands of the few but ink on the fingers of the many that made the final solution possible. There was a part for everybody here, and right at the heart of this tale of blood and sacrifice, there was a role for women which needed no special modern qualifications, no political power, or new organization — just women willing to be women and do the traditional things that women do. Thus, women in their classic womanly role, as wives and daughters of the death camp commandants, provided their menfolk with the necessary support, and enabled them to perform their inhuman task without being racked by doubt as to whether the daily slaughter of thousands of innocent women, men and children was a suitably manly role for them.

Should we focus on the 'betrayal' and 'victimization' of these women — or would it be more appropriate to focus on those other victims, male as well as female, who were dying in hell behind the fences only a few blocks away from their petty domestic paradises, those little orbits of 'women's sphere'?

Confronting these uncomfortable questions suggested to me that herstory in its crudest form is a consoling fantasy that conceals far more than it reveals. It is in danger of concealing from us the fact that though women certainly have been and are victims in history, they are not always purely and simply innocent victims, devoid of all responsibility for the crimes of history; they are, at times, both accessories and perpetrators; they can be both victim and victimizer. Thus, the clear bright picture of ideological fiction has become muddied. And here perhaps I was coming closer to that missing element in the feminist story which had so disturbed me. Women, so we had been given to believe, were equal to men in all things but sin; and in the matter of innate virtue, they have a head start on men, which however has never been allowed to show up on the historical stage because men have consistently suppressed women's potential throughout patriarchal history. Such was the herstory thesis. Yet a look at women's actual history, especially this painful period of the Third Reich, does not promote confidence in this account. On the contrary, it suggests rather forcefully that women are indeed capable of sin, and although the nature of women's sins is conditioned by the nature of their particular social and historical experience, they are not fundamentally different from what feminists would recognize and identify as men's sins.

It is I think significant that although feminist theology has been around since the 1970s, it is only fairly recently that there has been a serious interest in what could be called feminist ethics. This, I suggest, is because ethics has tended to be seen as a matter of the niceties of choice in grey areas of morality, which men who have cornered the main exercise of political and social power need to address themselves to. Women, on the other hand, who were fortified by the herstory thesis, tended to see themselves as placed by their special position in history to take up a somewhat different position. They felt more able, in good conscience, to present in black and white those matters which men tend to make into a murky grey.

However, the discipline of attending to some of the details of women's history is often useful as an antidote to presumptions of women's virtue. In considering women's response to the Nazi phenomenon, it is clear in retrospect that certain ethical questions were of profound importance for women faced with this situation; questions such as, when is it a matter of prudence to co-operate with those in power, and when is it a matter of betrayal? Yet, these were not the sort of questions that ideological feminism of the 1970s and 1980s was willing to address. The way the issues were presented tended to suggest that the answers were obvious or had been settled in advance.

I began to suspect that the actual role of the 'herstory' notion was the exact opposite of its declared purpose. Thus, rather than re-discovering women's history it served to prevent us from getting too close to the complex and murky reality of our history, to the extent that it is knowable. For the truth about women's history is that it cannot be rendered painless for us, nor can we pretend that it does not confront us with difficult dilemmas which women face in their historical experience. If we take our history seriously, we cannot hide behind the belief that ethical distinctions and niceties are for men — the ones with the power.

Traditionally, a woman's virtue was deemed to reside in her sexual purity, and her ethical concerns were limited to the necessity of preserving the same. By a strange irony, it seems that feminist politics has frequently employed a new version of this female ethics — a woman's first duty is to preserve her ideological purity against the threats to it from the tainted world of male politics and power manipulation — to remain, as it were, 'ideologically virgin'. Gender purity has been substituted for sexual purity. And the instinct, not unusual in feminists of this era, to make straight for the high moral ground is perhaps a legacy of the obsession with female virtue that has characterized our society, especially since the Enlightenment. It's as if the moral high ground is an enclosure specially set aside for ladies — a place where they can feel comfortable. But as feminists, perhaps we were a little too unsuspecting when we occupied this site on behalf of women. For what if female virtue and feminist purity alike are a kind of fiction that men and women, for their slightly differing purposes, have conspired to uphold? In a subsequent chapter we will examine this question in more detail. But in the meantime, let us look at another case of women's history (not Germany this time), where the question of the relations between women of different races is involved, and issues of purity are always present either implicitly or explicitly. As a result of my researches, I had begun to entertain a new sort of hermeneutic of suspicion; the suspicion that women's ethics of preserving a supposed purity can at times deflect them from dilemmas of a more painful nature; that is, those arising from a deep inequality of power between women of different races. In the next chapter, I shall address this question in an American context.

Notes

1 Gerda Lerner, 'Placing women in history: definitions and challenges', quoted in Julia Marina Hopkins, ' The understanding of history in English speaking Western Christian feminist theology', Doctoral thesis no. A2724, Bristol University Library (1988), pp. 63–4.
2 Hopkins, p. 272.
3 Claudia Koonz, *Mothers in the Fatherland: Women, the Family and Nazi Politics* (London: Cape, 1987).
4 Koonz, p. 31.
5 Koonz, pp. 32– 4.
6 Koonz, p. 28.
7 Koonz, p. 12.
8 Koonz, p. 68.
9 Quoted in Koonz, p. 62.
10 *Ibid.*
11 Koonz, pp. 62–3.
12 Koonz, p. 387.

6 *Alice in White Wonderland*

As feminists in the 1980s, we were, it seems, like a good many other people, willing to learn from our history only what we wished to know — or knew already. Yet perhaps it might be said, and with some justification, that even if it was not expressly articulated, the peace camp at Greenham could be seen as an 'answer' to the story of women under the Third Reich. Women under Hitler accepted the reality of male rule without question, women at Greenham questioned it fundamentally. German women sought freedom for the German race only, and only for those who were racially fit. Greenham women were concerned with the survival of the human race, not just the British race, and in the end they quarrelled and accused each other about whether they were racially inclusive enough.

It has been important for us that our feminist ideal, in precise contradiction to the Nazi one, is racially inclusive. This may help to explain what I will call 'the Alice Walker phenomenon' in feminist theology. By this I mean that it is virtually *de rigueur* for a feminist theologian these days to quote Alice Walker somewhere in her pages. In order not to fall below acceptable standards of a feminist theologian I shall follow suit. Here then are some quotations from the now famous conversation between Celie and Shug on the subject of God in *The Color Purple*:[1]

I don't write to God no more, I write to you.
    What happen to God? ast Shug.
    Who that? I say.
    She look at me serious.
    Big a devil as you is, I say, you not worried bout no God, surely.
    She say, Wait a minute. Hold on just a minute here. Just because I don't harass it like some peoples us know don't mean I ain't got religion.
    What God do for me? I ast.
    She say, Celie! Like she shock. He gave you life, good health, and a good woman that love you to death.

Yeah, I say, and he give me a lynched daddy, a crazy mama, a lowdown dog of a step pa and a sister I probably won't ever see again. Anyhow, I say, the God I been praying and writing to is a man. And act just like all the other mens I know. Trifling, forgitful and lowdown.

On the face of it, it is perfectly clear why this passage from *The Color Purple* should delight the heart of a feminist theologian. Walker expresses with great artistry both the particular difficulty feminists have with the patriarchal god-father image, god as old, white and male; and also, in the following passage, she raises the age-old problem of theodicy, the vindication of God, that any suffering or oppressed person may have:

She talk and she talk, trying to budge me way from blasphemy. But I blaspheme much as I want to.

All my life I never care what people thought bout nothing I did, I say. But deep in my heart I care about God. What he going to think. And come to find out, he don't think. Just sit up there glorying in being deef, I reckon. But it ain't easy, trying to do without God. Even if you know he ain't there, trying to do without him is a strain.

As Celie and Shug continue their playful but serious iconoclastic efforts, they go on to articulate a vision of God likely to find favour with most feminist theologians.

I decide to stick up for him, just to see what Shug say.

Okay, I say. He big and old and tall and graybearded and white. He wear white robes and go barefooted.

Blue eyes? she ast.

Sort of bluish-gray. Cool. Big though. White lashes, I say.

She laugh.

And Shug sums up her theological conclusions:

You come into the world with God. But only them that search for it inside find it. And sometimes it just manifest itself even if you not looking, or don't know what you looking for...

It? I ast.

Yeah, It. God ain't a he or a she, but a It.

But what do it look like? I ast.

Don't look like nothing, she say. It ain't a picture show. It ain't something you can look at apart from anything else, including yourself. I believe God is everything, say Shug. Everything that is or ever was or ever will be. And when you can feel that, and be happy to feel that, you've found it.

Shug's expression of God is very close to the immanentist female image of God preferred by feminist theologians as a replacement for the more male image of a God that seems to demand transcendence at the expense of women and nature. So it is clear that there are many very sound theological and literary reasons why these passages should be much quoted by us.

Nevertheless, I cannot escape the feeling that there is more to it than that. I suggest that it is not only Alice Walker's theological speculation embodied in her brilliant novel that interests us; we are also fascinated by the story that the author herself represents. It is a kind of Cinderella story, and at the same time, a very special version of the American dream. For here is a black woman who, by her own great talent and hard work has, against fearful odds, become a celebrated woman novelist, whose best known novel has been made into a successful Hollywood movie. And yet coming from the double marginalization of being black and female, she nevertheless dares to give voice in her novel to the experience and sentiments both of feminists and of lesbians. All in all, her triumph gives feminists something to celebrate. No wonder that American women are proud of her achievements, and want both to acknowledge them and associate her work with their own. British women in the field, taking their cue from their transatlantic sisters, have admired where admiration is due and duly followed suit.

But is there something involved in our love of Alice Walker that remains implicit, something which can't quite be told? Cinderella, as we know, gets to go to the ball and who does she meet there but her sisters? We her sisters are the white feminist theologians who fold her in a sister-ly embrace, and quote her warmly in our books. Those who read them will now be able to see that there is a convergence of views and interest between black and white feminists. And indeed it is extremely impor-tant for our self-understanding as feminists that this should be so, and be seen to be so. For isn't sisterhood that common bond between women forged from our experience of a common history of oppression and thus transcending differences between us of race and class?

However, one of the sisters, Susan Thistlethwaite has been listening to her black colleagues a bit more carefully than is usual for whites to listen to blacks. She notes that Alice Walker and her fellow womanists do not make so much of this common bond, but on the contrary are concerned to articulate their difference on a range of issues important to feminists — from housework to Christology. She quotes Dolores Hines, who says:

We are told that apples and oranges are the same, when we can see that they are not. You cannot easily substitute one for the other in a recipe. Their odours are different. They appeal to people differently. Even a blind person can tell them apart. Yet a steady stream of rhetoric is aimed at convincing Black women how much alike their lives, experiences, wishes and decisions are to those of our stepsisters.[2]

Stepsisters... so that's it. We recall that Cinderella's sisters were in fact her stepsisters. In her book, *Sex, Race and God: Christian Feminism in Black and White*, Thistlethwaite sets out to examine these issues of difference, and to take them seriously. At the beginning she tells how her original intention was to write a book called 'God and Her Survival in a Nuclear Age' and her first steps were to read the memoirs and biographies of Holocaust survivors. Her black colleagues' reaction to this was along the lines of: 'That's typical of you white people. Whenever you want to know anything, the only place you look is Germany.'[3] Her response to this reaction was to redirect her research — she began to look instead at why black women were jealous of their difference and resented being clasped in the embrace of their stepsisters. She found that the trail led back to the history of slavery in the US.[4]

When white feminism has looked for inspiration from the foresisters and mothers of the past, it was natural that they should come up with suffragists, women like the Grimké sisters who also opposed slavery. She shows how the opposition to slavery by such women was a result of their cultural re-shaping by Northern Enlightenment ideals, the same ideals which caused them to view their gender identity differently. But interestingly, the origins of the Grimké sisters had been in the South, where slavery took its classic form. Here indeed black and white women had a very intimate relationship — but it was not exactly one of common oppression. During the early period of slavery, the dominant Christian teaching was a form of Puritan theology. In this theology, the vast, wild expanse of the frontier was seen as a temptation to the bestial and barbarous in man, who needed to be brought firmly within the safe haven of a cultivated social state and the restraints of religion. Women's place in this particular theological configuration was a distinctive one. As Thistlethwaite says:

Fear of the uncharted possibilities of the wilderness aggravated misogynistic tendencies already resident in a Christianity that had declared sin and death to be the fault of women. Stringent regulation of women's chaotic sexual behavior was the ministerial prescription for the threat of the encroachment of the wilderness. Sex was a symbol of that which threatened man's rational control over his environment.[5]

But the presence of women on the frontier was of two kinds — the black slaves and their white mistresses — and each had a different but intimately connected role.

What the black slave woman provided was a buffer against the hatred of all women built up on the American frontier. She could become the bearer of the stigma of the physical, the carnal and the excess of women's lust that threatened the rationality of Christian civilization.[6]

White women were thus freed to play the role of 'angel of the home', the symbol of soul and spirituality. Thus their stake in slavery was two-fold. Not only were they relieved of the burden of punishing domestic and agricultural labour by the slaves, but they avoided the sexual terrorism of their menfolk that was the underside of the 'civilizing impulse'. This instead was vented on the slave women, and the whole system was kept in place by the psychological and physical threat of rape and beatings. And white women, as was expected of them, did their bit to uphold the system. Bell Hooks quotes from a collection of slave narratives the case of a white mistress who returned home unexpectedly to find her husband raping a thirteen-year-old slave girl. The mistress's response was to beat the girl and lock her in a smoke house. The child was whipped daily for several weeks.[7] Whipping — particularly of naked slave women, including the pregnant and nursing mother — was frequently employed against black women. White mistresses would send their female slaves to be publicly stripped and flogged for the slightest offence, such as when the bread did not rise or the breakfast was slightly burned.

It is clear that the endurance and resistance of black women to this sort of persecution and oppression was something of a different order to the opposition to it from white women. This, when it came, was a product of Enlightenment theories of liberalism, such as Mary Wollstonecraft had been inspired by and which also informed the Grimkés' work, especially that of Sarah.[8] The division of human experience into the rational and irrational, as in the previous Puritan theology, was retained — the difference being that Grimké, as an Enlightenment feminist, argued that women and men were intellectual and moral equals, and women should be treated as befits their equal status.

These two principles, the faith in human rationality and the assertion of the equality (in the sense of ontological identity) of men and women are, as Thistlethwaite shows, two of the hallmarks of liberalism; the other two were the view of the human being as an isolated individual who seeks truth and whose dignity depends on the freedom to pursue this search. Closely related to this is the doctrine of natural rights, the view that each individual has certain inherent or natural rights. The latter, of course, is consummately represented in the American Declaration of Independence: 'We hold these truths to be self-evident ...' And the pedigree of this can be traced back to the French Revolution, which, as we have seen, marks the origin of the modern notion of human rights.

Their belief in human rationality and in natural rights made it logical that the Grimké sisters should support the abolitionist cause as well as campaign for women's rights. But as Thistlethwaite comments, their faith in human rationality did not allow them to perceive the nature and function of the misogynist division of black and white women into body and soul. What they saw was the scandal of a situation where a Christian father might sell his own daughter, or the brother his own sister. Something of the kind may have happened in their own family since their brother had sired several children by a black female slave. But their appeals for an end to this disgraceful situation were predicated on an assumption of the white woman's 'enlightened mind' coupled with her moral purity, and they did not perceive the intimate dependence of this purity on the black women's degradation. Grimké, like later sisters, sees a kind of common suffering of the coloured woman, and the white women who experience psychological pain at this situation. It is a situation which, she feels, contaminates the moral purity of the white woman. But in her expression of pain at this, she is unaware of deeper anxieties about miscegenation and racial purity. As Thistlethwaite observes, her analysis does not allow her to grasp the white supremacist underpinnings of the 'Cult of True Womanhood' which formed the basis of the liberal ideal of woman on both sides of the Atlantic.

The Civil War was a struggle between the economic interests of the increasingly industrialized North and the agricultural system of the South.[9] But at the time many people including women's suffrage leaders like Elizabeth Cady Stanton and Susan B. Anthony believed that the war was being fought over the human rights of black Americans; that it was the result of 'enlightened' minds seeking to restore human dignity to those enslaved in the South. When the Republicans extended the suffrage to black men at the end of the war, the suffragists felt bitterly betrayed by what they saw as a male plot and drew the moral that woman should never 'labour to second man's endeavours and exalt his sex above her own'. From the liberal perspective of natural rights doctrine, Cady Stanton and other feminists could see their situation without the vote as one of slavery; the enfranchised black male had attained the 'kingdom' and they had been left out. This left the white female suffragist vulnerable to the all too prevalent racist atmosphere of the postwar period, and there was a widening gulf between women's rights activists, labour leaders and activists on behalf of racial justice. One of the latter, Frederick Douglass, was turned away from a suffrage meeting in the South, as Susan B. Anthony was anxious not to offend Southern women. The 1895 convention of the National Women's Suffrage Association urged the South to adopt woman suffrage 'as one solution to the negro problem'. Two years earlier they had passed a resolution which made it clear that white women suffragists had allied themselves with the white male and his system of industrial exploitation of foreign and black workers.

It is thus not surprising in view of this history that black women remain sceptical of white feminists' declaration of sisterhood and solidarity between black and white women, the transcending of all differences in favour of a common bonding on the basis of a common experience. Differences between women are not all, as feminists had tended to assume, just a matter of rational choice, and the experience on which they are founded cannot truly be described as 'common'. Yet, as Sheila Greeve Davaney shows in her paper, 'The Limits of the Appeal

to Women's Experience',[10] the works of the main 'pillars' of feminist
theology, Fiorenza, Ruether and Daly, all rest their case on the central
category of 'women's experience' and the claim that through this,
feminists can have access to knowledge of the truths of existence which
the patriarchs lack. For Ruether and Fiorenza this access is by means of
social struggles, whereas for Daly it is by virtue of their privileged
relation to nature.

And here we may remember that it was Daly who led the trend for
quoting from Walker. The passage she selected continues from where we
left Shug explaining her understanding of God:

She say, My first step away from the old white man was trees. Then air. Then
birds. Then other people. But one day when I was sitting quiet and feeling like a
motherless child, which I was, it come to me: that feeling of being part of
everything, not separate at all.[11]

For Daly, this aptly illustrates the movement towards the inexhaustible
'other', nature and the realm of pure being. She cites Adrienne
Rich's proposal that women's agenda should be a transformation of
the nature/culture distinction that does not place consciousness as an
abstraction.

We have been perceived for too many centuries as pure Nature, exploited and
raped like the earth and the solar system; small wonder if we now long to
become Culture: pure spirit, mind.[12]

But who is this we? Thistlethwaite reminds us that it was black women
who were raped and made to stand for Nature. White (middle-class)
women were the 'soul of culture', the civilizers of men. And if white
women, alienated from body and nature, are now seeking a reintegra-
tion, a return to the elemental, that is their agenda. For black women,
who were cast in the role of the exploited body, there is not the same
passion to return to the body. Both in fiction and theology, the womanists tend to stress a conflicted relationship between humanity and
nature. They take the conflicts of urban society as their point of departure. But for white feminist philosophers like Daly and Rich, it is urban
culture that is the source of our alienation, and the political institutions
of this culture that embody a politics of abstraction.[13] Thus they see the
task of feminist politics and theology as bringing this culture and politics
to accountability.

But for Daly's followers this bringing the culture to accountability
takes a rather different form from political struggle and analysis as most
black women understand it. Certainly Daly and her followers have
taken to heart the lesson of Cady Stanton that women should never
'labour to second man's endeavours and exalt his sex above her own'.[14]

Hence, the passionate search for sisterhood in the CR groups. But as Audre Lorde has written:

By and large within the women's movement today, white women focus upon their oppression as women and ignore differences of race, sexual preference, class and age. There is a pretense to a homogeneity of experience covered by the word *sisterhood* that does not in fact exist.[15]

If we look closely at the situation, it becomes clear that the liberal humanist assumptions of the nineteenth century have been revised and recycled in twentieth-century white feminist politics. Thus, in the CR groups, psychological theory tended to be the dominant mode, one which most black women have found alien to their more communal concerns. At root this theory reinstates the search of the lonely individual for the truth which shall make her free. The appeal to sisterhood and bonding appealed to white women who had been socialized to concern themselves with bonds — to avoid conflict, to foster dependence and the affective aspects of private life, creating a haven of peace and harmony from the harsh realities of competition in a capitalist society.[16] This, in fact, was the role that women in the Third Reich were reclaiming when they demanded 'emancipation from emancipation' and opted for Hitler's ticket for 'Kitchen, Church and Children'. Their version of his struggle for *Lebensraum* was domestic — the sanctuary of the living room.

On the face of it, our CR groups had nothing in common with such concerns. But at another level, they too were havens of privacy — the charmed space in which conflict is banished, a space in which middle-class women can somehow recognize their 'natural' role. Nor has the concern with purity disappeared, though it has been radically metamorphosed. Mary Daly now offers us the journey of pure lust,[17] where women can break through the sphere of potted passions and virtues and get in touch with Natural Grace. For it is in the realm of purity that all differences dissolve. But the irony is that such a realm is likely to be racially segregated too — pure white, since most of the black women (and a good many white ones too) have no access to her mystical spheres because of their economic and social and racial location. Daly's creation is that of a pure enlightened mind, such as the nineteenth-century women aspired to. She reinstates this dream, and in so doing she also reinstates the politics and culture of abstraction that she castigates. For what could be more abstract and remote from most women's ordinary concerns than her later works such as *Pure Lust*, *Gyn/Ecology* and *Outercourse*?

Yet the work of Mary Daly has been very influential and represents long-standing positions taken by white feminists. She is one of the mothers of the movement in the form in which it has been exported to the English-speaking world, laying the foundations of feminist theology in Britain and elsewhere. What is rather significant is that although the voice of Daly reached us loud and clear through the usual channels, the voices of her black critics were until recently screened out — either by us or by the exporters. For as they have observed:

White women have made a mistake parallel to that committed by white men — the assumption of common experience and hence the false universalization of what is only the experience of a particular group.[18]

As Thistlethwaite says:

The absence of an analysis of class and race in white feminist thought is not due to the fact that white women have no experience of class and race along with their sex, but to the fact that they have not allowed their consciousness of the interconnections of these social forces to become central. I believe that class and race solidarity have been a source of the bonding among white women, and what is often labelled as sisterhood is in fact sometimes economic and ethnic solidarity.[19]

Thus, it is not surprising that black women have rejected the desire of white women to bond with them as a 'pretense to [a] homogeneity'. And as we white stepsisters hug Alice to our breast at the Great Feminist Writers' Ball, we are desperately hoping that she will be so breathless and startled by the fervour of our embrace that she won't think to bring up the subject of difference. For difference is dangerous; like a dropped stitch, it may cause that whole feminist-ideological pullover to unravel. We are terrified lest Alice and her sisters force us to remember what happened in the slaveowners' kitchen; and worse still, to make us realize that though things have changed, certain things have a way of keeping the same shape.

So differences persist, despite our ardent desire to smooth them away — or stifle them at birth. Although Alice seems to confirm and endorse our passion for Nature (another reason why it is her above all that we love) it becomes clear that not all her sisters share our view of Nature as an 'exploited sister' with whom we should seek to reintegrate in the search for harmony and unity. For black women, as we saw, it was precisely as a result of being identified with Nature in the theology of both white men and white women, that they suffered cruel punishment and abuse. For this reason, Thistlethwaite suggests that the theological categories of sin and evil cannot simply be dismissed as unhelpful to women. It is necessary to understand very precisely how these categories have operated, and have been misused; and how women themselves have been party to the deceptions they embodied. Thus, she says, we need to see how both the white female slaveowners, and the white abolitionists and suffragists, failed to understand how the slave system enslaved them too; how they focused instead on an ideal world, a world before the Fall which diverted them from a true perception of their own capacity for violence. She believes that a white feminist treatment of the Fall should include an examination of the symbol of evil as the threat of the black woman as embodied 'other'. To do this properly means that we shall no longer be able to rest content with the theology of Daly and others who explore only their own objectification and means to resist this, and therefore repeat the historical error of women of their class of failing to understand that they also have an investment in the dominant culture that they criticize. White feminism has given insufficient attention to the Fall as a symbol of the depth of human intolerance for difference. As she concludes, there are no prelapsarian possibilities in contemporary American culture: racist, sexist America is unquestionably 'fallen'. And what we need to turn our attention to is the possibilities for idolatry that exist within our own experience as white women.[20]

Thistlethwaite tells the story of how in the course of presenting Valerie Saiving's theory about the nature of 'women's sin' to some students of hers she was challenged by a black woman student who informed her in no uncertain terms that sloth could never be construed as the besetting sin of black women.[21] As a result of this, she came to reconsider her endorsement of Saiving's views and to believe instead that 'Without a historically accurate definition of what it means to be female in different racial, class, and sexual role definitions, Saiving's contribution to understanding "sin for women" is misleading'.[22]

Thistlethwaite's re-setting of the theological agenda has been a very compelling one; but a further turn of the wheel reveals how deep-seated is the trope of purity in the feminist theological genre. For in some cases, white American feminist theology has taken on board her contribution to the extent that it has become necessary for new work in this field to ritually beat the breast about the inhuman treatment of black women by white. It has, in short, created a new requirement in the prescriptions for feminist purity rather than allowing us to consider the possibility that as women we are full participants in the sins of our race, class and culture. But before taking up this agenda more fully, I want to return to Greenham, to see if the result of these historical digressions may throw any light on the outcome there.

Notes

1 Alice Walker, *The Color Purple* (London: The Women's Press, 1983), pp. 164–7, quoted in Daphne Hampson, *Theology and Feminism* (Oxford: Blackwell, 1990), pp. 164–6.

2 Dolores Hines, 'Racism breeds stereotypes', quoted in Susan Brooks Thistle-thwaite, *Sex, Race, and God: Christian Feminism in Black and White* (London: Geoffrey Chapman, 1990), p. 58.
3 Thistlethwaite, p. 1.
4 Thistlethwaite, pp. 27ff.
5 Thistlethwaite, p. 30.
6 *Ibid.*
7 Bell Hooks referring to Feldstein, Stanley (ed.), *Once a Slave* (a collection of slave narratives), (New York: William Morrow, 1971), quoted in Thistlethwaite, p. 29.
8 Thistlethwaite, pp. 31–2.
9 Thistlethwaite, p. 36.
10 Quoted in Thistlethwaite, pp. 12–13.
11 Walker, p. 167, quoted in Thistlethwaite, p. 57, as quoted by Mary Daly in *Pure Lust* (London: The Women's Press, 1984).
12 Adrienne Rich, *Of Woman Born* (London: Virago, 1977), quoted in Thistle-thwaite, p. 57.
13 *Ibid.*
14 Elizabeth Cady Stanton, *Eighty Years and More: Reminiscences 1815–1897*, quoted in Thistlethwaite, p. 36.
15 Audre Lorde, *Sister Outsider: Essays and Speeches* (Trumansburg, N.Y.: Crossing Press, 1984), quoted in Thistlethwaite, p. 19.
16 Thistlethwaite, pp. 22–3.
17 See Thistlethwaite, p. 57.
18 Sheila Greeve Davaney 'The limits of the appeal to women's experience', unpublished paper (1986), pp. 2–3, quoted in Thistlethwaite, p. 13.
19 Thistlethwaite, pp. 45–6.
20 Thistlethwaite, p. 54.
21 Thistlethwaite, p. 78.
22 Thistlethwaite, p.79.

7 *The ghost writer of the Greenham plot*

For those who went to Greenham in the early 1980s, as I have mentioned, there was a sense of excitement in the events, a feeling that as women we were breaking new ground and somehow making history. And I do believe we were. And yet in retrospect, I am aware of a different picture emerging, one in which our 'free actions' are not nearly so free as they seemed at the time. And as the drama unfolds, it appears that it is not only we who were making history but history that was making us. From the foregoing explorations, it became clear to me that the stage was set for what took place at Greenham; and this was not only in the events of its immediate political and historical context, but also way back in the past, back in American and German history as well as in our own. As feminists, we were like new converts to a belief in the autonomy of the individual, for whom freedom of expression is the symbol if not actually the substance of this. Yet looking back, I feel that we could more accurately understand our role as that of actors who have to work with the lines they have been given in a play that was written before they were born.

It is interesting to recall that the events that immediately precipitated the great split at Greenham took place many thousands of miles from Greenham Common — in Russia. At the Congress of Women in Moscow in 1987, there was a delegation from the Greenham Women's Peace Camp, and this included some members of the Wages for Housework group, which had recently begun to establish a presence at Yellow Gate. Among the leading lights of this group were Wilmette Brown, an Afro-Caribbean woman originally from North America, formerly of the Black Panthers, and Selma James, another North American who had lived in the UK since 1960. In the course of the discussions, Lynette Edwell (a Greenham woman from Newbury) interrupted Wilmette Brown and asked her to get back to the subject of Greenham — as she was in the middle of a lengthy digression on the subject of her own writings.

Brown and her group chose to interpret Edwell's intervention as a racist attack. Reverberations of this incident followed the women back to Greenham where it lit the touchpaper to a tinderbox of tensions which erupted in a major conflict. The result was a bitter division at the peace camp, with Yellow Gate demanding unconditional support for Brown, and condemnation of Edwell's action. The other gate camps' refusal to do this resulted in them being labelled racist, and thus traitors to the Greenham spirit of solidarity between women of all races.

This incident with Wages for Housework, as it later turned out, was typical of the operation and tactics of this group. In November 1987, after a similar disruption at a CND conference, Jane Dibblin and Lyn Barlow carried out an investigation into the background of the group and its twelve-year history of 'guilt-tripping negativism'. In her article, Dibblin shows how the group's tactics were to latch onto other radical organizations (particularly in the women's movement and the peace movement) and use the issue of racism to exploit the self-doubt of its largely middle-class members, leaving trails of destruction in its wake.[1]

In order to understand why this group was able to disrupt the solidarity of Greenham women so successfully, I think we need to appreciate more fully the nature of the tensions it was able to exploit. Since I was not living at the peace camp there is a sense in which I cannot speak from firsthand experience. But the Greenham movement was wider than just those who lived at the camp, as the women themselves claimed in the slogan, 'Greenham Women are everywhere!' Of the tensions that developed in these groups I can give some account. To be present in the early days was to experience something in the nature of a baptism. We were immersed in the waters of a feminism that proclaimed us henceforth free from the sins that the patriarchal world had ascribed to us, and released us into a liberated perception of reality, where we would learn to trust those closest to us (other sisters) and to distrust those who had taught us to blame and distrust ourselves and other women (i.e. mainly men).

This then was the primary function of the CR groups to which many of us gravitated in those days and which were based on similar assumptions and philosophy to the peace camp. Here, in the intimacy of these groups, we were to taste and see the solidarity of sisterhood. And yet, as I recollect, how unsolid were these havens of solidarity! Products of our female, largely middle-class conditioning as we were, we entered these groups with our fragile self-esteem, together with our excitement and our fear. We were anxious to behave in the right way and to have the right feelings. Just as a subject race is wont to, we had unconsciously learned to identify with those who had more power than ourselves (i.e. men) and to desire to be like them, or at least to be secure in their favour. Those who were like us in being women were our competitors.

Yet in our feminist baptism, all that we had learned had to be unlearned. We could not admit to wanting to be like those who were, if not the enemy, at least the other side. We were now on the side of women and those with whom we had learned at best an ambivalent co-operation were now our sisters and our friends.

Yet, in reality, conditioning is not so lightly discarded. In these groups there was a tightrope of feelings to be walked, generating a great deal of tension which made many of us often feel anything but safe. To commiserate with each other in the slights and humiliations we had suffered at the hands of patriarchal society came easily to us — in that sense, support groups were often truly supportive. But how much more difficult it was for us actually to support any member who showed signs of achievement or leadership. For achievement on the part of one of the sisters was quite often deadly to the fragile self-esteem of the rest. It proved our worst fears — that they had mastered these terrifying tensions in a way we felt we could never do.

The other woman, our sister, may be the closest to us in her ideals, aspirations and desires. And because of what we share there is indeed scope for empathy and friendship. But precisely because of what we shared, and equally desired, there was also another possibility that co-existed in the sisterly bond — that of rivalry. The sister–friend as rival was not a theme that was much explored by feminist writings and theory in the 1970s and 1980s. Although there is plenty to suggest that this theme is quite familiar to women in their pre-feminist or non-feminist writings, it is as if it had been ruthlessly edited out of the feminist script. And yet anyone who has been involved in feminist politics or even just female friendship over the last decade can hardly have remained untouched by its occurrence in some way or other. More recent feminist writing has begun to observe this phenomenon, notably Rosalind Coward's book *Our Treacherous Hearts*, a very perceptive study of some of the difficulties of contemporary women around the issue of envy and competition.[2] And feminist psychotherapists Susie Orbach and Luise Eichenbaum in their book *Bittersweet* discuss the issue of women's difficulties in friendships with women.[3] They speak of the 'merged attachments' between women that provide security and support, but also subtly enforce fixed roles from which deviation is only possible at a price. When one partner in the friendship or support group finds opportunity in her life for growth or change, or the fulfilment of some aspiration or ambition that both may have shared or desired, then most frequently the other party suffers devastating effects — her confidence sags, her sense of self-worth is undermined, her very identity is threatened. Psychological theory, that was a familiar mode of analysis in the support groups, alerted us to the possibilities of conflict with male family members, and at least made us aware of ambivalent feelings towards mothers. But it had not much to say specifically about sisters except as siblings in general. And this, in any case, was overlaid by a climate of enthusiasm for this relationship, an absence of warnings that it too could contain pitfalls. Like Christians before us, washed in the waters of baptism, as feminists we were to find that not all stains of inadmissible feelings and desires were capable of being washed out forever overnight. What humiliation then, to discover feelings of fear and resentment caused by Mother resurrected in one of the sisters; or of helpless rage and envy provoked by a 'younger sister' in the group who seemed to manage all the hurdles so much better than we did.

Thus, the ideal of sisterhood, it seems, could give rise to as many repressions as the ideal of femininity that radical feminism had so fiercely exposed. Presented as a struggle against men's power, the truth is, as Coward observes,

that the deep struggle of feminism was with the previous generation of women. Feminism could be called the daughters' revolt, so central has been the issue of women defining themselves against the previous generation and distancing themselves from their mothers. It is no accident that feminists used the language of sisterhood, evoking an image of siblings in revolt against parental authority. Much more important than women's relationships with men were the hidden agendas existing between the different generations of women.[4]

Thus, one can begin to see how a little hermeneutical suspicion is also appropriate for the script of women's freedom as radical feminism presented it to us. One can appreciate how the gap between our feminist ideals and the reality of our feelings and fears could generate a growing tension that would eventually pose a major threat to sisterly peace.

There was another area too where the aggregate of tensions indicated further hidden agenda. I gradually began to suspect that there was a reason for the fiercely anti-authoritarian rhetoric of feminism that did not appear at the level of ideological acknowledgement. It was not just men's misuse of authority that was being disapproved; it was also women's actual or potential use of authority that was being discouraged. The unacknowledged task of many of the CR groups was to maintain Men as the enemy in general, but to ensure that members did not have to mount a real challenge to any actual exemplars of patriarchal authority. For this the ideology of structurelessness served us very well. It meant that any move to the exercise of effective leadership by women in these groups was often blocked by what could be presented as impeccably good ideological reasons. Any move to set up a committee, for example, to get a particular task done could be seen as 'playing male politics' and treated as if it presented a dangerous occasion of sin! By this means, we sometimes rendered our endeavours quite harmless to those we had designated the opposition. Thus we allowed ourselves to operate within the traditional confines of our female conditioning of not challenging male authority, while at the same time maintaining a good radical-sounding anti-male rhetoric.

Yet for a while, there is no doubt that the peace camp did indeed pose a very considerable challenge to the male authorities, and an effective witness to the suicidal insanity of the nuclear arms race. And for this reason, if for no other, it is essential that we examine the factors that led to its fatal weakening through internal dissension.

Women at Greenham were proud of their ability to operate apparently without leaders. But it was this 'open door' policy that allowed Wages for Housework to operate so effectively and with such destructive re-sults for the peace camp. Moreover, one can appreciate with hindsight that it might have ultimately strengthened the challenge of the peace campers if they had also understood that it is normal for women to fear women's authority more than they do men's. The fear is that those of their own sex will be less protective towards them — and less manipula-ble by them. Women's deeply ambivalent attitude to women's power may help to explain the attitude to feminism of those women who do not become feminists. But it also has to be reckoned with as a factor that is powerfully present among feminists themselves, and serves to set limits to their effectiveness.

Women's relations with women, in the fiercely separatist days of the eighties, were problematical and guilt-generative at least in part because they were not supposed to be. Women's relations with men, on the other hand, were so over-problematized that they often ended up by mount-ing a replica of precisely the situation which feminism was supposed to have liberated women from — where the desires and needs of actual women were such a threat to the ideology that they became candidates for repression. Women who desired to work with men, sleep with them, marry them or just enjoy their company would soon feel that it was not safe to acknowledge such desires in a feminist environment.

When feelings and desires do not measure up to the self's ideal, then there is always the problem of what to do about them. For feminists, guilt itself is a feeling they are not supposed to feel, for we are supposed to have been liberated from that too. There is of course a time-honoured way of dealing with inconvenient guilt, and with desire that disturbs but which cannot be fully admitted. It involves the ejection of our violence and that which we are forbidden to feel on to the Other, the one who can be safely cast out from the bonds and bounds of the community.

A reading of the feminist theory of those times would seem to suggest that it was men who would be cast in this role of scapegoats — but this is a trifle misleading. For those who are socially powerful are not really suited for the role of scapegoat. This role has to be played by someone who is lacking in social power. Thus, in feminist struggles of the last decade, it was usually women to whom the lot fell, though occasionally it might be a man who for some reason could not or did not resort to the normal means of patriarchal protection. Thus, in a charged situation like Greenham, women in the feminist ranks who could be found guilty of thinking like men, or desiring to associate with them, were in danger of being deemed ideologically impure, and therefore unfit for the work of feminist endeavour and practice.

Scapegoating usually happens when the existence of a group is threatened by the presence of irreconcilable conflict and the imminence of dissolution. It is the means by which an individual or weaker section of the group can be made to 'carry away' the guilty weight of the community's self-destructive violence. It is the price that must be paid, by someone other than ourselves, for preserving our self-image of spiritual or ideological purity. As Fergus Kerr says, paraphrasing the French philosopher René Girard, 'If we go on saying "*we* have no sin" we shall be resisting the terrible truth about ourselves that we need scapegoats to keep ourselves at peace.'[5]

One of the forms this 'saying that we have no sin' took in the feminism of the 1980s was focused on the issue of rape. Radical feminists like Susan Griffin and Susan Brownmiller and feminist theologians like Daly have described how rape is the fundamental mechanism by which men establish and maintain control over women. Though the majority of men do not actually commit rape they benefit from the position of power established for all men by the rape threatened and committed by the few. This theory is one that many women can relate to without difficulty, feeling that it articulates what instinctively they know already. As we have seen, the anxiety about violent sexual attack is also a strong feature of right-wing women's politics.

I think that there is something of importance in this theory, which I do not want to deny. Nevertheless, there is a delicate matter here which it is vital for us to confront — and that is the role that this theory of rape has played in our claim to female innocence and 'not guilty' status. Sin in most modern minds usually has connotations of sex — wrong sex, sex that is disapproved of by the church. Rape in radical feminist theory is the primary expression of the victimization of women, the symbol of all male violence. And because it is the sin which women are not capable of committing, it comes to stand for the sinlessness of women, their exoneration from the charge of violence. The accusation of rape to men as a whole is, you might say, the radical feminist answer to the church's ascription to women of the guilt of Eve. For the peace camp at Greenham, which had invested heavily in the ideal of the non-violent women, it came to have a particular significance.

On 25 December 1981 a new peace camp was founded at Molesworth, modelled on Greenham except for the fact that it was a mixed camp —

including men and women. This fact made it offensive to many hardline Greenham women, whose view of patriarchal society was that there could never be any 'peace camp' between men and women, because in this society, men will always victimize women. This issue came to a head when it was alleged that two female peace campers had been raped by male peace campers. The *Spare Rib* article on the events claimed that it was only after a third rape took place that two of the women who had been raped 'felt that they had kept quiet for all the wrong reasons, and had to do something'.[6] So they, and some other women from Greenham, returned to Molesworth and spray-painted some of the benders, dismantled others and axed a peace camp sign — 'because of all the hypocrisy about peace and love' — as one of the raped women is reported as saying.

Theresa Sunflower also wrote an analysis of the events at Molesworth, in which she observed that the Molesworth issue had produced a polarization in the peace movement in which women felt forced to take up a 'for-or-against-us' position: either they had to come out against the rapists and support a women-only peace camp as the only way to ensure women's safety: or else they felt they must condemn the 'violent' response of the women and defend the 'innocent' majority of men who were getting blamed for it all. But many women, she commented, were in fact somewhere in the middle, feeling alienated and confused, unwilling to take up these positions and dismayed by the bitter strife that had overtaken the peace camp.[7]

It is interesting, as she notes, that the polarization was taking place *not* primarily between women and men, but between different groups of women. Many women at Greenham found themselves under strong pressure to support the first position along the lines: either you support us or you are guilty of collaboration with the rapists.

The outcome of the Molesworth rapes is uncertain as they never came to court — nor presumably would the Greenham women have wanted them to, since all the workings of 'male' justice were considered to be, by definition, a foregone conclusion. Thus, if the courts had found the rapes to be proven then they would only be confirming what the women believed they already knew, hence an unnecessary verdict. If, on the other hand, the courts had found the rapes to be unproven, then they would conclusively prove the radical feminist case — that women can never expect justice from men.

The net result of these events was that a climate was created in which women had begun to accuse each other of betrayal. The poison that eventually became manifest in schism had already entered as the issue was posed in terms of guilt and innocence, and women found themselves either in a guilt-manipulating or guilt-manipulated position. From here, it was only a short route to discovering that one or some of 'us' should be treated as the Enemy.

The conflict that had erupted at Molesworth soon found its way back to the camp at Greenham. As we saw, the trigger for the great schism was the arrival of the Wages for Housework group — a group which centred on two black women wielding a forceful feminist rhetoric. At Greenham, there were always rumours about secret and sinister plots by the establishment, like 'zapping',[8] for example, designed to break the strength, confidence and unity of the women which more direct and open methods had failed to do. But who would have suspected that black women coming to the aid of the party — a scenario devoutly to be wished by any true feminist — was to be the source of rout? But if the government had set to work the full might of its counter-intelligence division, it probably could not have come up with a better device for the undermining of its female opponents at Greenham. To suggest that this is what in fact happened is perhaps to credit the intelligence operation of the establishment with too much intelligence. But ironically for the non-violent women of Greenham, deeply committed as they were to racial solidarity, the entry of black women (albeit on a very small scale) into the arena was the event that effectively undermined the peace camp.

It is here perhaps that the connections with the history that we examined previously begin to fall into place. There is a sense in which the ideal of the non-violent woman at Greenham can be seen as a descendant of the cult of True Womanhood. Our ideological foremothers such as Wollstonecraft and the Grimké sisters were much concerned with what woman's virtue truly consisted in. And so too were feminists at Greenham — only the terms of reference were different. For them, the true woman was the non-violent woman, eternally victimized by men in history, whose mission was to champion the cause of non-violence, forswearing all forms of male defence and desiring only to engage in mutually empowering relations with her sisters. And in the hierarchy of virtue based on degrees of oppression, black women were thus well placed. If they adopted this particular feminist rhetoric (and most of them had other more pressing concerns and were fighting on a very different terrain) they were 'better placed' than their white sisters to wield the weapon of guilt manipulation. White sisters who had been able to play the 'Virtuous Victim' game in relation to the brothers, now found that when black women entered the lists, the issues were no longer so black and white! As we saw, black women in the US exposed the feminist fiction of a 'natural' female solidarity. Now at Greenham, the presence and operation of black women served as a catalyst for existing tensions to explode into open conflict.

It was part of the original commitment of feminism that guilt manipulation was a strategy to be resisted. What happened at Greenham demonstrated how difficult this was to adhere to in practice, and how feminist women as well as non-feminists were capable of falling victim to it, black women as well as white. There were also those at Greenham who resisted guilt manipulation and discovered how costly this could be. One woman who stayed on at Yellow Gate after she had refused to acknowledge uncritically the charge of racism against herself and women at the other gates, remembers how she was sent to Coventry, pointedly ignored by her sisters and former friends. Groups fell silent as she approached, no one would sit near her. On one occasion, when friends came to visit her, and felt the chill of this treatment, they decided to move away a little and make a new fire. The other women responded to this by moving in, in the manner of the bailiffs, and stamping out the fire.[9] In the context of Greenham, this was a very symbolic act; it was the treatment of a 'sister' as enemy, using the methods of the enemy. What our feminism of those days failed to remind us of is that our kinship with women of different eras can be traced not only through our acceptable feelings and behaviour towards other women, but also in our betrayals. Scapegoating in particular evokes the memory of those betrayals: those Jewish women in the 1930s, for instance, who found themselves suddenly excluded from women's organizations of which they had been loyal members for years — like the BDF for example in which they had worked shoulder to shoulder with their 'sisters' for entry into the male world, and which now quietly accommodated itself to Hitler's requirement of a Jew-free and compliant women's movement.[10]

What these women experienced, you could say, was the price of someone else's peace. For a brief period millions of formerly demoralized and defeated Germans were uplifted and united, Protestants and Catholics, women and men united in passionate devotion to the Führer. Millions of another race, picked out as the internal enemy of German nationhood, paid the price for this unity. But the peace that was bought at the price of the scapegoat was temporary — as it always is. In Germany, there was war — and ultimately defeat. At Greenham there was schism; two sides with different versions of what happened.

I am not saying, of course, that Greenham women were no better than German women who supported Hitler — far from it. Unlike fascism, Greenham was a genuinely radical movement of women, which for a brief time glimpsed a new and exciting mode of women's political action. That it contained powerful contradictions present in women's politics, as indeed in all politics, which eventually worked towards its undoing does not mean we should dismiss or underestimate its achievements. What it does mean, however, is that if we wish to develop a political wisdom from out of our engagement with women's politics, it would be as well to understand better some of the forces that are at work in them.

Thus, as we begin to be aware, none of the language we use in our search for the answer to women's oppression is innocent. It has a history.

And if we try to use it 'innocently', that is without awareness of its ambiguous nature, the 'ghost writer' of history has a way of pitching in and spoiling the script. The drama that eventually takes place is not the one we planned. Thus, at Greenham, the language of 'women's space' was a significant one, an expression of the idea that the 'special nature' of women was their essential non-violence. Yet this idea of 'women's sphere', her special nature and virtues, is also not 'innocent' language. Its antecedents include its use in Germany in the 1930s. Here it served to reassure men that women did not aspire to challenge men's power or enter the sphere of male politics. At Greenham one could say that the intention was exactly the opposite — to challenge the basis of men's political and military power. And yet, it is arguable that both these manifestations of womanspace/women's realm were at times used to obscure from men, and from ourselves, the use of women's power. It is odd that those of us who were living through the decade of Thatcherism in the 1980s should ever have needed a reminder that women do have and do use power — and not always on behalf of women as a whole. But much feminist theory at the time seemed almost to 'forget' this fact, thus testifying to the power of ideology which allows us not to know what we do know, and not see what stares us in the face.

The feminism that prevailed in and around Greenham at that time did not deny that women were concerned with power. But they made a distinction. The power that women were concerned with was their individual autonomy. It was not seen as the same as the 'dirty' form of power which men handle, strive and kill for. Autonomy is creative and fulfilling, and it is this which men have wrongfully deprived women of under patriarchy and women may now strive to regain. This feminism had much to say about the universal limits to women's autonomy imposed by patriarchal order; but the protective fiction of herstory prevented us from examining the relatively large distinctions in autonomy between, say, the protected women of the slaveowners' society and their slaves: or the wives and daughters of the Nazi state, and Jewish women in the death camps. Thus we tended to stare past these unseemly divisions unseeing, and to be unaware of the new gender dualism we were creating in our thoughts about women and men's use of power. We believed that we were making a new space for women — but were we perhaps redecorating, sometimes with colour and imagination, an old space that had already been set aside for us?

It has been vital to the feminist project to depict the female sex as almost by definition the victims of male violence. We have at times presented this almost as the basis of unity between women — our common inheritance as it were, of male violence. And this in a sense is hardly surprising. For the victimization of women by men defiles the history of humanity in every age and every society. And yet, even here where we feel we can be most certain, it seems to me that we are in danger of succumbing to a dangerous and illusory logic. We need to ask: how does the fact of our victimization make us pure? Perhaps those who have died of it could be said to have expiated their sins by death. But those who have survived, the black as well as the white, given the nature of human history, share in some sense in 'survivor guilt' — though it is clear that the price of survival has been higher for some than for others. They/we are participators in the inheritance of the violators: or as it has been said, 'Only the damned learn to survive'.

Secondly we need to ask: how have we (white feminists) been so readily persuaded that women are at all times the enemy of violence? There is in fact not a lot of evidence to suggest that women are always 'put off' by violence and rather more to suggest that they are 'turned on' by it, when they perceive that it is directed to the Enemy, the Other who is the outsider. Much has been said in feminist circles about women's relational skills and their preference for relational modes. But this, it seems to me, is somewhat disingenuous. It ignores the fact that the relations that women have been much exercised with in their history and concerned to preserve have been relations of protection — protection for themselves and for their children. And for this end, as Jean Bethke Elshtain shows in her book, *Women and War*, women have usually been happy enough to enlist male violence — less happy, naturally, when they are the victims of it. The historical evidence does not seem to suggest that women, on balance, are less bellicose than men, and as far as war is concerned, they are not averse to joining in and joining up where circumstances permit. It is as much men as women who — for their own purposes — have wanted to preserve the image of women as the non-violent ones who do not press the trigger or push the button. For men, women are to be the ones defended, in whom are reposed the values they are called upon to defend. And women, by allowing themselves to be defended, give value to the whole enterprise whereby men commit violence (not universally 'natural' to them) and suffer as well as inflict it, in their own bodies, as the price of war.

As Elshtain shows, men and women have always been allotted different cultural roles in relation to war; the warrior versus the weeper and keeper of the home fires. And with the defeat of religion by the Enlightenment, and its replacement by the religion of the nation state, war has become the central rite of blood sacrifice of the state, with the obligations to sacrifice incumbent on each citizen according to gender. And women of modern times, taken as a whole, have not been slow or unwilling to perform their obligations.

Radical feminists took it that the non-violent role of women was fundamentally at odds with the violence of men; and that, fully articulated, this must represent opposition to the war games of men. But they failed to see that the 'opposition' of women's non-violent role is of a rather special kind. It is the opposition of contraries that complement within a single picture. And however sincere the opposition is in its own self-understanding, as Elshtain shows, in the grand cultural pageant of the nation state, even the opposition is included, and indeed required to play its part. This is the part of the 'Beautiful Soul' — an idea originally articulated by Hegel, it applies to all those who, by artistic or religious profession or gender, have been allowed to 'opt out' from the demeaning realities of power, politics and the corrosion of history. Their role is to enshrine and preserve the noble ideals and highest ethical aspirations of their culture — which the rest of the nation finds rather inconvenient for daily use. In this role, they are encouraged to preserve a personal purity, for theirs is a kind of culturally permitted innocence. Although they may be individuals of either gender, it is, according to Elshtain, women in the West who have been cast in the role of the collective Beautiful Soul, representatives of the True Womanhood, the burghers' daughters. For it is, of course, the female children of the Enlightenment who are eligible for this role. And the Beautiful Soul is usually a white not a black one.

It is this essentially modern (i.e. post-eighteenth-century) cultural role of women, Elshtain suggests, that has doomed them to lose certain battles over and over again. For Beautiful Souls are too good for the world — but absolutely necessary to it. Thus, it has become clear to me how, in our female separatist and peace commitment, as at Greenham, we were playing a version of this role to perfection. Just when we believed that we were scaling the walls of the patriarchal citadel, we were in fact engaging in a necessary and permitted activity that served to shore up the fundamental structure. Our failure, in political terms, was perhaps a foregone conclusion.

The outcome of events at Greenham can be read as an ironic rebuttal of the idea that women have a special, non-violent nature. For it demonstrates that all the roots of violence, anger, rage, rivalry, guilt manipulation and scapegoating — all are present in women as they are in men. If patriarchal culture ordains that women do not normally shed blood through violence, this does not make us innocent of the blood that has been and continues to be shed in our history. Relative virtue cannot be assessed on a body count. 'He who looks on a woman with lust has already committed adultery with her in his heart' (Matt 5.27) could well be adapted for women, 'She who endorses male violence for her protection or profits from it, has committed violence in her heart.' Sacrifice, and the high price of war, is the means by which men create an artificial value for themselves. But by the same token, it also gives value to women who thus gain a vested interest in being the repository of the precious, those for whom the bloody sacrifice is made. Women's consent to protection continues to legitimate and sanction the whole bloody and futile business of war. The insight of the Greenham women was a truly radical one — but their investment in women's innocence was a fatal flaw that ultimately undermined the radical nature of the enterprise.

If feminists can no longer sustain their claim that women be considered not guilty of history, we need to ask where this leaves feminist theology which, as we saw, presupposed a level of female innocence, a kind of untainted alternative herstory to which we can turn to find salvation. As Julia Hopkins says: 'The re-writing of history as herstory places the scheme of salvation history in jeopardy because it demonstrates the ideological and social nature of history writing.'[11] But what if herstory demonstrates even more conclusively the ideological nature of certain uses of history, especially by those cast as the Beautiful Souls?

The story of the events of Greenham shows rather well how the personal is political, if by that we mean that the way in which we are conditioned as female persons has political origins and political implications. But because of the 'ghost writer' of history we discover that the personal is political in ways we did not quite expect. We are left in the dark as to why the realm of the political so often cheats us of the liberation that we seek. Perhaps it is time to see if our theology can throw more light on these matters.

Notes

1 Jane Dibblin, 'They play such terrible head games', *New Statesman* (27 Nov. 1987), p. 20.
2 Rosalind Coward, *Our Treacherous Hearts: Why Women Let Men Get Their Way* (London: Faber and Faber, 1992).
3 Susie Orbach and Luise Eichenbaum, *Bittersweet: Facing up to Feelings of Love, Envy and Competition in Women's Friendships* (London: Century, 1987).
4 Coward, pp. 91–2.
5 Fergus Kerr, *Theology after Wittgenstein* (Oxford: Blackwell, 1986), p. 182.
6 Barbara Norden, 'Utopia is dead', *Spare Rib* (Jan. 1987), pp. 40–3.
7 Theresa Sunflower, *Conflict Resolution and the Peace Movement: What Can We Learn from Molesworth?* (unpublished booklet, Nov. 1986), p. 10.
8 Zapping refers to the alleged use of some new form of radiation by the military against the Greenham women, which some believed was causing sickness and debility among them.
9 Personal conversation at Greenham with the woman concerned.
10 Claudia Koonz, *Mothers in the Fatherland: Women, the Family and Nazi Politics* (London: Cape, 1987), p. 357.
11 Julia M. Hopkins, 'The understanding of history in English speaking Western Christian feminist theology', Doctoral thesis no. A2724, Bristol University Library (1988), p. 75.

8 The post-Christian myth of original innocence

In the previous chapter, I discovered in the Greenham context that secret symbiosis which existed between the rhetoric of radical feminism and the patriarchal structure of male violence that it critiqued. In this chapter, I want to explore the possibility that these apparent opposites are related by means of the common myth of origin which the two sides both share and at the same time dispute — like parties to a will who are in dispute about their inheritance. I also began to realize that the dispute itself had been inherited by feminists, and that its origins lay further back in both the Enlightenment and in the Reformation.

The emergence of feminist theology in the 1970s, as we saw, was a product of the rise of radical feminism, and this connection is evident in the language that is used to talk about matters of guilt between the sexes. To describe the radical feminist case seems to involve, sooner or later, using imagery from the Genesis story of the Fall. '*Spare Rib*', the title of the magazine that articulated the radical feminist cause in Britain in the eighties, is a good example of this. Radical feminism identifies the story of Eden as the source of the guilt that is imputed to women. The basis of its case is to deny this guilt by contesting the judgement and laying the blame elsewhere. Men, not women, were the archetypal sinners, the ones who ruined the purity of relations in Eden by violating sex, and introducing sexual violence. Thus, the church and its theology is present in radical feminism as the archetypal male accuser, the inquisition; the one who holds woman in bondage, guilty by virtue of her bodiliness. It is hardly surprising that this language, which is so much a product of reaction to the church, should find its way back to its implicit target; and that women within or on the margins of the church should take up the cry of 'not guilty'.

This stirring among the women in church has had a two-fold movement; first, as women received the news that they were no longer

under the curse of Eve as defined by the church, they began to rise up
and declare that they too should be allowed to enter the holy places and
celebrate the sacred mysteries, as well as preach and teach the Word.
Men in the church have been divided in their response. Some, being
children of the same Enlightenment that has shaped women's thinking,
have acknowledged the validity of the claim. But others have reacted
with deep alarm. In earlier times, like the nineteenth century, when the
vicar and his ilk had been demoted to the lowest rank of the masculine
hierarchy, he could at least find solace of a sort taking tea in the ladies'
drawing room. Here he was a person of some importance for the ladies,
who liked to think that God might be available to them when men failed
to be, and the vicar might help them get in touch with Him. But alas for
the vicar — the ladies have become women, there is tea and coffee as
they sit on the bean bags in the sitting room, but the vicar is no longer
welcome; and worst of all a number of them are after his job. As Dowell
and Hurcombe prophesied in 1981,

If the church does not recognize and bless the vision of many of its women, if it
closes the parsonage door and seeks the solace of the sweet familiar face by the
fireside, it will find that she has either fallen asleep or gone to join the monstrous
regiment who are breaking down the gate.[1]

This is the situation we find ourselves in now — at least for women in
the Church of England. As I have been writing this book, measures to
ordain women have finally been passed and the first women priests are
beginning their ministry in England. But in the long struggle that pre-
ceded it, and still continues for Catholics and others, there were many
who became weary or disillusioned by the slamming of the door in their
faces and have turned away in disgust. Why waste energy and time on a
futile effort? Why not leave the old men prisoners in their tiny castle?
And so, answering the summons of radical feminism and Mary Daly,
they walked proudly and scornfully, out of ecclesiastical enclosure, to set
up a women-only camp on the margins of the male stockade, and pour
contempt on those who remain within — the women who still concern
themselves with such unworthy opponents, or are foolish enough
to seek 'peace' with them or reconciliation. This then is the origin of
'post-Christian' theology and its message has been that the home of
true radical women is nowhere within the pale of male religion and
spirituality.

In Britain, one of those who represent this movement of post-Christian
theology is Daphne Hampson — for many years a campaigner for the
ordination of women, who became disillusioned with the intransigent
sexism of her church, and left it. She has concluded that Christianity is
irredeemably patriarchal in the very nature of its thought and structure
and she directs us instead towards a religion that is 'gender free', one in

which the feminist belief in the fundamental equality of women and men in all things is taken as axiomatic. Anything less than a radical re-conceptualization of God along these lines and 'transcending' Christianity is, to her mind, backward and benighted, a kind of superstition (that which is left over when Meaning has moved on). As she says, modern thought has relativized religion, and shown up the very particular, hence partial, nature of Christianity. According to her, modern women, schooled in more sophisticated, universalist ways of thinking, are — and should be — rejecting Christianity as a myth which is both immoral and untrue.[2]

But what does it mean to say that something is a myth? Hampson uses it here in a derogatory sense, as synonymous with 'untruth', and in distinction to another sort of language that she assumes can speak truthfully and directly about the subject — in this case God. But what sort of language can speak truthfully and directly about God? This is the real issue. And feminist theology has made a very important contribution by pointing out that much theological language, which appears to be at the service of the user, is not as innocent as it seems. Wasn't it feminist theologians who pointed out to men — who thought they were innocently speaking about God — that they were in fact much of the time speaking about themselves and attributing to God the attributes of men? Not such an innocent activity in the eyes of the feminist theology pioneers, who first explored the patriarchal character and androcentric focus of much traditional religion, and undertook the quest for new religious symbols in place of the divine patriarch. They called for a language that would reflect more of the everyday experience of women. It is to this trajectory that Hampson belongs.

But as we have already seen there are a few problems with the idea of women's experience. Hampson has characterized Christianity as a myth. A myth might be seen as a way of approaching the truth — and holding on to it. And perhaps it is also a way of holding the truth at arm's length, making sure that it doesn't come too close, which would partly explain the ambivalent space that myth seems to occupy — somewhere between truth and falsehood. The idea that what we as women think is somehow naturally pure, and purified through 'our' suffering during our history of oppression, was fundamental to the whole enterprise at Greenham. And as we witnessed, the whole project foundered on the rock of a reality that finds women indeed formed by their history but not as 'pure' victims. The history that has formed feminists, like that which has formed Western women as a whole, has left them standing with a foot in both camps, the camp of the oppressor and of the oppressed. In the outworking of our history, women's experience has had a nasty way of becoming entwined with the ideologies and politics of men, and taking forms which sometimes make it difficult to distinguish fundamentally from men's historical projects.

What characterizes myths is not just whether they are true or untrue — they usually contain some important aspect of truth — but what function they play for those who subscribe to them. Thus for every truth they reveal, they also contain a truth that is concealed, invisible to the naked eye so to speak. Thus, it was the myth of women's experience which inspired us to consider our own experience as a source of truth. And indeed there is some truth in it. But there is also some concealment. I suggest that it also makes sense to consider it as a concealed dogma, whose function could be described as the feminist answer to infallibility. By this I mean it has a built-in 'not open to challenge' quality about it. This is because as *women's* experience the implication is that it cannot be subject to criticism from men. And because it is women's *individual* experience, the implication is that it is unique and therefore cannot be subject to the criteria of public discourse. Thus, cleverly, it achieves a quasi-dogma status while fiercely denying connection with dogma of any sort. It represents women's claim to authoritative utterance.

Now the suggestion that a feminist theologian might be guided by a dogma is enough to send a shudder through her soul which is, as we shall see, an interesting clue to the origins of her theology. It is the pernicious influence of dogmas that feminist theologians like Hampson see as being part of the harmful nature of the Christian myth to women. But could it be, as I have suggested, that we have substituted or supplemented the Christian myth with one of our own — one that is quite possibly not as helpful or liberating to women as it is made out to be? For the price of this neat move in the form of a concealed dogma is that the articulation of women's experience remains in the end firmly contained within the realm of private discourse — the place where women have traditionally been contained. Contrary to the declared policy of feminist endeavour, it serves to shore up the familiar gender divisions that limit the role of women, and operates a new dualism in place of the old — one that permits women to indulge pure and wholesome dreams of a world where 'female values' rule, while remaining uncontaminated by the world of political power and public discourse.

The radical feminist myth of women's original innocence was born from its polemic against the myth of women's original guilt which they believed was the creation of patriarchal Christianity. Yet, I suggest that the rendering of the Genesis story that radical feminism seeks to refute does not come directly from the text as they suppose. And that the corrective version which they substituted, far from challenging the dominant patriarchal code as they believed, in a curious way actually confirms and complements it. For the myth of women's innocence (and therefore their special need for protection) pre-dates feminism and has its origins elsewhere. Perhaps I can clarify this by looking further at the work of Daphne Hampson.

As Hampson would no doubt agree, any language used for speaking of God must fall short of comprehending that of which it speaks. The real problem with the language of myth is mistaking it, or any language, for the Real Truth. And it seems to me that despite her awareness of the problem, she falls into the trap. She privileges her own mode of God language without being aware of its specific human and historical origins — precisely what she thinks Christianity is guilty of doing. Hers is the characteristic Protestant reverence for the individual soul, who needs no intermediary between itself and God. But she has, it seems, reckoned without the invisible (to her) intermediary of her own language of the soul. Hampson's soul shows signs of being shaped by the Enlightenment — both in its secular and religious aspects — and in this respect she is not unique. Now horrifying as it must seem to think of something so personal as one's soul being shaped by anyone but God, the fact is that this is probably the case for most of us modern women, and worse still, particularly for those of us engaged in feminist theology. The fact that some of us would greet with horror the suggestion that a feminist is guided in her theological investigations by a doctrine or dogma is, I think, something in the nature of a giveaway as to the origins of our presuppositions.

Protestant religious individualism was born in reaction to the idea that revealed religious truth could only be mediated through the authority of the church in the form of dogma and priestly magisterium. Protestant-ism contested this authority and relocated 'true' religious experience in the relationship between God and the individual, mediated through the Word. Originally the Word was the Bible and reflection on it. But in its secular derivative, philosophical empiricism, this was replaced by the data of individual sense experience. Feminists have made use of these religious and philosophical antecedents to produce the doctrine of the theological self arising from the data of women's experience.

The overthrow of patriarchal Christianity by this new theological self, formed upon the data of individual experience of God, did not begin with feminism — it also has a precedent. The band of soul brothers who gave us the Enlightenment ditched Christianity because it was, to their mind, inherently irrational. Like some of the sisters who have come after them, they wanted to get rid of priestcraft and all its works, for they recognized no valid role for any so-called mediators of the Divine. But once the Divine Patriarch had been toppled by the work of the great critical intellects of the Enlightenment, some of them experienced a bit of an ethical chill — and an urgent need for a replacement of the clothing of religion which they had given away. For although they had got rid of God, they saw themselves as good and decent men, and they had no

intention of dispensing with morality. They believed that moral innocence was possible without God. But as Alistair MacIntyre shows in his
brilliant study, *After Virtue*, the various attempts of Enlightenment
thinkers to provide a rational vindication of morality failed. Once the
shared background of religion had been lost, secular rationality was
unable to provide a substitute — a universally acceptable foundation for
moral discourse and action.[3]

The project of justifying morality failed according to MacIntyre because of the rejection of the old consensus about human nature — what
it was and what it was destined for. As Catharina Halkes says in her
book *New Creation* the medieval and Renaissance view of nature and
society observed a hierarchical order in cosmos and society in which
there was an organic relation between the human body and the greater
world.[4] Medieval Christianity inherited the philosophical system of
Aristotle, in whose hierarchical scheme the apex was man, whose ideal
destiny was the life of rational contemplation, and for whom the rest of
humanity are instrumental.

But with the coming of the Enlightenment, this teleological view
of human nature, and of nature in general, was shattered. The development of a scientific-technological world view led to a rejection of
Aristotelian philosophy. The view of nature as alternatively nurturing
mother and chaotic destroyer of human hopes and schemes gave way to
a view of nature as a terrain to be conquered, a female being whose
secrets could be wrested from her by science, as the instruments of
torture could extract her secrets from the witch. Halkes quotes Bacon:

> The way in which witchcraft, magic, and all such superstitions are prosecuted
> and run aground ... not only sheds useful light on how people accused of such
> things should be treated, but we can also borrow from it useful directions for
> unveiling nature's secrets. No one need have scruples about penetrating these
> caverns and corners when interrogating the truth is his only object.[5]

But it seems that some of those who were fully committed to this new
mode of scientific and empirical investigation with its ideology of objectivity nevertheless did eventually begin to develop some scruples. One
of the reasons may have been that the absence of God was rather embarrassing. What was to stop women and servants getting the idea that they
too could investigate truth and pry into what was hitherto marked
Secret, and even — perish the thought — come up with different
answers to those of masters, husbands and fathers? Who was to ensure
that the very foundation of morality, which all these free-thinking philosophers subscribed to, would be held in place? Marriage, the family,
promise-keeping and keeping women in their proper place — who was
to guarantee all that now? And so some of them attempted to invent a
rational alternative to religion. Deism, or natural religion, was brought

in to fill the breach, and God, who was fatally compromised by His association with the *ancien régime* and its stupid and venal clergy, was replaced by something much nicer: the idea of benign Nature who must be worshipped and honoured as the great moving principle behind the universe. The Cult of the Supreme Being was one version of this endeavour. Perhaps a kind of nostalgia for the old organic understanding of nature was at work. Purified and reformed, Nature could be let back into the drawing room.

This nostalgia for Nature begins to have a familiar ring about it — the little stream of Deist nostalgia for nature has become a torrent in our own day, as the tide of ecological ferment rises, and many people, often with feminist theologians in the forefront, are urging us to worship and revere Mother Earth, now so abused and exploited by her children, particularly her male ones. Earth has been ripped apart and raped in the name of progress and technology, they say, just as women have been raped and abused and victimized by men. Throw out the old patriarchal god and bring back the goddess...

Yet for feminist theology to take this stance is full of ironies. For it is the same Enlightenment that brought us the scientific method and progress that also made it possible for women to seek truth on their own initiative, question that which was never questioned before, demand their rights and equality. It was the Enlightenment that provided them with the language to do this. Hampson is somewhat old-fashioned in the extent to which she reposes confidence in this slightly dated version of the scientific paradigm and its objectivity. The post-modern view is aware of science as a way of doing things according to our own interests, a way of interpreting Nature according to the questions we put to it. The rather grandiose idea that we are revealing Nature's purposes gives way in post-modernism to the recognition that science is a human idea, and that 'scientific facts' exist within the context of a human hypothesis.

Like the Deists, Hampson has also displaced the God of the *ancien régime* of patriarchy with a religion that is rationalist. She cannot accept a Christianity that is rooted in the past, and preaches a revelation that reaches us in the language of the past. To her mind such a concept of God is neither reasonable nor ethical. She seeks therefore to substitute a new version of a 'natural' God — who wouldn't be so uncouth as to accept sexist language from anyone in praise of the Divine. However, being a decent Protestant woman, she distances herself from some of the wilder margins of the goddess worshippers and doesn't align herself in an uncritical way with the back-to-naturists. She is anxious to stress that she isn't trying to propose anything that smacks of goddess worship: 'I had no interest in finding female figures, or "feminine motifs" in the religion. I just wanted a religion in which gender was not of significance.'[6]

What a modest and sober ambition! — no images, no idols, no interfering male clergy or goddesses or female popes — just the simple, sober purity of the Word. And yet the Word is perhaps the greatest deceiver of them all. The theological word is far from innocent, for language is a double agent. Behind its seeming purity and simplicity lurk all the riches and the horrors of human history and culture. The word of truth for Hampson is linked to the scientific paradigm — only this, she believes, can truthfully describe reality. But as we have seen, this scientific mode had its beginnings in a new relation of domination — one in which Nature must be tortured to yield up 'her' secrets — science which conducted the inquisition of nature in the name of objectivity. And it is us, those sweetly reasonable people, who believe our modern minds to be objective, who are called on to discard the ancient myths, and to reinvent God with the aid of the brand new vision of feminism — 'a total vision, involving different ethics, a different politics, a different ecology, and not least a different spirituality'.[7]

Her vision, in company with many feminist theologians, is one of salvation through connectedness — women weaving webs of life against the fear of death; women celebrating creation as the profound connectedness between humankind and the rest of nature; it echoes all the sort of language, in fact, that was used by women who frequented Greenham in the 1980s. Hampson, unlike Thistlethwaite, does not develop a critical perspective on the Saiving–Plaskow thesis about the nature of 'women's sin' — in fact she endorses it strongly. She makes the interesting point that Saiving's thesis is very similar to the view of Kierkegaard that there are typically 'manly' and 'womanly' ways of sinning. But she goes on to query whether 'the failure to take responsibility for self-actualisation' should be deemed to be 'sin' at all:

If we think of women's typical 'failings', as Saiving names them, they can hardly be said (in the way in which this is true of male pride) to be actively destructive of others. Rather have women been destructive of themselves and their own potentialities.[8]

Thus, Hampson in her reluctance to concede that women are normally guilty of human sin typifies to a high degree the post-Christian myth of original innocence. She prefers to refer to the possibility of female sin by the euphemism of a 'break in connectedness'. But the theology of connectedness has its own 'underground' connections which feminists do not always make explicit, because they might seem to connect us where we don't want to be connected. As Susan Thistlethwaite says:

One of the sources of a theory of connectedness in white feminist theology today is process theology and its ancestor in the faith, Protestant liberalism. It may be more accurate to say that rather than a *source* for white feminist theology, many feminists (*sic*) have found process theology to be largely congenial. Many aspects of process theology make sense to white middle-class women. Since women's (*sic*) experience has been denied as human experience, white feminist theology usually begins by claiming the validity of that experience and process theology has a framework that permits this claim... the androgynous God concept of process theology is attractive to those who are tired of fighting the 'God the Father' battles.[9]

But God-the-Father is rather more sneaky than feminists may have realized — perhaps not quite the silly old fool they took Him to be. More like the GodFather. Thistlethwaite tracks Him down in an area which some feminist theologians have wrongly assumed to be 'safe'. As she says:

Dominant process perspectives in theology need to be critically reexamined because they sustain both an alienated picture of humanity and a dualistic worldview. This alienation manifests itself in an implicit identification of the *imago dei* in humanity with mental process, betraying its rationalist roots.[10]

She notes that no black theologian or ethicist has chosen a process perspective for her work, and advises white feminists to be extremely wary of this type of theology as a benign face of patriarchy. For the rationalist mode of thought in American history, as we have seen, rested on a particular anthropology in which the black woman symbolizes the body and materiality and the white woman stands for the soul of culture, while the white male takes pride of place as the symbol of rationality.

Thus, Hampson believed she could find a God beyond gender — and yet she has ended up opting unwittingly and uncritically for a gender cultural stereotype in its 1980s feminist form — one that posits women's special nature and experience, oblivious to the profoundly particular nature of that experience, based as it is on one ethnic and class cultural group. And so, this thoroughly mediated cultural thought form becomes the basis for the unmediated Divine presence that is the goal of her quest.

The search for God in most people is not wholly separate from the search to be accommodated, to find a role in the community that claims to represent God's affairs on earth. But as we saw, post-Christians such as Hampson have largely abandoned the search for accommodation in the church. For they have felt that the church was incapable of offering them a role that would accord with their status as rational post-Enlightenment women, entitled to equal authority with their brothers. They have turned instead to authorship as a means for claiming this birthright. Hampson sees her concerns as being ethical as well as theological — and both are subsumed under the feminist ideal. The individual articulation of moral truth through authorship has become the new terrain of women's moral authority. Freedom is the possibility of finding a publisher. Publication is the priesthood that the post-Christian woman may aspire to.

And yet... the brave new world of authorial freedom is deceptive; here too we are in fact as bounded by the past as we were in the patriarchal church we seem to have escaped from. MacIntyre shows how the failure of the rationalist project of justifying morality has led to a situation where, since there are no objective, rational criteria for moral choice, moral argument is doomed to be interminable.[11] There is no court at which morality can be fully authorized or vindicated. There is only a market-place for moralities, a 'supermarket of the self' with each seller pushing her wares. Thus, it seems, our job prospects in the big wide world outside the church are to become saleswomen in the great pluralist bazaar where it's not moral choice that is on offer but consumer choice among moralities. A feminist may harbour secret and sometimes half conscious dreams of speaking an infallible truth, or guiding the flock with episcopal gravitas. Yet the democratization of moral agency means that this is likely to be unfulfilled. For as MacIntyre says, everyone is a moral agent now.[12] We have been liberated from hierarchy and authoritarian control. In the West, at least, freedom of speech is ours — we can say what we like. But who will listen? Why should they listen to us rather than another? We seek to speak our truth, but we live in a culture where truth has been displaced as a value and replaced with psychological effectiveness — mind management by the new breed of 'human technologists'. And this in turn leads to a breakdown of the distinction between manipulative and non-manipulative relations.[13] We seek to protect our own autonomy, not to be manipulated. But we also want to incarnate our own standpoint and modes of practice. How else to do this except by engaging in the manipulative modes which we want to resist in our own case?

Thus, our much prized individual autonomy is apparently limitless — yet in reality profoundly conditioned. In matters of morals, pluralism reigns, the 'rational' quality of debate is illusory. This is because, in the realm of fact, nearly everything has been decided. What kind of choice is open to us has already been decided. We live in a highly corporate state, where individualism is the ideological partner of bureaucracy — the culture of bureaucratic individualism as MacIntyre calls it.[14]

A feminist might be tempted to say that in this culture of bureaucracy the choices are all controlled by men, and it is therefore another name for that which we have already defined as patriarchy. But this is an over-simplification, for as Christopher Lasch says, in an article 'Recovering Reality', cultural radicals have been attacking 'bastions long since surrendered' — such as the patriarchal family and repressive sexual morality.[15] These were the targets of G. E. Moore and the Bloomsbury set who exposed the whole pompous paraphernalia of the Victorian age

which concealed the arrogant self-will of fathers and clergymen. Some of
the heat and steam of feminist polemic seems to have these nineteenth-
century characters in mind, and not to notice that things have moved on.
Lasch's contention is that the corporations, the advertising and mass
culture industry have long ago co-opted these demands by replacing
patriarchy with 'friendly' paternalism, and the work ethic with a
consumer ethic that is not only tolerant of, but deeply dependent upon
constant innovation and novelty, hedonistic morality and the rage for
sexual and creative fulfilment. According to him, in the New Paternalism, the managerial and professional élite comprises both men and
women, but all are given the degraded status of women — oppressed,
dependent, selfless and therefore in constant need of others to reassure
us of our existence.[16]

The distrust and suspicion of moral authority has helped to create the
distinctive moral feature of the age in which modern feminism exists —
namely protest. Protest is the mode in which it is expected that we assert
our individual moral autonomy, and indignation is the predominant
emotion. But as MacIntyre observes, the mode of protest goes along with
a repressed consciousness of the futility of doing so. The 'shrillness' of
protest is caused by the fact that it can never win the argument — nor
lose it either.[17] It is ineffective to unmask the arbitrary will and desire
that lie behind the masks of modernity. We cannot unmask the manipulators because we ourselves are trapped in the same ideological modes
as they operate. This helps to explain that secret symbiosis which I first
observed at Greenham, between the radical rhetoric and the structures
which it critiqued.

Hampson's work, I suggest, belongs to the genre of protest theology,
and thus exhibits this distinctive moral feature of the contemporary
scene. And in her case, as for much feminist theology, its specific origins
can be traced through the genealogy of Protestant theology. For Protest-
antism was, you might say, the original protest theology as it reacted
against the corrupt institution of the Catholic church that appeared to
have smothered the gospel in a mass of priestly privileges and clerical
perks. No wonder the reassertion of the value and validity of the
individual soul seemed such a liberating doctrine. For it attempted to
call a halt to the exploitation of human guilt for ecclesiastical profit. But
at the same time, the protest theology of feminist theologians like
Hampson also crosses another boundary that Protestant theology does
not necessarily cross. For it grounds itself in a myth of Enlightenment
origin — the implicit perfectability of our essential nature. And this
conformity to our true nature — in the case of feminism our female
nature — can be achieved by means of a right consciousness or a correct
rationality. There are of course many varieties of this modernist myth of
which feminism is one, sometimes, as we've seen, in alliance with one of

the others like faith in the scientific paradigm. But its distinctive feature, and that which makes it post-Christian, is its polemical relation to its genesis — in Genesis. Thus, in one way or another it proclaims the myth of our original innocence. That is the essence of its good news. But I think we need now to consider whether this doctrine of our innocence is really so much more liberating in the long run than the doctrine of our 'original sin'. Could it be that paradoxically this dogmatic attachment to our innocence can leave us open to an even more dangerous and cynical manipulation of unacknowledged guilt?

Notes

1 Susan Dowell and Linda Hurcombe, *Dispossessed Daughters of Eve: Faith and Feminism* (London: SCM Press, 1981), p. 111.
2 Daphne Hampson, *Theology and Feminism* (Oxford: Blackwell, 1990), p. 3.
3 Alasdair MacIntyre, *After Virtue: A Study in Moral Theory* (London: Duckworth, 1981), pp. 35ff.
4 Catharina J. M. Halkes, *New Creation: Christian Feminism and the Renewal of the Earth* (London: SPCK, 1991), p. 22.
5 Francis Bacon, *De Dignitate et Augmentis Scientarum*, quoted in Halkes, p. 28.
6 Hampson, p. 71.
7 Hampson, p. 145.
8 Hampson, p. 123.
9 Susan Brooks Thistlethwaite, *Sex, Race, and God: Christian Feminism in Black and White* (London: Geoffrey Chapman, 1990), p. 87.
10 Thistlethwaite, p. 87.
11 MacIntyre, p. 8.
12 MacIntyre, p. 30.
13 MacIntyre, p. 29 and p. 66.
14 MacIntyre, p. 33.
15 Christopher Lasch, 'Recovering Reality', quoted in Janice Doane and Devon Hodges, *Nostalgia and Sexual Difference: The Resistance to Contemporary Feminism* (London: Methuen, 1987), p. 49.
16 Lasch in Doane and Hodges, p. 59.
17 MacIntyre, pp. 68–9.

9 The Puritan politics of the modernist myth

In 1987, the Geneva talks between the USA and the USSR negotiated the removal of the cruise missiles at Greenham thus removing the main *raison d'être* of the women's camp. At the same time as they were rolling up the barbed wire in the background, the big split that had begun at the Women's Congress in Moscow was gathering steam, shattering the unity of the women on which the success of their cause so much depended. On the microscale, it seemed that feminist ideology had failed to provide a solution to the bankruptcy of moral authority. On the macroscale it became clear a few years later that communism had also failed to achieve this.

As one of the great ideological legacies of the nineteenth century teetered and collapsed, moving us into the decade of the nineties and the ending of the cold war, it may be that there is more of a revelation here for feminism than we have cared to recognize. Properly observed, I suggest that the history of our politics in action can indeed function as a site of revelation for us — but only if we don't make the facile assumption that these will be affirmative in some uncritical way, or that women's stories will be neatly separable from those of men in the same culture. As Diana Fuss has usefully suggested:

While experience can never be a reliable guide to the real, this is not to preclude any role at all for experience.... If experience itself is a product of ideological practices, then perhaps it might function as a window onto the complicated workings of ideology.[1]

On the one hand, the collapse of the cold war showed up the total absurdity of its 'logic' which Greenham women had been trying to get across to the nation since the beginning of the peace camp. We (the West) had threatened Them (the Soviets) with annihilation because, officially, They would not be like us, accept our ways of thinking. Yet events now made it clear just how like us they really were all along, how ardently they were straining at the leash to be able to jump onto the consumer bandwagon. And perhaps that was the real problem all along — they threatened us not because they were radically different from us but because they were frighteningly similar; they wanted what we wanted.

But at another level, these events were not so reassuring for feminists. Perhaps it was not just historical accident that led to the crumbling of the Iron Curtain and the break-up of the peace camp to coincide. For both were societies (on a hugely different scale) that had opted for salvation through ideology — that characteristic myth of modernity which the twentieth-century vacuum of moral authority has given rise to. For when moral utterances merely mask somebody's preferences or bid for power, a widespread cynicism is generated and a deep-seated hunger for a new access to purity of purpose. This then is what ideology provides — the stains of cynicism and self-doubt are swept away, the enveloping fog of endless liberal guilt is cleared, the sun of a wonderfully simplifying truth shines on those ready to receive it. By means of ideology our innocence can be re-born, the pristine purity which we believe we had in childhood can miraculously be ours again.

In the groups, movements or societies that have made this option, the search for ideological purity becomes the distinctive form of politics. Thus, at Greenham in its later stages, the rule of radical separatism at the camps began to insist on a diet of only 'pure' foods, and on a politics and personal/sexual relations that eschewed all collaboration with men. Certainly not all women who participated in the camp subscribed wholeheartedly to the separatist philosophy, yet a good many accepted its more puritanical fiats literally for the sake of peace. Perhaps too, the insistence on the strict diet of purity in matters of food, sex and politics helped the women to cope psychologically with the appalling conditions of mud, damp, cold and squalor, as well as the perpetual vulnerability to invasion whether from the constant stream of well-wishing visitors or the hostile intrusions of the 'male' world of law and order — bailiffs, police, etc.

But whatever the cohesive potential of the politics of purity, there is a sort of fatal inevitability about their outcome. Sooner or later the language of treachery follows. In Communist societies it was the identification of 'class traitors' or the 'running dogs of the imperialists'. At Greenham there were those who were deemed to have sided with the rapists and racists. For ideology is an attempt to short-circuit the terrifying problems of the moral vacuum created by the Enlightenment. And in the end, its failure becomes apparent, leading to an even bleaker version of the same crisis. Vaclav Havel, perhaps the most perceptive and well-known critic of the distortions of ideology in its communist form, refers to the 'tragic story' of this sort of mental short circuit:

Why bother with never ending, genuinely hopeless search for truth when a truth can be had so readily, all at once, in the form of an ideology or a doctrine? Suddenly it is all so simple. Think of all the difficult questions which are answered in advance! Think of all the laborious existential tasks from which our minds are freed once and for all! The essence of this short-circuit is a fatal mistake: the tacit assumption that some ingenious, universally applicable artefact — and is a doctrine or an ideology ever anything more than a human artefact? — can lift from our shoulders the burden of the incessant, always unique, and essentially inalienable question and utterly transform man [*sic*] from a questioning being into an existing answer. This is the illusion that the demanding, unending, and unpredictable dialogue with conscience or with God can be replaced by the clarity of a pamphlet, that some artefact, like a set of pulleys freeing us from physical effort, can liberate us from the weight of personal responsibility and timeless sorrow.[2]

Thus, the ideological society with its roots in the myth of original innocence soon runs into trouble. On the basis of the 'original goodness' of their adherents, they have set aside the old structures of authority. Purity is deemed to have its own kind of authority, which gives it the power to stand in judgement on the old society operating under the normal auspices of institutionalized authority and power. Thus, purity is what the new movement seeks to preserve at all costs — because its purity *is* its power. Yet it is an endeavour by its very nature impossible to achieve — for purity of this nature cannot be preserved in the human community at large. And so purity has to be formalized, institutionalized, to be no longer the result of virtue or grace, but of reason/rationality — a rationale. The threats to internal purity which arise through conflict and fallibility in a normal human community have to be displaced on to outsiders — those terribly necessary outsiders. Whether by means of show trials or scapegoats, power has to dress itself in a cloak of radical purity. And as we know, who have witnessed the ignominious collapse of communism in our decade, the institutions constructed over a radical ideological purity have an inbuilt time-bomb.

Feminists may find it hard to see any mirror of themselves in the fate of communism. What were they but men with their hierarchies of power? But differences of scale and gender should not blind us to our similarity of cultural inheritance. We did not find an answer to what happens when there are differences of opinion between those who are radically pure, those who had believed themselves to be 'saved' by right thought, ideology. We who had affirmed the freedom of the individual woman, now discovered that this faith in the power of individual moral autonomy wasn't enough to save us from the threat of disintegration. We had developed no communal procedures for coping with the irruption of the mad and the bad in our midst, for we held loyally to the belief that all women were equal and did not presume to judge between one another. We had dispensed with authorities as being untrustworthy and patriarchal, and there was thus no one to whom we could turn to help us resolve our differences, and protect the space and the lifestyle lovingly created by many sincere and devoted women. Ideology in which we had put our faith had let us down. The purveyors of purity are the greatest con-merchants of all. For the possession of autonomy in the form we desire it is not compatible with a return to innocence.

It is curious and revealing that in our politics we 'play out', as it were, the flaws in our thinking. Though it may not have been apparent at the time, the outcome of Greenham could be seen as marking the collapse of the politics of radical separatism. If women passionately in pursuit of peace could end up behaving in a way remarkably similar (on a small scale) to the men who conducted the cold war, then the claim that women's culture and politics are fundamentally separate from men's begins to seem implausible. Could it be that men and women, formed in the same cultural tradition, are not as radically different as both sides like to think, but embarrassingly and frighteningly similar in certain respects?

Implied in the designation of movements of the radical left and of radical feminism is the claim that their analysis 'gets to the roots' of the problem. Thus, in feminism of this sort, the problem is seen as oppression by men, and so the further the separation from men and male institutions, the more pure and the more radical. Thus, post-Christian feminist theologians have tended to see themselves as more radical than those who remain within the Christian orbit, closer to the sources of pollution. But I suggest that the radical designation of this sort of feminism is a misnomer. It does not get to the root of the problem at all because its concern is with uprooting, separating from ancient roots now seen as a source of impurity. In the act of separation, it denies its own roots. And yet in that same act, its own roots are powerfully present but unrecognized. They may be present for example, in the adoption of the scientific paradigm that analyses, takes things apart, reduces reality to empirically examinable facts, and sets up a dualistic universe which fundamentally separates the knower from the known. These roots are present in a mind-set which scorns the old myths as the mystification of an illegitimate authority, but always fails to perceive the function of its own ideological myth that sustains its own power and machinations. As Havel observes:

When traditional myth was laid to rest, a kind of 'order' in the dark region of our being was buried along with it. And what modern reason has attempted to substitute for this order has consistently proved erroneous, false, and disastrous, because it is always in some way deceitful, artificial, rootless, lacking in both ontology and morality. It may even border on the ludicrous, like the cult of the 'Supreme Being' during the French Revolution, the collectivist folklore of totalitarian systems, or their 'realist', self-celebrating art. It seems to me that with the burial of myth, the barn in which the mysterious animals of the human unconscious were housed over thousands of years has been abandoned and the animals turned loose — on the tragically mistaken assumption that they were phantoms — and that now they are devastating the countryside.[3]

He goes on to suggest that these phantoms or demons make themselves at home in places where one least expects to find them — in the secretariats of modern political parties, where they are able to co-opt the tools and authority of modern reason — and thus their plunder is sanctioned by the most scientific of world views. Because the project of justifying morality failed, we are left with a deep sense of taint, and no means of ridding ourselves of our guilt. And so the nation state has arisen to justify the unjustifiable; the religion of war, whose idols are sited at places like Greenham, takes the place of the old gods, and blood sacrifice is once more the order of the day. And whereas the old myth demanded at most the sacrifice of animals, the new purity myths of ideology may demand human sacrifice in millions to ensure a happy future for all.

The demons simply do what they want while the gods take diffident refuge in the final asylum to which they have been driven, called 'human conscience'.[4]

Feminism of itself is perhaps unlikely to become the ideology of the state, and radical feminists may rejoice at this as being further proof of our inherent purity. Yet this fact should not blind us to our kinship in language and concept with ideologies of the left — and also of the right — which do not hesitate to assume the mantle of state power. Koonz' story of the Mothers in the Fatherland makes it clear that women are anything but immune to the allure of totalitarian rhetoric and millions saw fascism as home to their traditional concerns. We tend to assume that once a woman has undergone a feminist or radical conversion, she is proof against seduction by such distorted rhetoric. But the borders between opposing ideologies are rather easier to cross than we may have realized, since at one level their fundamental purpose is very similar. Thus, Rosie Boycott passed over from being the founder editor of *Spare Rib* to being editor of the men's magazine *Esquire* without too much apparent ideological pain;[5] and a recent television programme showed how a female Russian party apparatchik underwent only a short period of disorientation before going on to become an enthusiastic manager of the free enterprise economy.

Thus, as feminists, we need to consider whether the myth we have opted for is really more liberating than the one we have renounced. Those who are convinced by Hampson's story will have concluded with her that the Christian myth is backward and benighted, not suitable for modern minds like ours. But, I wonder, what do we really mean by this? Do we by any chance mean that it is written in a language we do not understand? The Jewish and Christian scriptures are in many ways like the past — another country, and they do things differently there. And we, as true daughters of the empire, have a way of expecting the natives of this country to speak English — at least when they are speaking to us, their master-mistresses. We then judge them on the inhibited and restricted communication they have with us, and remain ignorant and oblivious of the richly nuanced conversation that takes place among themselves. We meanwhile, in our knowledgeable superiority, have settled for a simplistic idea of the source of evil that gives us a sense of spiritual security, and a justification for our own particular being. But what it does not do is to warn us of the dangers of our situation. For wherever the scientific spirit and apparatus is combined with the passion for purity — whether it is racial or sexual, gender or ethnic purity — the smell of corpses is not far off. And when sweet modern reason, even sweet feminist reason, subjects God to a purification process, to purge the rottenness of former times, can we be sure that it is God we shall liberate — or the demons?

The ancient stories that we are willing to trash contain many narratives about the dangerous passion for purity, stories which both endorse this passion and ruthlessly deconstruct it. They are stories which also know of the existence of demons and do not underestimate them. But if we wish to understand fully the stories on which the Christian myth is based, we may have to undertake a longish period of residency among the scriptures, not as colonialists or missionaries but as guests. And in this capacity, we may have to undergo the slow, perhaps painful process of confronting our own ethnocentricity as we learn a new language, a language which, unlike ideology, cannot be instantly acquired but requires patience and a change in the ways of our knowing.

Notes

1   Diana Fuss, *Essentially Speaking: Feminism, Nature and Difference* (London: Routledge, 1990), p. 118.
2   Vaclav Havel, ed. Jan Vladislav, *Living in Truth* (London: Faber and Faber, 1986), p. 174.
3   Havel, pp.160–1.
4   Havel, p. 161.
5   See Ian Katz, 'Rosie's crown of thorns', *Guardian*, 24 Feb. 1992.

10 The fallacy of walking out as a model for theological courage

The widespread diffusion of the modernist myth, and its characteristic ideological features and effects, suggested to me that it is something transmitted to us not so much by the conscious option of belief but through the unconscious inheritance of the structures of language. There is a sense in which our language is the genes of culture. Depending on the soil of the particular sub-culture, the myth can take either a crude or a highly sophisticated form. It can inform not only our political preoccupations but also our theological and spiritual quest.

Characteristic of the cultural genes that feminist theologians inherit is a particular concept of the self that is fundamentally a product of the Enlightenment. As Fergus Kerr says in his book, *Theology after Wittgenstein:*

> With the age-long emphasis on rational and autonomous consciousness, the metaphysical tradition entrenches the myth that there has to be an element of reflection or deliberation in every respectable human action. Otherwise actions fail to be intelligent or free — and the people in whose daily lives reflection or deliberation seldom occur drop into the margins of history.[1]

According to this model, the self must be constituted by a 'right consciousness' — hence one can see how this privileges the recourse to ideology, the effects of which we examined in the previous chapter. Feminist social criticism and feminist theology have concerned themselves in many ways with women — seen as those who have 'dropped into the margins of history'. Yet, ironically, this rescue from oblivion has been undertaken on the basis of the doctrine that truly human behaviour depends on reflective consciousness. Thus, typical of the 'mission' of the Women's Liberation Movement in the seventies and eighties was, as we saw, the spread of the 'consciousness-raising' groups. The rationale of these groups was to pass on to women a thorough-going critique of their role and position in patriarchal society. Yet, retrospectively I am beginning to see them in a different light. Could it be that they were the means that Western educated women, such as we were, devised to ensure that they fully appropriated the basic doctrines of their Enlightenment heritage — notably the Western doctrine of the self with its rational and autonomous consciousness? To appropriate these doctrines was in a sense to penetrate to the inner mysteries of Enlightenment culture. By this means, educated women became fully initiated — but lacked only the recognition of their new status by their male counterparts.

The concerns that have occupied many feminist theologians reveal how firmly they stand in this particular tradition of the theological self, in which the mind is seen to be radically private and inaccessible, steeped in what Kerr calls 'epistemological solitude'[2] and beset by a yearning for total intimacy. This yearning for intimacy was evident in the inspirational ideal of sisterhood, as it was also in the nostalgia for spiritual purity, that featured so strongly in the feminism of this period. It was fundamental to the whole enterprise at Greenham — and to much of the feminist theological project, based as it has been on the modern Western notion of the self. According to Kerr interpreting Wittgenstein, this notion is part of the metaphysical tradition which disavows 'the mundane world of conversation and collaboration in which human life consists'.[3] He shows how we are wedded to the idea that the primary act of meaning is representing — conceptualizing — but this depends on the nature of activity within which the connection between words and their referents is established in the first place.

In the particular feminist version of this tradition which I have been exploring, it took the form of a belief in the primacy of private, subjective female experience, which was set against objective measurable male thought. Thus women's 'subjective' experience was deemed to be in touch with reality and therefore really 'objective', i.e. true; whereas 'objective' abstract male thinking was shown to be based on male prejudice and self-interest and therefore to be 'subjective', i.e. untrue. A neat reversal. But there was a snag. Feminism was committed to the liberation of women's creativity, the breaking of the rigid moulds that society makes for women. So why was it that so much of feminist writing and activity based on these assumptions followed such a very predictable stereotype? Could it be that the original presupposition about language was false — that language does not mysteriously bubble up from some pure and private place in the soul, but is acquired out there in the bustle and bodily contact of daily life? If this is true then it also followed that however 'high' our consciousness was raised (in terms of comprehensive abstractions) it was bound to be, at another level, a warmed-up version of the same old cultural stuff. Newness, it seems, has to wrestled out of the bad old, mucky, messy world that is not just male but common to humans.

Thus, while being sceptical and critical about large sections of the superstructure we have inherited, as feminists doing theology we often took on board without question this transcendent self of Western tradition, which is in many ways its taproot. And so, unwittingly, we reinstated the dualism that we criticized so fiercely in the first place. As Ruether observes in a recent paper, the tendency in recent feminist theology has been to develop a 'reversed dualistic ideology' whereby 'those regarded as "oppressed" and the "victims" become paradigms of indefectable nobility and goodness, while those with historical power are capable only of vicious meanness'.[4]

Thus, theology, whether feminist or otherwise, that is done on the basis of the transcendent self is inherently idealist. It posits an ideal self — which in the nature of things is unobtainable. Thus, feminism had produced the new ideal of the peaceable, non-violent, sisterly woman. And when she failed to live up to this ideal she became a prey to guilt exactly as she was under the old ideals of femininity. Feminist theology had diagnosed women's problem not, as the old teaching would have it, in the temptation to prideful self-assertion, but rather to a deep lack of self worth. Yet ironically the remedy it proposed became in its turn the problem. It made pride of self into a goal, and the inevitable concomitant was guilt. The threat of chronic guilt and self-dissatisfaction generates in the individual the need to project these distressing emotions on to one who can take them away from the self, i.e. the scapegoat.

Hampson boldly sets herself the task of reconceptualizing God from a feminist point of view, and on the basis of her own experience. But as Iain Torrance concludes in his article on her book:

One can only meaningfully refer to God on the basis of one's private experience if one presupposes the grammar (rules of use) of the name 'God' [referring to Wittgenstein's *Philosophical Investigations*]. And grammar is in the public domain. What I am saying is that I find it hard to see how Hampson's reconceptualizing of God on the basis of her own experience makes sense. To do theology, it seems that one needs a community.[5]

And this identifies part of the problem for post-Christian thought. Post-Christians, like all good post-Enlightenment people, pursue autonomy — the self as law, a law unto oneself. Yet what is a law that binds only oneself? A law implies that which binds us in common, into a community in which there are structures of authority, even if they are only grammar rules. In fact, Hampson's thinking is bound by the language and thought forms she uses. In speaking of God, she makes light of the context within which the connection between the word and its referent was established — a context which for her, as for almost all feminist theologians, has been in the dominant Western Christian theological tradition. Thus her concepts are not simply rooted in some

alternative private female experience — they already exist i̇
domain of existing theological language. Neither female experie.
the Western scientific paradigm is or can be such a pure sour̄
language to re-conceive the divine. What happens then, is that s.
detaches herself from one part of her Western cultural inheritance in
order to critique it; but in order to do so she stands within the structures
of another aspect of that inheritance, without subjecting it to the same
critical scrutiny. To do so would be to uncover the unpalatable truth that
there is in fact no moral high ground for us to stand on.

Theologians, whether feminist or not, intend that their pronounce-
ments should be authoritative, carry moral weight in a community of
souls who confirm their insights. Both Christian and post-Christian
theologians seek to achieve a certain purity of purpose and authority in
the work they do. But this search for authoritative utterance, among
feminists, has sometimes run into trouble because of our fear of owning
it for what it is. Our doctrines and teachings have been concealed —
even from ourselves, because of the fear of the critical, ridiculing,
exploitative male gaze, or the fear that both male and female Christians
will refuse to accept that discussing doctrines of God is a woman's
proper business. Whatever the understandable reasons for this deep-
rooted desire for concealment, we need to acknowledge that we have in
fact accepted and adapted certain doctrines (that is, authoritative teachings) about what we believe to be true. And the reluctance of some
feminist theologians to acknowledge the existence of these doctrines or
to own their connection with existing structures of thought has had the
effect of confirming the exclusion of women from theological conversation that hitherto has been imposed.

This is one reason, I think, that it is necessary to look again at the
model of theological courage that is implied in the work of feminist
theologians like Daly and Hampson. This is the model of walking out of
the church in judgement and high dudgeon. It may seem a very appealing and logical response to the hurt of exclusion but ultimately I suggest
it is in danger of leading us up a theological and spiritual cul-de-sac — a
danger of being stranded on a rock of moral high ground as the tide
goes out. It is as if we were to look in the mirror and, appalled by what
we see, walk out in protest. For that which we, as women, see in the
church is not so neatly separable from what we ourselves are. The
church has been concerned to preserve her purity and to speak authori-
tatively. So have we. The church has, on the whole, been ruled by men
usually claiming divine legitimation — we have also been so ruled. The
church has, at various times in her history, tried to throw off the rule of
men and be ruled instead by the law of the Spirit — so have we. The
church has often failed to preserve her much vaunted purity, and has
submitted to grave political and moral compromise (as for example in

the Third Reich). The same could be said about women. The church has at various times in its history both resented and envied the power of its priesthood and clung to its protection. Our relations with men have been similar. The church has upheld an ideal of unity, yet been continually subject to splits, fissures and strife of all kinds in the course of her history. Our politics betray the same pattern. It may seem strange that women's history and politics are so like that of the church. But the reason we are like the church is because we are the church. And the spectacle of women walking out of 'men's church' is both absurd and tragic, because it means that far from being ultimately liberated they are the ones who have been ultimately conned by men into accepting that the church belongs to men.

By seeking to remove the feminist project from corrupting contact and limitation of the 'male' church, we were in fact playing right into the hands of men — those men, that is, for whom our departure comes as a great relief. They are delighted to see the back of the trouble-makers — foolish and misguided women, people with a chip on their shoulder; delighted that they plan to hold their meetings elsewhere — not in our church; so we don't need to worry what goes on there any more — just the usual women's talk...

And so, with this strategy, it's business as usual — and no pressure on men to clean up their act. Women have kindly removed themselves from the scene and let men get on with it. By stalling and prevaricating and outright obstruction where possible these men (and the women who loyally support them) were able to persuade many feminists that they had no inheritance in the ministry of the church — or at least not one that is worth waiting around for or trying to claim.

When Daly made her grand gesture of walking out of the church and declaring herself 'post-christian' she took out a patent on the designation 'radical feminist'. And since then, a steady stream of feminists have been trooping out after her as a means of displaying their radical credentials, and looking with scorn on those who try to remain within the tainted patriarchal church. But perhaps the time has come to question this claim to radicalism — to suggest that her famous gesture of walking out might just be a little old hat — decidedly old hat, in fact. For members of the Western intelligentsia have been doing it for centuries — since the seventeenth, to be precise. And in Western Europe large sections of the population have walked out of the church ages ago and have been existing in a largely post-Christian society ever since. Daly, who lives in a rather more church-going type of society than we do, might not have noticed these things. She rests her claim to radicalism on the fact that she acknowledges no roots, no origins in anything that would connect her to male values — for she has been born again in her head. Yet as her critics have observed, the origins of her thought are not thereby invisible to those who look on — a case of the Empress' invisible nudity (the Emperor's new clothes in reverse so to speak). Her thought betrays the indelible marks of its origins in the concept of liberty that was current on the American frontier. The liberty of the individual as a law unto herself — the values of the Wild West transposed into a female key. Such a concept of liberty has plenty of roots — roots in the slave-owning society where the master was free to impose his arbitrary will on the slave — and the mistress likewise, either through him or on her own account. It has roots in the nineteenth-century idea of the survival of the fittest, a kind of racial biology that has borne such accursed fruit in the holocausts of the twentieth century. There is nothing particularly radical or pure about these roots — they are as tainted as anything we might find in the church.

A feminist theology which insists on pursuing the defence of female purity, albeit in ideological form, is, I suggest, unable to break out of its nineteenth-century childhood. It is a childhood that is also re-enacted in the romanticism about nature, especially female nature, and in the lingering attachment to the idea of progress. These romantic tendencies in feminism have recently been critiqued within the movement itself[6] as well as in Thistlethwaite's work. Thus, the task that confronts us now if we wish to come of age theologically is to face up to our theological origins. Yet this exercise of self-knowledge may be more painful and difficult than we have hitherto allowed for. We are likely to encounter resistance — resistance to the idea that at least some of the ancestors of feminist theology are to be found in the narrow souls of our Puritan forebears, with their compromising collusion with the brutal rule of the frontiersmen. The pilgrim fathers and mothers set out on the *Mayflower* in much righteous indignation to found a new world where God could be worshipped in freedom and sober truth. Yet in that new world, purged and separate from the reach of the ancient and false privilege of unholy powers, the worm once more appeared in the communities that budded from the *Mayflower*, and blossomed in the cruel flowers of genocidal violence of the frontier.

Our own brave new world in feminist theology has been marked by similarly unspeakable connections with our origins; for us too there has been a maggot in the apple. For the knowing of our true origins is, I think, a kind of knowledge that is hardly achieved — in both senses. As enlightened parents, we tend to think these days that our children would prefer to get the facts of life straight out, and not be messed about with silly stories of storks and gooseberry bushes. But latterly I have begun to suspect from observing children that the prevalence of such myths in times past was not just the result of embarrassed parents but also of children's own need not to know too much too soon of how they came to be around.

Officially, as feminists we are enthusiastic about self-knowledge. Hampson recommends Schopenhauer's injunction to self-knowledge as one of the few values to be recycled from the patriarchal rubbish heap. But in practice, we are likely to meet with resistance, not only to what may emerge from the cave of our own personal unconscious but also from the dark recesses of our racial and cultural history that has been passed through the genes of language. It was the explicit aim of the CR groups to raise our consciousness to new heights; yet in reality it was their function to permit a greater degree of unconsciousness about all that in our cultural body with which we shared a history but which did not form part of our ideal. The new consciousness denied this bodiliness and enabled us to float free from the pain of these connections and walk out proudly from the compromised church.

And here we encounter the crux of the theological error that we are in danger of perpetuating. We have believed that beautiful flowers grow out of pure elements. In fact, as the lotus reminds us, their roots go down into every sort of impurity and rottenness. Thus our theological quest must proceed not by means of separation, of walking out on ourselves, but rather by staying on and going deeper. For we are also descendants of those who never made it to the shores of the 'new' world, but were nourished even as they were compromised by the rich compost of the rotten old world that the pilgrims left behind.

Walking out is apt to be the strategy of angry adolescents, arrogantly ignorant as they seek to resist the knowledge that they too were conceived and born in sin and suffering; not sin and suffering as some grandiose theological hypothesis but as a mundane reality inscribed in the lineaments of our history both personal, cultural and sub-cultural, and transmitted through the genes of language and education. Walking out on all this is not an act of courage, a radical departure. It is a refusal to face the facts of our cultural and theological life. We cannot get to the root of these facts without discovering how we are implicated in them. To attempt to separate ourselves from these origins is to lock the error and the pain into place and to ensure that sooner or later it will be repeated in history. As the Buddhist teacher and poet Thich Nhat Hanh says: 'If we do not liberate our ancestors, we will be in bondage all our lives, and we will transmit that to our children and grandchildren.'[7] And as Saul Alinsky used to say, quoting the French philosopher, Jacques Maritain: 'The fear of soiling ourselves by entering the context of history is not virtue but a way of escaping virtue.'[8]

Thus I think we must question the claim of the post-Christian feminists to a teaching that is uniquely modern, radical and unmythical (i.e. true) compared with the hoary old sexist myth (untruth) of Christianity. They pride themselves on a modern universalism, compared with the dated particularity and obvious irrelevance of the Christian tale to modern woman. Yet the 'relevance' of post-Christian feminism is largely contained in its ability to disguise from its adherents the ethnocentrism and class confinement which it shares with its liberal parents. As for its uniqueness, it is indeed unique, in the sense of having a precise historical form and particular cultural determinants; but *not* unique in the sense that it has common features with all the Western myths of modernity, and common features with all myths ancient and modern that dispatch the demons from the living room. Like all myths, it indulges our willing ignorance and permits us not to know that which we do not wish to know about ourselves. A genuine theological radicalism is that which can enable us to penetrate the snare of myths that lure us to a false consciousness of self with their ideals of womanhood. And theological courage may be that which enables us to discover that the root from which we are ultimately derived has a far greater richness than we have imagined with our moralistic version of the spare rib story.

Notes

1   Fergus Kerr, *Theology after Wittgenstein* (Oxford: Blackwell, 1986), p. 115.
2   A phrase coined by J. M. Cameron — see Kerr, p. 44.
3   Kerr, p. 140.
4   Rosemary Radford Ruether, 'Dualism and the nature of evil in feminist theology.' Address given to the Annual Conference of the Society for the Study of Christian Ethics, Oxford, September 1991, p.14.
5   Iain Torrance, 'Is Christianity irredeemably sexist? A response to Daphne Hampson', in Richard Holloway (ed.) *Who Needs Feminism?: Men Respond to Sexism in the Church* (London: SPCK, 1991), p. 84.
6   See Sandra Schneiders, *Beyond Patching: Faith and Feminism in the Catholic Church* (Mahwah, NJ: Paulist Press, 1991).
7   Thich Nhat Hanh, *Touching Peace: Practising the Art of Mindful Living* (California: Parallax Press, 1992), p. 36.
8   Quoted in Kenneth Leech, *The Eye of the Storm: Spiritual Resources for the Pursuit of Justice* (London: Darton, Longman and Todd, 1992), p. 180.

11 The trial of faith at the court of tradition

Of course, many women who have not followed my own sort of tortuous peregrinations on these matters have probably reached similar conclusions rather more economically. There are signs that the gesture of walking out of the church in judgement is being superseded as a useful paradigm for feminists. As the first women are ordained in the Church of England in the UK, the symbol of ministry within the church begins to have new possibilities and a new appeal. If walking out is not, after all, the passport to radicalism and purity, what is there to be gained by staying on? Might it be that by some strange means, the real access to the spiritual treasure we desire is hidden, here in the heart of the citadel of reactionary sexism?

If walking out has proved an unviable solution in the long run, this does not mean that the problems of women's life within the church have been solved. All the problems that were identified in the early days of feminist theology are still around. And nowadays, they are even visible to bishops (at least in a few select cases). As Richard Holloway says, in the introduction to *Who Needs Feminism?: Men Respond to Sexism in the Church*,

Behind the vacillations and timidity of Christian bodies as they respond to the challenge of the women's movement there lies a deep faithlessness that is rooted in a peculiarly male type of insecurity that has to keep things neat and tidy and nailed down, with everything in its place, especially women.[1]

As Richard Holloway speaks about the 'faithlessness' of the men who are so desperate to keep women out of celebrating the mysteries, there is something here that should make us pause. If 'faithlessness' on the part of men is at the root of the problem, could it be that faith is what is required for the job of staying in the church whether as priestly minister or not? The question of faith might just be a problem for feminist women as well as for sexist men.

Faith is a rather less talked about concept in the women's movement
these days, whereas the concept of spirituality is booming. This may be
because faith is seen as a rather dubious thing — you don't know exactly
what you're getting. Whereas with spirituality you do know what's on
offer and there's something for every taste and type — feminist spirituality, gay spirituality, Christian feminist spirituality, New Age spirituality. You can have off-the-peg or designer spirituality — you get what you
pay for of course; and the beauty of it is you can always discard a particular spirituality when it no longer suits you. Whereas with faith — well,
there's always the danger that you'll get more than you bargained for —
or possibly a lot less. And the worry is that in the end you'll find you've
signed away your liberty to an old celestial autocrat who doesn't even
realize that you've got an individual right to life, liberty and the pursuit
of happiness...

So the question is, if we are not simply to take the timid men's word
for it, how do we find out what faith implies? Well, you might say the
safest place for a feminist to explore the concept of faith is in the work of
feminist theologians. This I have endeavoured to do. But I have to
confess that, although in the process I have learned a lot and gained
much to stimulate and edify me, yet, in the end I have come away with a
sense of spiritual undernourishment. And I fear that if I had to subsist
on a diet consisting purely of feminist theology, I should be close to spiritual starvation by now. The reason for this has been summed up rather
well by Hampson, who says: 'What seems to have replaced talk of God
is largely talk of women's experience. It is not even women's experience
of God: it is simply women's experience.'[2] In this matter I think she is
entirely correct, and it helps to explain my spiritually hungry condition
— the fact that in all my feminist theological explorations I don't seem to
have come much further in understanding what faith is all about.

This has brought me to the conclusion that what I am missing is a
feminist theology that takes as its subject women's experience of God. If
we were to define our quest thus, I ask myself, what would follow? I
realize that one consequence might be that suddenly, from being rich
women, with our exclusive possession of new and hitherto unrealized
feminist perspectives on God, we might suddenly become poor women,
who live and are shaped by an age of great spiritual poverty, raised in
the great spiritual slums of the twentieth century. It seems not impossible to me that women whose experience of God was rich and vivid lived
in a different age to ours — or lived in another culture. But one might
argue that this is exactly what feminist theology has been about —
reclaiming women's religious experience from the past. Officially yes,
that is what we have been about. But what I have noticed is that where
women of the past have articulated their experience of God, we haven't
given too much attention to what they actually said; or what we have

received of their thought has been a selection of 'bites' which are suited to our taste and preconceptions. This has enabled us not to notice that what they are saying about their experience of God is in some cases wildly at variance with the claims that we are making about God. Could it be that we are not so much 'reclaiming' the religious experience of women from other ages as colonizing it — in a way that the universaliz- ing language that we inherit is so well able to do? We have not, it seems, been willing to let their experience teach or shape or puzzle or question us. It's not so much dialogue with them we seek as confirmation of our pre-conceptions. As Donna Haraway has said: 'The feminist dream of a common language, like all dreams for a perfectly faithful naming of experience is a totalising and imperialist one.'[3]

Much of our 'identification' with women's experience from the pre- modern period is, as Hampson has observed, thoroughly bogus. And she thinks that because it is so alien we should admit that it is largely irrelevant to us. But I think that, on the contrary, precisely because it is so alien to us, it is profoundly necessary for us, because it presents us with the challenge we need to re-found our theological thinking. We have been in the habit of marching in with truth on the banner and demand- ing to set free all those prisoners of the past who are held in chains by the patriarchal heresy. We couldn't wait to break the good news to them that God has now been decently re-clothed in something less offensive to female sensibilities. God is not now totally Other and unknowable, but has become for us a warm, woman-friendly being, personal, com- munal, and 'ecologically dynamic towards transcendence over alien- ation, injustice etc.'.[4] Three cheers for God! And if God has been revealed in Jesus Christ, we have to understand that Christ is now to be under- stood as 'the communal symbol for the messianic, pneumatic activity of groups struggling for liberation'.[5] And as for the Resurrection and the Last Judgement, well that's all a bit passé, definitely not in line with God's new image.

At this point it might be worth stopping to consider: how would our spiritual sisters in the past react if they were able to respond to this good news of ours? What would Teresa or Julian, Hildegard or Catherine have to say when we brought the God of the twentieth-century feminist theology to their door? Would they welcome the news with open arms and say, yes, this was the good news we were waiting for but never received in our benighted times? Or would they pale, and turn away in horror and incomprehension, being unable to recognize the designer- God we proclaim as we weave our web of wonderful abstractions? Would they see it as having any relation to the God they knew as the object of their faith? Or would there be no common ground on which to start a dialogue of faith with their post-Enlightenment sisters? And if they attempted to speak to us of the God they knew, a God of revelation who demands absolute surrender of our will and autonomy, would we wince and also turn away in disillusion, thinking: what can you expect from those who still use the old language about Him, who are still trapped in the structures of unfreedom?

And so it seems we can safely greet our spiritual foresisters from a distance — but, as in the case of our Third World sisters too, it is better not to get too close lest we expose ourselves to the cultural shock of realizing just how utterly alien they are to our mode of thinking. This is true, of course, not just for feminist theology but for a good many varieties of modern theology, not only those claiming to be radical but also those which believe themselves to be 'preserving' the truth from the past and protecting it from the radicals.

Perhaps it is only those of us who are driven by spiritual undernourishment who will want to proceed with this risky enterprise. On the other hand, if feminists are going to concern themselves with the function of teaching what is true about God, it seems desirable that they be willing to consider the testimony of female (and male) witnesses in other ages who spoke a very different language from our own. Yet as soon as we take this on board, it becomes clear that we have begun to tangle once again with that hornet's nest — the problem of authority. How shall we decide who is right in their speaking of God — them or us? And how will the decision be reached?

This, it seems to me, is the context in which a re-evaluation of tradition is essential. Feminists in the early days at any rate were wary of tradition, and post-Christians in particular treated the whole concept with profound suspicion. But this rejection of tradition is full of irony. For as we womanfully and scornfully separated ourselves from patriarchal religious tradition, we somehow failed to notice that we had delivered ourselves gagged and bound into the arms of the Enlightenment traditions — as if these were somehow cleaner and more woman-friendly than the ones we had abandoned. As we walked blinking and dazzled out of the darkness of the patriarchal church, we stumbled into the arms of the consumer society, which was only too happy to receive us, to greedily suck out our souls. And because we had not learned to listen seriously to our foresisters in the faith, we could not have been aware of their warning — that this bold action (as we saw it then) of walking out of the church in judgement was one of the greatest spiritual danger to ourselves, one that could literally blind us and prevent any further development on the spiritual path. I suspect that they would have been amazed at our belief that women, subject as they are to a lack of self-worth, are incapable of the sin of pride; amazed that we could have fallen for such matronizing claptrap.

The fact that we found it fashionable to kick away the traditions that have formed and shaped us may be part of that particular

Enlightenment dream that we have not yet awoken from. By the very act of proclaiming ourselves independent of tradition, we identified ourselves immediately in the specific tradition that has made us what we are! The problem is the image we have had of tradition — inherited no doubt from the timid and faithless men — of some great grid that will force us all into the same shape. Unwittingly we have bought their version of it. But tradition does not have to be a stifling authoritarianism. To believe this is to allow the timid men to con us out of our inheritance. For tradition is the preservation of arguments about what is true, and to some extent the passing of time makes it easier to see which side has found greater acceptance with the community — the jury of time. It is the continuation of this same enquiry, together with evidence from our own times, that makes us members of the particular community of truth-seeking. As the feminist enquiry mounts up its own arguments and counter-arguments over time, we may be better able to appreciate this than in the iconoclastic days of our beginning.

Tradition can be compared to a court in permanent session. We cannot simply assume that the most modern evidence is conclusive — and that all witnesses from the past should be discredited because they didn't have the latest scientific or empirical evidence that is available to us. As we have seen, the scientific and empiricist paradigms have their own etiology, with roots in a past which we do not wish to own uncritically. Yet, that past is responsible for the type of evidence selected — it too is partial and limited, as partial and limited as the evidence of the witnesses from the past whose testimony we have either cavalierly rejected, or cleverly pre-selected.

Thus, if the 'whole' truth is to be found in any age, it may require that we continually take the evidence from witnesses from the past and compare it with the evidence from witnesses from the present in order to arrive at a true verdict — that is, as true as we can manage given the limitations of historical being. Such a method requires patience and painstaking application to the past. Its results are not instantaneous and clear cut like the results of ideology. Ideology also subjects the evidence of past and present to examination in the nature of a trial; but this trial is a sort of show trial — its verdict is always a foregone conclusion. Its truth is not so much whole — can there be a 'whole' truth? — as total. This totalizing truth of ideology has a seductive allure with its specious promise to us of the conviction of innocence.

If as I suggest it is time for feminist thought to come of age, it must be time that we extricate ourselves from the love affair with the image of our innocence. We may have to acknowledge that traditional 'loss of innocence' involved when children find out the facts of life. The facts about the origins and destiny of human life are often deeply disturbing and unpalatable to them because they are not abstract facts but ones which touch them personally, intimately. They have to take on board this new self-knowledge — that they are the result of the sexual congress of their parents, and that the destiny of those same parents, as well as themselves in due course, will be death — the cessation of bodily natural life.

There is I think a similar process at work in the spiritual journey, similar deep resistances to be encountered as we acquire self-knowledge that is a threat to the self — as we discover that the discourse of faith is a decomposing one. To follow deeply the connections and contradictions of our own thinking takes us not only back to our sexual and cultural origins, but also forward to the destiny implied by our mortal nature. In their celebration of embodiment, feminists have had much to say about sexuality — but less about its twin sister mortality. Indeed, a good many of us would not be aware of any obvious or immediate connection. But the Judeo-Christian tradition through which we have been formed has always posited a connection between the two. And if we are going to try making use of tradition in the manner I have suggested, then this might be a useful place to begin.

Notes

1   Richard Holloway (ed.), *Who Needs Feminism?: Men Respond to Sexism in the Church* (London: SPCK, 1991), p. 10.
2   Daphne Hampson, *Theology and Feminism* (Oxford: Blackwell, 1990), p. 170.
3   Donna Haraway, 'A manifesto for Cyborgs: science, technology and socialist feminism in the 1980s', *Socialist Review*, vol. 80 (1985), p. 92.
4   Julia Marina Hopkins, 'The understanding of history in English speaking Western Christian feminist theology', Doctoral thesis no. A2724, Bristol University Library (1988), p. 271.
5   Hopkins, p. 273.

12 *Sex and mortality*

In 1988, as the forces of disintegration were gathering at Greenham, I found myself being dragged away from the perimeter fence — not by police this time but by the advent of an unplanned pregnancy. With a new baby and a re-constituted family I was washed up for a while on the shores of Ireland, and removed from any immediate involvement in feminist politics in Britain. Before this sudden re-routing of my life, I had planned to commit to paper some of my reflections and doubts about feminist theology which I have charted in the foregoing chapters. My new circumstances were far from ideal for embarking on such an endeavour. But ironically, from another point of view they were rather well suited for taking the project further. My poor state of health after childbirth, together with those intimations of mortality that are a feature of life after the age of forty, combined to produce a new basis for my thinking on the subject of embodiment.

When I returned to England, the political scene had shifted quite significantly. With the ending of the cold war the nuclear threat had abated somewhat in popular perception. But the other part of the message from Greenham, that our environment is fatally threatened, was beginning to be quite widely received. A large number of people in the Western world, outside the immediate borders of feminism, were more ready to believe that the earth has been fearfully abused, that technology has become a Frankenstein monster out of our control, and that if we are not careful we shall destroy our inheritance in the natural world and the very processes of generation which sustain the whole future of the human race.

The fierce puritanism of the radical feminist position, whose contradictions had emerged at Greenham, was giving way to a new more inclusive ecofeminism that laid less stress on the need for separatist purity, but still relied on the common identification of women with nature to justify the special contribution of feminism to the new approach. Many of the goals and assumptions of eighties feminism were taken on board in the new movements of creation spirituality, such as that propounded by Matthew Fox. Fox more or less accepted the critique of much radical feminist writing that traditional Christianity was irredeemably sexist. The answer for him was to propound a re-vamped version of it, in which the old symbols were taken over and given a new interpretation in line with his doctrine of creation spirituality.[1] Certain parts of religious tradition — for example the mystical writers like Hildegard, Julian and others — were reclaimed because they were seen to affirm the holiness of all creation and thus confirm the insights of the 'innocent' native cultures on these matters. But the kind of theology that was unreservedly rejected was that associated with Augustine, the 'Fall and Redemption' model of theology, in which (according to Fox) it is taught that humans are born fallen and corrupt into a world that is fallen and corrupt, and the only hope for salvation is in the life hereafter. This was now regarded as the invention of a dualistic and patriarchal society, which keeps us all in check by its emphasis on guilt, asceticism, duty, control, and denial of the body.

Augustine's doctrine of Original Sin was now seen as the headwater of all the anxiety, shame, guilt and moral confusion we have about sex. If it wasn't for this unfortunate legacy, people would be able to be natural and loving in their sexual relations, their erotic passions would fuel a great and generous passion for life and justice which would lead to the overthrow of the death-bearing repressions of our civilization. Without this unnecessary guilt and shame to torture and distort them, they would be able to appreciate and respond to all the beauties of creation, and would naturally begin to care for and preserve our threatened planet. For sex as it should be is the image and symbol of natural bodily love between people, non-violent, expressive and not repressive, fruitful and generative, a holy force in fact, symbol of God's good creation and original blessing.

Many feminist and non-feminist women responded to Fox's gospel or some version of it. The new feminist spirituality championed the ethics of ecstasy and mutual non-competitive relationships. Augustinian theology was seen as responsible for the legitimation of the physical and sexual abuse of women. According to Mary Ann Rossi:

Augustine locates the source of original sin in the male erection and women are the cause of it. The depersonalization of women into whore, wife or mother can be traced to his writings.[2]

The task was now to subvert his pernicious influence on our erotic lives and our relation to nature. Thus Melissa Raphael in her article 'A feminist spirituality of gardening'[3] offers her version of the challenge to the patriarchal myth that the primal paradise of Eden was forfeited by women's sinfulness. Her vision of woman as a spiritually expressive gardener presents her as eating the secret knowledge of the tree of life, cheerfully indifferent to divine judgement. She also refers us to Phyllis Trible's exegesis of the Song of Songs according to which human sexuality is imaged as a fragrant garden and the actual garden is the setting for sexual joy.[4] The garden of this text, according to Trible, subverts the myth of the Fall by celebrating labour as a function of the erotic. The pain of work is transformed by woman into the pleasures of unalienated sexuality. The flaming sword is not to keep women and men from the tree of life but to discourage those who would control and exploit. The cherubim are there to welcome lovers to romp and roam in the pleasures of eroticism.

As I read some of the texts of ecofeminist and creation spirituality, I realized that despite their distinctive novelty there was a slight sense of *déjà vu*. I seemed to recognize what I will call the Californian gospel of Good Sex, a philosophy that had been popping up in one form or another ever since the 1960s and probably before that — but that's when I first came across it. It is, you might say, the quintessentially American exegesis of Freud. It is the idea that sex is a thoroughly natural activity which is, or should be, guilt-free. The presence of guilt or hang-ups spoils sex, and should be got rid of by various means which range from primal screams to mysticism, according to fashion. Since sex is a natural, pleasurable and some say God-given activity, it is primarily pleasure that needs to be the criterion about what is good. And guilt is a notorious pleasure-spoiler.

Since the discovery that Augustine was responsible for the doctrine that all evil is passed on in the human race by sexual transmission, people have found a theological topic that excites their wrath, and allows them to vent a torrent of righteous indignation. Here at last is the culprit — the one who can be blamed for all those nagging guilts and moral worries and confusions that sometimes persist despite all our earnest efforts to be rid of them. So the Californian gurus and their world-wide groupies, who are passionately convinced that people — like breakfast cereals — are just stuffed with natural goodness, are now (metaphorically speaking) digging up the bones of Augustine and anathematizing him for his heresy of Original Sin.

However, it might be as well for feminists to pause at this point and recall that there were a few problems with some of the earlier versions of this gospel. Women in the sixties, as we recalled previously, were rather disillusioned to find that men were perversely unaware of Nature's blueprint for loving relations between the sexes. Despite the sexual revolution, it seemed, things hadn't changed much and women were still expected to be available for sexual servicing and making tea. It was partly out of this disappointing experience of the sexual revolution that new-wave feminism came into being. But the new wave had themselves been weaned on this gospel and were unwilling to give up on the blueprint entirely (such is often the way with revolutions). So they adjusted it instead to produce the radical feminist version of sexual paradise. Here hopes for liberated and 'natural' sexual relations were transferred to same-sex love — a garden from which men must be excluded because they were the violent and violating sex. Maleness was present in the serpent who seduced women into heterosexual slavery. And it was men and not women who were responsible for the Fall. The fallen world is the patriarchal world, where women are held in check by the threat of rape.

According to this doctrine, women, though marginalized and silenced by patriarchal culture, have an alternative available to them. Unlike men they retain a capacity for Edenic harmony with Nature, and they have access through their experience to a world of 'natural wisdom'. Salvation for women involves making connection with this world by means of empathy with nature and right relation with other women, including right sexual relation. Thus, lesbian sexual love became the orthodox form for radical feminists. In the works of Susan Griffin, such as *Pornography and Silence*,[5] we find that the male, obsessed by the natural world that he has forfeited, continually seeks to bind up, abuse and torture the body of woman in pornographic image and practice because it reminds him of his own body, whose weakness and vulnerability he can never truly accept because it threatens his masculinity.

The radical feminist solution to sin then was to exclude men from the garden altogether. But the trouble at Greenham — and similar strife in other women-only settings — began to sow the seeds of doubt about the reliability of this solution. And perhaps there were a few traitors around — sisters who secretly found it a bit dull in the garden without Man. Whatever the cause, there are signs that ecofeminist spirituality is willing to re-admit him — on condition that he curses Augustine and renounces the baleful theology of Fall and Redemption.

Griffin contested the gospel of the sexual libertarians, and unmasked the pornographic pursuits of men as a form of slavery not of liberation, in which men are the enslavers and women the enslaved. But as women with newly-achieved social and economic power begin to demand a pornography of their own as the 'last step in emancipation'[6] this latest development seems to raise questions which Griffin did not ask. For example, is it the case that female nature, unlike male nature, is not tormented by the dualisms of our inheritance? As we saw, in the history of the American frontier, it was black women not white women who primarily stood in for 'Nature' whereas white women played the part of 'Culture'. And black women, as we know, didn't find playing Nature in the patriarchal play such an amusing role, nor do they have much confidence in the salvific quality of Nature and her harmonies. But those who played 'Culture', according to Thistlethwaite, have also had a price to pay — the price of experiencing the alienation from our bodily selves that is part of the legacy of a dualistic culture.[7]

But even if we agree for the sake of argument that all women have in some sense been identified at some level with nature, as Griffin and the ecofeminists suggest, then there is still a problem. Surely we are not meant to see Woman, the creature of Nature, being a helpless victim, bound and gagged and abused by Man the creature of Culture/Reason. No, of course, Griffin also wants to say that we/she can escape, get out from under and survive to write books about how women's bad experiences of being cast and castigated as Nature can be transformed into good ones. But the process of getting out from under and writing books about one's experiences tends to make one into a creature of culture, even if one wasn't before. And similarly, to approach one's sexual life with a particular doctrine about women and nature is rather a sophisticated cultural thing to do — not quite the same thing as just living along with the birds and the bees.

As the Women's Liberation Movement has moved on from the eighties, it becomes clear that the feminist quest for sexual liberation is part of a much wider movement for sexual freedom. The simple and reassuring dualisms of radical feminism have broken down. Now it is possible to find feminists, including lesbian feminists, as well as female sexual libertarians, for whom the routine sado-masochism of everyday life is not enough; they desire to introduce the rituals of bondage, submission and domination into their sex lives, and to claim this as part of their right as liberated women. Could it be that, men apart, woman's relation with her own flesh is not entirely natural and problem free? Is her flesh too 'naturally' heir to the craving for bondage? Is it perhaps that our sexual relations are not some little haven of doing what comes naturally — that they are, in fact, another area of culture? And whether heterosexual or lesbian, the culture that has produced us stamps its indelible mark upon them. Thus, Jane DeLynn, who explores the American lesbian scene in her novels,[8] has observed that those who speak in a 'politically correct' way are apt to tell another story in the bedroom — where who has what negotiating power to indulge their own particular narcissism and fantasy is the operative reality, and relations between women are frequently governed by the same codes of 'lookism' (i.e. what you look like) as are the relations between men and women.

In our anti-dualist outrage against original sin we defiantly proclaim our love for the body. But in reality it is only bodies of the approved variety that attract us — well fed but slim, curvaceous but not bulging in the wrong place, muscular if masculine; bodies that are too thin, too fat, the wrong colour or wrong shape in any particular do not attract our love. Like fruit in the supermarket for our consumption, they must be subjected to a rigorous quality control — breast expansion, nose reduction, tummy tucks. We shudder with abhorrence at the female mutilation practised in societies like Africa and China, yet unconsciously assume, even if we disapprove of it, that our rather more technologically sophisticated procedures of body mutilation for the sake of the ideal are more acceptable because they are not only more hygienic but also 'self-chosen'. Meanwhile, young women starve themselves to death in pursuit of an absurd ideal of slim-body perfection. In such circumstances, one can't help feeling that a healthy obsession with the state of the soul would be quite an improvement.

Thus, while performing our vows to 'nature' we proceed to consume each other according to ideal consumer standards — the 'lookism' which Jane DeLynn noted among gays. The pleasure that we assume to be physical is more in our minds than we care to realize. And as we have already discovered, our minds are not those pure altars to embodied reasonableness that we have presumed them to be. So if, in our fantasies of sexual escape, we invariably reproduce the modes of the dominant culture, and a selection from its infinite variety of cultural bondage, then we may ask: what exactly are we escaping from? Are we really yearning to embrace the natural — or is nature implicated in that which we seek to escape? For women involved in same-sex love, there is one very obvious area in which such relations provide the chance of escape — that is the escape from bondage to reproductive function. For those who remain within heterosexual relations, the possibility of this ancient bondage, the connection of sex with childbirth and child rearing, is still present. But as we have begun to realize, bondage is not something that is only feared but also that which is desired. And here we are reminded that it is not only radical feminists or ecofeminists who have worshipped the goddess nature. For the not-particularly-feminist middle-class women, who haven't given up on heterosexual relations, also pay court to her as they seek to discover and experience the beauty of nature in natural childbirth. (Even lesbian couples have been known to endure the 'unnatural' practices of the medical profession so as to conceive and be eligible for the fulfilment of natural childbirth.) In this realm, we are in favour of letting Nature take its course, so that the whole experience can be pure and beautiful instead of being dominated by male medical technology.

There are indeed many good reasons for restraining the excesses of medical interventionism, and curbing the arrogance of consultants who regard childbirth as merely the stage for their own superior operations. But the natural childbirth movement is not without some delusions and excesses of its own. If we are really so keen on the presence of unadulterated Nature at our births, should we not arrange a swap with women in the Third World? They are rather in favour of our Western medicine, and could offer us a mass of natural childbirth in return. Perhaps our new fund-holding health services could buy in some of it for middle-class mothers. No, we won't take the poverty as well — that can be classed as man-made. Of course, you realize you will have to cope with rather more dead babies... and quite a few maternal deaths as well. Ah, well now, that's a bit different... Yes, yes, as you say, 100 per cent natural but all the same, we need a bit of time to think about it first.

Looking again at the slavery of heterosexual relations, as radical feminism posed it, reminds us that it is not only the patriarchal bondage that menaces our liberty, but its root in the reproductive role of women. And here at this root, nature is represented, albeit distantly to those of us protected by Western technology; she is represented in a form in which we don't much care to recognize her these days — the role of pain and death. To us moderns it seems particularly outrageous — not natural, but a perversion of nature — that the shadow of death should intrude upon the area of sex, the area where we focus our hopes for pleasure and comfort, fulfilment and escape. But it seems that in the end, our fantasies of escape are just that — fantasies. Nature does not provide a real escape. The 'natural' blueprint for innocent and loving sexual relations has proved difficult for either or both sexes to achieve.

Thus it becomes clearer that the Californian gospel of Good Sex, whether it appears in sixties sexual revolution, or in radical feminist orthodoxy of the seventies and eighties, or in the creation spirituality and ecofeminism of the nineties, does not owe all that much to Nature. Rather it is a thoroughly culture-bound concept that reflects the privileges and preconceptions of those who hold it. This may help to explain why people of the past and of other cultures, who in theory share with us a common human and sexual nature, do not appear to share our attitudes to sexuality. We have concluded that in the past, Christians lacked our enlightenment on these matters, and often seemed to be neurotically concerned with the connections between sex, sin and mortality. But for people of Augustine's day, for example, and before that, the connection between sex and bondage to mortality was not some obscure religious connection, it was a fact of life. Peter Brown, writing about Latin society in the early Christian centuries, describes it as one that was more helplessly exposed to death than even the most afflicted underdeveloped country in the modern world.[9] It was a society in which the average life expectancy was less than twenty-five years, and death fell savagely on the young and those who survived childhood. It was a population 'grazed thin by death' and both young men and women were discreetly mobilized to use their bodies for reproduction. The pressure on young women was inexorable — for the population even to remain stable, each young woman needed to produce an average of five children. They were recruited early for this task — as young as fourteen was average. Yet as many of these fourteen-year-olds went to their marriage beds, they went also to their death beds. In the days before contraceptive and birth technology, every pregnancy could be life threatening. The 'carnage of the marriage bed' among young women was every bit as grim as the carnage of the battlefield was for young men. Only for women there were no 'times of peace' unless or until they survived their reproductive years. Even without a violent husband, or poverty, the domestic scene was never a safe and protected zone. It was menaced by that same Nature whom we Western women are about to define as women's saviour and protector.

It is little wonder that virginity, which seems to us so bizarre and 'unnatural', came to have a strong appeal for many women in Christian tradition. As Brown observes, the Roman world is one that is known to us from a resolutely male viewpoint; but it was from a Christian treatise on virginity[10] that we learn something of the physical state of the married women — their danger in childbirth, the pain in their breasts during suckling, their exposure to children's infections, the terrible shame of infertility, and the humiliation of being replaced by servants in their husbands' affections 'and all this they endure, seeing no end to their labours'. Had they not married, the treatise comments, 'they would be blessed, even if there were no Kingdom of Heaven for them to receive'.

To women in these circumstances, it's not hard to see how virginity must have seemed a vivid symbol of life, of freedom and of the life eternal that could cheat death and bondage to death. Yet we, in our superior wisdom and belief in bountiful Mother Nature, see it as evidence of a 'negative' attitude to sexuality. Yet they would no doubt be amazed at the naivety of our belief that sex could be separated from the bondage to mortality; that we could claim such reverence for nature while apparently displaying such a profound ignorance of nature's domain.

They might also find it strange to hear that we think them to be negative about sexual pleasure. When we hear that Augustine opted for the celibate life after many years of a satisfying sexual relationship we find it hard to believe. For we mostly understand the option for celibacy as one made either by the benighted (i.e. Catholic priests) or the frustrated and those who for one reason or another must make necessity into a virtue. But Augustine it seems was well aware of the 'sweet joys' he was leaving behind when he finally made his decision. He felt them

plucking at my garment, my flesh, these my past sweet joys softly murmured 'Are you dismissing us? From this moment, you will never be allowed to do this, to do that?' And oh my God, what was it that they suggested in those words, 'this' and 'that'?[11]

If for people of his day perhaps the pleasures of sex were taken for granted, its terrifying dangers were equally obvious. Augustine was well
aware, it seems, of the consequences to women of some of these 'sweet
joys'. In his writings he reflects on the nausea, illness and pains of pregnancy and labour that women suffer, as well as the 'tortures inflicted by
doctors, or the shock and loss of giving birth to an infant stillborn or
moribund'.[12] As Elaine Pagels says,

> Augustine catalogues these sufferings like a man who has felt and witnessed
> them: some babies, he says, are born blind, deaf, deformed, or without the use of
> their limbs; and others are born into such forms of human suffering as demonic
> insanity or chronic and fatal disease. Even the fortunate ones, the children born
> normal and healthy, evince the terrifying vulnerability that pervades nature;
> every infant is born ignorant, wholly subject to passions and sensations, bereft
> of reason or articulate speech and entirely helpless.[13]

How different this is from the rosy picture that seems to inform much
middle-class child rearing — a picture of children as innocent beings
who, given the right conditions, will painlessly unfold according to the
blueprint that benevolent nature has implanted in them. Thus, armed
with a plausible rationale for our failure to undertake the painful and
difficult task of their moral education, we abandon them to the mercy of
their own passions and to the merciless pressures of the consumer
society, which will be only too happy to shape and manipulate their
desires in its own image and interests.

Thus, people of Augustine's day might well be astounded at our
idealism about sex, coupled with earnest efforts to make it live up to all
we have invested in it. Is it possible that having separated sex from all
that made it dangerous, we may have lost much of what made it intensely pleasurable? In the course of our 'enlightened' desire to throw
over ancient morality, we may have introduced a new moralism into sex
which is capable of being as stultifying as we perceived the old one to
be. And in the act of celebrating our sexual liberation, we may not notice
that we have become in fact erotically illiterate.

In the Enlightenment revolt against the fathers, the brothers effected
their sexual revolution by throwing off the traditional sexual morality,
together with the mystifying rule of priests. They wanted no more of
hocus pocus (*hoc est corpus meum* — this is my body) for now all that was
to be replaced by reason. Rational morality, in the libertarian tradition,
was absence of censorship, the freedom from sexual restraint, the freedom to explore your own sexuality. Many of these assumptions have
been firmly established in the feminist canon of belief. Yet, how interesting it is, as Griffin shows, that a major part of the obsession of the porno-
grapher is to transgress the sacred. Somehow the power of the father-
priests is still there, and the modern sexual self needs to establish its

identity by negating it. The sisters have continued their own version of the brothers' revolt against the fathers, re-defining these latter as all men. But we have become ensnared in the same trap as the brothers before us — of needing to 'find' our sexual selves by outraging what are seen as moral norms of the fathers.

Thus, the desire to escape from the prison of the cultural mind-sets we have inherited and seek the pure and liberating re-enactment of sex in Eden before the Fall is part of a Western paradigm that is wider than its appearance in feminist thought. But this quest for sexual liberation has frequently ended in bondage of one sort or another — bondage to a never-ending search for the ultimate orgiastic fulfilment or for the elusive embrace of natural pleasure. It is, I suggest, part of our specifically modern illiteracy about sex that we are unaware of its capacity to enslave. In our love affair with nature, we seem unwilling to seriously consider the possibility that the pursuit of 'natural pleasure' may also at some stage subject us to the tyranny of obsession. Christian tradition has quite a lot to say on these matters, but with our new-found faith in natural wisdom we have ignored this as a hopelessly reactionary source.

But Nature as a teacher of wisdom, sexual or otherwise, is apt to be problematical. To take one example, Nature is not a very good role model for mothers. Mother Nature has a habit of sometimes getting the cord round the baby's neck and strangling her offspring at birth. Not from any malice, you understand, but just casually, naturally. But is it natural for a mother to strangle her children? It's all a question of how natural is natural? Birth is natural and good and a few labour pains we can take on board. But what about the complications and consequences of birth? How about backache and piles? Are they natural and therefore good? What about miscarriage, stillbirth, fetal deformity, perinatal mortality of all sorts — is this all part of natural childbirth? In a word, death, and all the mortal aspects of nature. We have to decide if we think that these are part of nature — or are they, as Augustine thought, part of nature gone wrong? And if nature has 'gone wrong', how did it happen? How did that paradise, which one way or another we repeatedly posit in our dreams of free and loving sexuality or natural childbirth, get lost?

Notes

1 Matthew Fox, *Original Blessing: A Primer in Creation Spirituality* (Santa Fe: Bear and Co., 1983).

2 Mary Ann Rossi, 'The legitimation of the abuse of women in Christianity', *Feminist Theology*, no. 4 (Sept. 1993), p. 59.

3 Melissa Raphael, 'At the East of Eden: a feminist spirituality of gardening: our way past the flaming sword', *Feminist Theology*, no. 4 (Sept. 1993), pp. 101ff.

4 Phyllis Trible, *God and the Rhetoric of Sexuality* (Philadelphia: Fortress Press, 1978), p. 157.

5 Susan Griffin, *Pornography and Silence: Culture's Revenge Against Nature* (London: The Women's Press, 1981).

6 Catharina J. M. Halkes, *New Creation: Christian Feminism and the Renewal of the Earth* (London: SPCK, 1991), p. 147.

7 Susan Brooks Thistlethwaite, *Sex, Race, and God: Christian Feminism in Black and White* (London: Geoffrey Chapman, 1990), p. 60.

8 Jane DeLynn, *Don Juan in the Village* (London: Serpent's Tail, 1991); *High Risk.*

9 Peter Brown, *The Body and Society: Men, Women and Sexual Renunciation in Early Christianity* (London: Faber and Faber, 1988), p. 6.

10 Eusebius of Emesa, Sermon 6.5, quoted in Brown, p. 25.

11 Augustine, *Confessions*, VIII.11.

12 Augustine, *Opus Imperfectum*, 4.114.

13 Elaine Pagels, *Adam, Eve and the Serpent* (London: Penguin, 1990), pp. 133–4.

13 *The unoriginality of sin*

Augustine was deeply preoccupied with the question of nature gone wrong. He, like us, speculated about what sex in Eden would have been like. Women, he thought, would have enjoyed painless childbirth, and marriage without oppression and coercion.[1] The fact that he believed that the primacy of man over woman was part of the natural order of things immediately alerts us to the fact that his vision of nature was very much conditioned by his cultural presuppositions — a state of affairs from which we are hardly likely to be immune.

For Augustine, it was in particular the sufferings of innocent children that had to be explained — he could not conceive that they could be part of the design of a just God. God would not allow suffering where there was no prior fault.[2] Thus, he came to the conclusion that it was human sin from the beginning that must be responsible for our condition, and it was this that lay behind his interpretation of the story of the Fall in Genesis. Eve's sin brought suffering on women, and Adam's brought punishment to men.

The entire human race that was to pass through woman into offspring was contained in the first man, when that married couple received the divine sentence condemning them to punishment and humanity produced what humanity became, not when it was created, but when having sinned, it was punished.[3]

This doctrine was by no means universally accepted in Augustine's own times. Julian of Eclanum, a younger contemporary and admirer of Augustine's great learning, became convinced that on the matter of nature he was making a great error.[4] He defended Pelagius' views and also made use of the ideas expressed earlier by John Chrysostom and other Christian teachers. He believed that Augustine was totally wrong to regard the present state of nature as punishment; and although he accepted that Adam's sin brought death and moral corruption on the human race, he could not accept the idea of a physically transmitted, hereditary condition which had infected human nature, and nature in general. Both Julian and Augustine referred these questions back to Genesis, each claiming its authority for their own approach.

Thus, through Christian tradition, if we bother to examine it, we inherit not only Augustine's doctrine of Original Sin, but the doubts and counter-arguments of other Christian scholars. As the wheel of time turns, Original Sin is again under suspicion. It's clear that anyone holding the Californian gospel of Good Sex, or even a mild version of it, is likely to find Augustine's teaching very unhealthy. But amid the heat and smoke of our disapproval, it might be well to examine his actual beliefs more carefully. It is true that he saw the primacy of man over woman as part of the natural order of things. But interestingly, what Augustine saw as a *consequence* of the Fall — the blight of male domination on the whole structure of sexual relations — has often been identified by feminists as the *cause* of women's ills. According to the radical feminist version of the Fall mythology, and some ecofeminist variants of it, human sin is essentially and primarily male sin — the sin of raping Mother Earth by means of the violating technology of the patriarchs. As Ruether has commented:

The ecofeminist myth is also problematic as myth or symbolic parable. It allows contemporary Western women to imagine themselves as heirs to an original innocent goodness, projecting the cause of an evil culture of patriarchal domination of women and nature on to evil 'outsider' males.[5]

Further reflection on the doctrine of male sinfulness/female innocence makes it seem a little unconvincing. For example, there is something a bit specious about the attribution of technology to men. The fact that we can contemplate sexual relations which do not issue in children is possible because of contraceptive technology. It is only this separation of sex from reproduction that makes it possible for us to associate it primarily with freedom and pleasure, and to ignore the bondage to mortality that is the inevitable concomitant of biological sex. The fact that we can choose 'natural' childbirth is a result of the backup of Western medical technology — however unaesthetic we find it at times, or however much we may wish to challenge the arrogance or inappropriateness of its procedures. The powerful protection of the all-embracing technology of our culture surrounds us from conception to our last hours and till death. It protects us from exposure to nature as it is known by our less fortunate sisters, till in the end we see nature only through romantic spectacles.

Of course we are right to revere the bodily. But isn't it quite 'natural' that we should love our own well-protected bodies? We seem to take for granted, however, what has been central for their protection, and fail to notice that in so many of our intimate and erotic moments, technology is present. Contraceptive technology has liberated some women from the mortal stresses to the female frame of unremitting fertility. But it also distances men from the consequences of their begetting. All our technology has this ambiguous quality. The distance it makes possible for us from the consequences of our weapons of destruction or from the sources of our food supply mean that we can preserve the façade of innocence about what these structures entail. Since we know of it at second hand, we can continue to feel that though regrettable they do not involve us personally. Much of what we relate as good news, therefore, like feminism and green spirituality, has the implicit and unacknowledged protection of this technology as its unseen foundation.

It may well be that Augustine's doctrine of Original Sin can be considered, as some have suggested, a kind of myth. The idea that sin is, as it were, sexually transmitted, seems to us moderns absurd and we feel able to dismiss it with cheerful scorn. For one thing, we have a different relation with the word 'sin'. Sin was the device that the fathers used to keep us in our place, to stop us having sexual pleasure which we now know is our God-given right. In the libertarian strand of our Enlightenment heritage, sin has associations of sexiness — and sexiness with liberation from the deadening hand of an outworn morality. The false connection between sex and sin is seen to be the essence of this old-fashioned morality that is the baleful legacy of Augustine.

So is he guilty as charged? Peter Brown comments at the end of his chapter on Augustine: 'He created a darkened humanism that linked the pre-Christian past to the Christian present in a common distrust of sexual pleasure. It was a heavy legacy to bequeath to later ages.'[6] But perhaps even so, it is not quite as simple as that. If Augustine really cared so much about women's pain and bodily love and nature and the suffering of children (like we do) why did he come up with this crazy idea of Original Sin? Earlier Brown says:

The *concupiscentia carnis* [lusts of the flesh] ... was such a peculiarly tragic
affliction to Augustine precisely because it had so little to do with the body.
It originated in a lasting distortion of the soul itself. With Adam's Fall, the soul
lost the ability to summon up all of itself, in an undivided act of will, to love and
praise God in all created things. Concupiscence was a dark drive to control, to
appropriate, and to turn to one's private ends, all the good things that had been
created by God to be accepted with gratitude and shared with others. It lay at
the root of the inescapable misery that afflicted mankind. Sexual desire was no
more tainted with this tragic, faceless concupiscence than was any other form of
human activity.[7]

Ironically, it turns out that it is in the vision of a spoiled Eden that we find ourselves on common ground with Augustine. Like Augustine, we look around and see the beautiful garden of Earth ruined and desecrated by human activity and realize that the scope of our technological hubris has extended even into the process of generation and birth. And we also know, as Augustine concluded, that this condition cannot be attributed to Nature; it is a result of human sin.

Augustine, like us disturbed and tormented by the evidence of human sin at the heart of Nature, provided an account of how the rot set in. We have done the same, but our own account is distorted by the fact that from our protected situation, the mortal nature of our bodies seems to have slipped our notice — in a way that is more difficult for people whose situation is rather less protected. Feminism has identified how men try desperately to forget their bodily nature by projecting it on to women, by flirting with immortality, through dynasties, through art and authorship. In contrast, we have declared our desire to reclaim bodily nature. But it is often a rather intellectualized bodiliness we celebrate, and I suspect that the real implications of our mortality are as alarming to us as they are to men. On closer inspection, it appears that we want not so much to recall men to what they are so desperate to forget but rather to share their amnesia.

Death remained for Augustine the most bitter sign of human frailty, for it tore apart the 'sweet marriage bond of body and soul'. It could never be, as his former Manichean colleagues believed, a freeing of the soul to which it had been joined by accident. It was an unnatural occurrence.[8] He was well aware that merely having a body, a body that is subject to decay as well as desire, is not what corrupts us. He was not disturbed by the prospect of human society where people married, made love and begot children, for this, as he understood it, would have happened even if Adam had not fallen. But what remained a dark enigma for him was the corruption of the human will.

The twisted human will, not marriage, not even the sexual drive was what was new in the human condition after Adam's fall. The fallen will subjected the original, God-given bonds of human society — friendship, marriage, and paternal command — to sickening shocks of wilfulness, that caused these to sway, to fissure and to change their nature; it was the present twisted will that had led to the development of slavery and to the sinister emergence of the state as a necessary agent of coercion.[9]

Thus, Augustine saw in this derangement of the will a race condemned and justly punished by God. And for him, the way sexual drives escaped the control of the will was a peculiarly resonant symptom of the frailty that was inherited by humankind from Eve/Adam's first act of disobedience. It was a punishment to fit the crime. And although, compared to humankind's other ills, sexual temptation was not very significant, nevertheless it had a high symbolic value. Sex and death stood at either end of the life of every human being, and formed ineluctable symbols of our loss of the primal harmony of body and soul.[10] And so it came about that in Augustine's teaching, sexuality was effectively taken from its physiological context and made to represent a continuing, unhealed flaw in the soul.

We recoil from these dark conclusions, not least because they seem to implicate us in a state of affairs which we heartily abhor and from which we wish to disassociate ourselves. Yet, if Augustine's doctrine was flawed, some of those which we have preferred may also contain a few imperfections. What we have been taught is a bowdlerized version of his teaching about the 'lust of the flesh' where the latter stands only for sex and thus comes out as the crude equation, sex is bad. Thus, our good news, our Californian gospel based on an evangelistic reading of Freud, is equally simplistic — sex is good. The result is that our whole understanding of what sin is about is narrowed down to questions about sex. And conveniently, the issue of sin as the lust for privatization, for the enjoyment of privilege, is shifted off the agenda. We fail to recognize how the inverted moralism of our obsession with sex obscures some of the real moral issues of our situation. As D. J. Taylor says in an article on 'Sex and the Singular Novel':

Whether we like it or not the decline of the traditional morality has invalidated great areas of the traditional British novel. It is up to writers to start acknowledging that there are more engrossing subjects — power for example — than the tedious recapitulation of the sexual act and the pointless adulteries currently disfiguring the shelves of books which even now are held up as faithful reflections of contemporary life.[11]

If our conflation of sin and sex and misunderstanding of the nature of both has badly affected our contemporary literature, it's possible that this confusion has had an equally disastrous effect on other areas of our life. I think we need to examine sceptically the idea that sin is sexy and exciting. The fact is that sin, whether original or personal, is really very boring, deadly boring in fact. Sin is about compulsive repetition, about never being able to do a new thing or reach a new place. Sex may be God's gift — but the trouble with gifts is that they depend on the will of the giver. God it seems may not have been informed of our right to expect continually satisfying homoerotic union or enduring heterosexual bliss. God obviously assumes that if it's a gift, it can be given if and when God pleases. God is unaware of the obligation to make sure it turns up fresh every day on our doorstep like the milk.

Thus, as we dream of ourselves as champions of rational freedom and sexual liberation from Augustine's bad dreams, we may have made ourselves instead the authors of bad fiction, and the guardians of stultifying ignorance and ethical and erotic monotony. If we take seriously the commitment to self-knowledge and reflect on some of our deepest experiences including our disappointments in sex, or politics or even prayer, we might well begin to find evidence of the impotent will that Augustine spoke of, the groove that frustrates our efforts and mocks our idealism.

To make such discoveries could serve to open a proper discussion with Augustine on the subject of sin — not necessarily to agree but to argue seriously as Julian did. But this of course would mean that he would no longer be available simply as a dumping ground for all that unresolved anger and resentment we have about God, sex, our fathers and the church. But this loss of a convenient scapegoat might be compensated for in other ways.

I confess that from my own experience of embodiment I have found the doctrine of Original Sin, whatever its defects, a better starting point for discussion than the Californian doctrine of Good Sex and all its derivatives. Sex in a scented garden is all very well, but it doesn't seem to deal with the fact that kids have a way of messing up our gardens of ecstasy, and ruining the impeccable mutuality of our relationships. Somehow I find Augustine's anguish over the pain of mortality, the afflictions of motherhood and the suffering of infants rather more theologically illuminating than the fragrant fantasies of eco-erotic spirituality. These do not address the problem of that which conditions us from infancy, and how the genes of culture distorted by sin pass from one generation to another. The idea that sin entered the human race through the first human pair, seems to me to be a way of speaking about the fact of the corporate nature of sin. For the ways in which we are sinful are historically and culturally conditioned, as we have seen, and sin is patterned according to race, and gender and class. Thus there are patterns of sin among the powerful and somewhat different patterns among the powerless. Those with power use it to exploit and manipulate the weak; and those without power sometimes find ways to manipulate the powerful by means of their weakness. Women in the Western tradition, to which feminists largely belong, have a foot in both camps. The inadequacy of much of the feminist doctrine that I have encountered has been its refusal to deal with this question. It has resorted instead to that device which it has identified in male theology — that of shifting the blame for the origin of evil. If Eve's first sin was the will to power through appropriating knowledge, it was Adam, so to speak, who invented and perfected the technique of buck-passing. But radical feminism was instrumental in making sure that women have a go at this too.

Feminism (in company with other modern ideologies) stresses the power of choice for women, and sets much store in the liberation of our capacity to be creative and original. But the humiliating truth about 'original' sin is that it is really desperately unoriginal. Man (shall we say 'man' here for once?) is always trying to make something new, to create something new by technological invention. But nothing fundamentally new is ever created by such means. What happens is that our existing capacities are enlarged — including our capacity for destruction. So in this century we have witnessed the slaughter of the Somme, of Auschwitz, of Hiroshima — all in their own way ⟨the technological triumphs of the back-room boys. And now the destruction of the whole world, of creation as we know it, is only the press of a button away. But still there is nothing which has the newness of new life, no new lilies of the field, no new species, and the only new human beings are ones that have been generated by very ancient means. All the ideologies of autonomy produce only monstrous growth, weird forms based on massive scale repetition, like computer art. The culture of post-modernism is based on this endless recycling of images. The 'inheritable' quality of sin seems to commit us to ever new forms of destruction, of each other and the environment, while on the micro-level it holds us fast in sadomasochism of the ordinary relations of everyday life.

Thus, in much modern spirituality, feminist and otherwise, sin has been abolished as a kind of false consciousness. Augustine's account of sin has become suspect because he is identified as a misogynist patriarch who hated sex and women. Yet curiously, we don't seem to mind that our own understanding of sexuality has its roots in the work of another patriarch — one whose record in relation to women was equally if not more suspect. For it was Freud who was willing to suppress (by treating it as fantasy) the testimony of his female patients about their abuse in childhood, so as not to embarrass or scandalize the scientific fraternity whose good opinion mattered most to him.[12] And this suppression has a certain logic about it, for as Peter Gay, his biographer, has written:

Freud, the man who above all others is supposed to have destroyed the justification of Enlightenment rationalism, was the greatest child of the Enlightenment which our century has known. His fundamental assumption was that the search for truth must never stop, that only knowledge allows reason to function, and that only reason can make us free.[13]

Thus, we accept Freud's account of our sexuality because he inhabits the same mythological landscape as we do, whereas that of Augustine is alien and threatens to undermine the sources of our wisdom. And yet ironically it seems possible that it is Augustine, rather than Freud, who has taken a better measure of those 'animals in the barn of the human unconscious' and, unlike Freud, does not overestimate the power of unaided human reason to bring them under its control.

Freud, it seems, has earned our gratitude for revealing to us the mysterious paths of our desire. For it is to these we turn to escape the prison house of our systems of rationality. The urgency of our desire for escape from the latter has blinded us to the possibility — which Augustine was aware of — that these desires also have the capacity to enslave us. And there is another reason too why we cannot afford to question seriously our commitment to the desirability of unrepressed sex. For the fact is that the Western culture of capital needs these assumptions about sex to stimulate unceasing desire for consumption, and especially to exploit the market of youth culture and its purchasing power.

Thus, we have adopted — and adapted — a theory that the repression of our sexual inclinations is bad for us, and that the expression of our sexual desires is both innocent and natural and necessary for our health. But at the same time, we have failed to notice that the uncritical acceptance of this theory has involved us in the repression of certain other things about ourselves. We search for our true selves in the 'Supermarket of the Self' as Stanley Cohen and Laurie Taylor designate it, giving ourselves goals of meaning and progress the attainment of which

would reflect our individual transcendence over the meaningless, repetitive, soulless nature of the many life-worlds we inhabit. By our diligent use of escape routes we seek to construct in our minds that which does not appear to us in the world. We attempt to create free areas in which, our individuality having been wrested from society, we may now enjoy a certain immunity.[14]

But we do not reckon on the ability of society to continually co-opt and subvert those very areas which we had hoped to hold sacred for the attainment of meaning and progress and self. 'No sooner has a new road to the true self been encountered than it is boxed and packaged for sale in the escape attempts supermarket....'[15]

In many ways, it seems to me this accurately describes the cul-de-sac that much of our theology has run into. We embraced it as offering us new hope for the liberation of the self. Yet because we have repressed a true understanding of the will, we have implicitly accepted the consumer society's definition of this as our power to choose. We were unwilling to perceive the fatal limitation in our wills that ensures that all our strenuous efforts to discover our 'true selves' are destined to futility. Like African chickens, whose feet are tied on their way to market, we are doomed to a series of desperate and hopeless flutterings towards freedom. For we have repressed that part of our cultural inheritance that would provide us with knowledge of an aspect of the self that is quite as fundamental as that of our sexuality. It is our sexuality, as it issues in the process of generation, that provides the most intimate and powerful experience of the flawed will that undermines our idealism. As daughter becomes mother, the inadequacies of our dreams of sisterhood are sharply exposed. My own experience of motherhood has brought home to me that particular loss of innocence, that sad wisdom which comes with being a parent. For neither child nor parent is 'innocent' in the sense of being free from wilfulness, but as child becomes parent her fantasies are bounded by the reality of her power — and powerlessness. Once confident in her power to remake the world for the child in the image of her ideal, she discovers painfully that the brave new world of the next generation comes already marked by the scars from the previous one. The terror and the tragedy is to know oneself as the intimate agent of this process. As we have been mothered so we mother, and what we pass on is, at one level, as little determined by our conscious choices as the genes that we pass to our child. It became painfully clear to me why this image, culled from Augustine's thought, of sin passed on by sexual transmission, despite its offensiveness to all our sense of natural justice, has had such a hold on our imagination.

Notes

1 Augustine, *Opus Imperfectum*, 6.26.
2 Augustine, *Opus Imperfectum* 6. 23.5.
3 Augustine, *City of God*, 13.3.
4 Elaine Pagels, *Adam, Eve and the Serpent* (London: Penguin, 1990), p. 132.
5 Rosemary Radford Ruether, 'Before and beyond patriarchy: rebuilding healing cultures', *Feminist Theology*, no. 2 (Jan. 1993), p. 105.
6 Peter Brown, *The Body and Society: Men, Women and Sexual Renunciation in Early Christianity* (London: Faber and Faber, 1988), p. 426.
7 Brown, p. 418.
8 Brown, p. 405.
9 *Ibid.*
10 Brown, p. 416.
11 *Guardian*, 9 Jan. 1992.
12 Jeffrey Masson, *The Assault on Truth* (London: Fontana, 1992).
13 Peter Gay, quoted in H. Stuart Hughes, *Consciousness and Society: The Re-orientation of European Thought, 1890–1930*, quoted in Susan Brooks Thistlethwaite, *Sex, Race, and God: Christian Feminism in Black and White* (London: Geoffrey Chapman, 1990), p. 21.
14 Stanley Cohen and Laurie Taylor, 'The supermarket of the self', *Guardian*, 26 Aug. 1992, p. 32.
15 *Ibid.*

14 The jellyfish babies and the genetics of sin

Back in the UK after a brief but fruitful excursus, I prepared myself to face the post-cold war era of feminist thinking. I found that the feminist theological understanding of sin was undergoing development. The problems of a theory of male-only sinfulness were becoming apparent to some, and it became possible to suggest that women might also be capable of human sin, rather than just the female variety. Ruether had identified sin as present in the choice we make for or against the well-being of creation and fellow creatures.[1] For as she says, humans alone can sin and invert the evolutionary process. Other varieties of ecofeminist theology gave it a similar role in their productions. And as I became acquainted with some of these, I saw how the seeds for this new direction of feminist theology had been present in the previous era.

In 1985, the women at Greenham had received some visitors from the island of Rongelap, one of the islands in the Pacific. Since the eighteenth century, these islands had been the focus for the romantic and escapist fantasies of Enlightenment Europe. Travellers' tales created it as a place of silver sand, blue lagoons and whispering coco-palms; the home of the noble savage, of beautiful women, and guilt-free eroticism; a repository of dreams for all those disgusted with the sophistries and repressions of European civilization.[2]

But while this timeless paradise lived on in Western fantasy, the real Pacific islands had entered the world of the twentieth century, a world of de-colonization, Coca-Cola, cars and TV and above all of nuclear testing and its effects. It was the terrible effects of this testing that eventually forced some of the inhabitants to try and escape from their role as figments of the European imagination. In 1984–6, nine indigenous Pacific women came to Europe on a mission of their own. In March 1985, they were welcomed to Britain by the women of Greenham. They told how fifty years ago their 'paradise isles' were colonized by Americans who, in 1946, began to use the islands for nuclear testing. Soon after, the women of the islands like Rongelap began to give birth to babies so deformed they seemed scarcely human — babies with no eyes, no heads, no limbs. They came to be known as the jellyfish babies.[3]

The existence of phenomena like the jellyfish babies has put the question of 'sins against creation' on the agenda of modern consciousness, and ecotheology and the feminist version of this can be seen as a response to this. In her recent book *The Body of God: An Ecological Theology* [4] Sallie McFague attempts to address the ecological crisis by means of a re-visioning of 'our common creation story' based on a reading of post-modern science. Though like Hampson she bases her theory in the premises of modern science, there are some significant differences between her approach and that of theology of the previous era. Mindful, no doubt, of the critique that has been developed on this subject, she does not presume overmuch on the category of 'women's experience'. She is aware, no doubt, of the scepticism articulated by black women writers about the whole presumption of innocent and universal sisterhood that was implicit in the theology of the earlier era. Nor does she stress women's greater innocence compared with men. She is conscious that it is human sin in the form of greed that has led to the ecological crisis and that it is those in the well-off nations like herself who are most responsible. She also distances herself from what she sees as the naive utopianism of some of the advocates of creation spirituality. But in company with other ecotheologians, her project is concerned with the restoring of sacrality to nature, in the hope that this will provide a powerful barrier to its exploitation.

Clearly we have come some way from the walking-out posture of Daly. McFague does not identify herself as a post-Christian, nor does she stress the superior virtue of feminism. Yet it is clear that in other ways she shares all the assumptions of the modernist myth, as well as something of Hampson's distaste for the uncouthness of the Christian story. She is, you might say, a post-modern Christian feminist who perceives that the old stories are ripe for redevelopment by a more sophisticated designer. This she offers with her version of 'our common creation story' premised on the big bang theory of the universe and its subsequent development. Her 'organic model' of creation as God's body is the substitute she provides for the biblical story of creation and incarnation.[5] For as she says, that a first-century Mediterranean carpenter should be claimed as the creator and redeemer of the fifteen-billion-year history of the universe with its hundred billion galaxies, is not only offensive to the integrity and value of other religions, but incredible, and absurd even in the light of post-modern cosmology.[6]

Aware of the charge of ethnocentrism against some forms of feminist theology, McFague is emphatic about the need for respecting difference and abolishing all hierarchies of value among cultures and creatures. She points out that previous theologies, both traditional and modern, have been too 'anthropological' in failing to acknowledge the importance in creation of all those other non-human life forms. Modern science, as she points out, does not put human beings at the centre of creation, nor does it provide evidence of a cosmic teleology as the older theologies imagined. Thus, her concern is that all hierarchies of creation dominated by 'man' are to be replaced by a consciousness of the mutual dependence of all life forms on each other. Thus, her key metaphor is of the 'crazy quilt' where each culture or species has its allotted space, and none is allowed to overreach its own area and dominate the designerless design.

But there is something disingenuous about the seeming modesty of her approach. In eschewing the evils of hierarchy, McFague has ignored the fact that the whole paradigm of Western thinking, and certainly of Western science, is based on a concept of hierarchy of value. A library is an example of ordering of knowledge according to a certain hierarchy of value. Thus, at its most basic level, a hierarchy of value is an inescapable part of our intellectual and spiritual endeavours. And science is the mode of Western thought *par excellence,* which has emerged top of the hierarchy among world cosmologies. To see it as simply one patch among others in a crazy quilt is to engage in a certain amount of self-deception.

As many feminist critics are well aware, science represents a particular set of values and interests, and these determine its approach to those problems it elects to solve. Thus, its claim to be value-free is a form of self-legitimation of the biases within its value system. As Sandra Harding has shown in her book *The Science Question in Feminism,*[7] the adoption of mathematics as the measure of objectivity was crucial to Enlightenment thinking. Science adopted this standard which was based at least partly on a Platonic ideal of knowing, with its particular assumptions about gender. As she shows, science became a totalizing system in which the highest priority was assigned to those problems which it is best equipped to answer, thus more or less guaranteeing that it would impose on Nature 'the very stories we like to hear'. For what scientists tell us about nature is not nature itself but a representation of nature.

McFague would no doubt say that she is aware of the androcentric biases of science, and that she has been careful to distinguish between science which understands being in terms of mechanistic hierarchies, and that which portrays it in terms of organic interdependence. Yet ironically, our situation within the cultural paradigms of our inheritance is perhaps more organic than McFague has bargained for. In taking her stand within the inheritance of Western scientific rationality, she may not be able to separate herself so completely as she intends from the side of it she rejects — the culture of control, the Baconian legacy. For as Catharina Halkes has observed,[8] 'technology is the genetic code of our society'. And technology, the handmaiden of Western science, is essential for the apprehension of that 'common creation story' on which she sets so much store as the basis for a vision of unity in diversity. It is through the microscope and the telescope (not to mention the TV camera, underwater camera, etc.) that we have been privileged to see into the wonders of evolutionary history. And this technology issues from the same matrix as that we have used to order Nature and protect us from her ravages. It is the same technological capacity that produced the testing of nuclear devices in the Pacific — undertaken for the sake of our security.

This 'privileged' aspect of our seeing is relevant to the question of how 'common' is this common creation story that she advocates. She hopes that this new version of the old dream of paradise — the restoration of the harmony between nature and humans — will provide us with the sort of security that won't compel us to destroy the earth in order to obtain it; that it will cause us to leave behind those contaminated politics of the past that produced Rongelap and Hiroshima and Auschwitz, and unite in a final struggle to save our common home, the earth, from ultimate destruction. But our position as the victors through technology may mean that we fail to perceive that what we regard as 'common ground' may otherwise be regarded as disputed territory.

McFague would no doubt claim that she has informed the 'stories of science' with her own theological vision of creation as the very Body of God. It is a vision which she believes takes up some of the highest values of Christianity while not being limited by its narrow historical bias. Thus, through her model of divine embodiment in creation we may acknowledge our shared bodiliness with the poor, and particularly with the 'new poor' — those species and life forms whose existence we threaten with our greed and lust for control. To have a care for the inclusion of the outcast and oppressed is a scandal by conventional standards, she says, and makes no sense in the process of selection in evolutionary biology. Yet she commends us to this traditional Christian vocation — to feed the body of God and nurture it in the form of those who are threatened or oppressed.

It sounds like a truly innocent and radical dream. But I confess there is something about her language that makes me suspicious. It reminds me how easy it is to contemplate the sufferings of others before the ageing ache, the cancer or the hunger has become a stubborn lodger in one's own body. But when that happens, the talk of holistic embodiment somehow loses its shine and develops a sickly quality. One cannot quite escape the feeling that, however much they are stressed, the sufferings of the poor in McFague's work have an aesthetic function. They are the black and red in the grand design of the quilt that has no designer.

But there is another aspect too. Embedded in her highminded ideal-ism about the 'new poor' — creatures and species that are threatened with extinction — it seems to me there is a contradiction the implications of which she does not explore. Like her, we may yearn to wander in the forest at our leisure, to contemplate the huckleberries and the redwoods, and be confident that their future is not terminally threatened. We have come to see it as part of our right as enlightened citizens to enjoy the beauties of nature. Much of our ecological outrage stems from the fact that this privilege is being eroded. As we drive or fly out to see Nature's beauty spots, we are dismayed to find so many others with the same idea. Pollution and tourist abuse are spoiling Nature's beauty, and she is no longer 'virgin' just for us. And so we seek places further and further afield, we crave the lost wilderness in which it is traditional to seek God.

But it seems there may be some conflict between the poor and the not-quite-poor, and those who want to re-create the wilderness in order to restore the spiritual harmony with creation. The poor do indeed need to be fed; and like other ordinary people they aspire to feed themselves, to gain a livelihood from the land.

On America's old frontier a drama is currently being enacted that suggests that there is a factor in our ecological concerns that we have tended to underplay. In Montana, where once the cowboys hunted down the Indian tribes, their descendants are themselves being invaded. Americans tired of urban sprawl, crime and pollution are moving to Montana in droves. But the ranchers resent the invasion which threatens their own lifestyle and livelihood. There is conflict over the use of natur-al resources, as the newcomers push for millions of acres of the land to be protected in perpetuity from all commercial activity. To the ranchers' horror, the good-to-be-green people feel that their wilderness will not be complete without the re-introduction of wolves — which are, of course, the natural enemy of cattle. And so the lines are drawn up between the new invaders with Nature on their banner, and the old settlers who are more concerned with making a living in the time-honoured way. The latter have begun to resist this 'Californication of the wilderness'[9] which they see as, in effect, the creation of a rich people's park.

What has begun to happen in the USA may prefigure a similar conflict on a global scale — in which the greens and eco-spirituals unwittingly become the gamekeepers and wardens for the lords of the New World Order, preserving their grounds in all their glory so that they may take their ease there, and scaring off the 'poachers' whose short-sighted concern is only for their next meal. It is not surprising that the Third World nations are sceptical about our earnest concern for the preserva-tion of bio-diversity, when the West has for so long been so little concerned to preserve the human diversity of the poor and their need for habitat and livelihood in order to flourish.

Thus, in the midst of the lamb-like innocence of our ecological ideals, we discover the 'wolfish' aspect of class interest that is still lurking; the well-meaning green guardians of creation are also those who are willing to defend the threat to their recreational resources. Our noble care for the future of creation begins to appear in a different light. All those new wildernesses-plus-wolves could be seen as the film sets for the great Hollywood drama we are making; the post-Enlightenment version of life in paradise, the garden of Eden for those who can afford it. In the re-created wildernesses of this paradise, nature no longer rules, for it has become part of the park of the New World Order, where the well-off get to select the best apples.

Despite her concern to uphold the mutuality of all life forms, and challenge anthropocentrism, there is a sense in which McFague and other ecofeminist theologians implicitly present ourselves as a sort of ethical summit of creation, a critical crossroads where the whole future of the evolutionary process hangs on the outcome of our choices. But I suggest that we subject this picture to a little of the hermeneutical suspicion that we have employed on other theologies. We shall note that feminists are not all agreed as to the means by which creation may be restored. There is a spectrum of opinion ranging around three poles; from those who favour a Goddess/Mother Earth cosmology, those who support a distinctive feminist ethics, and those who see the way forward through science purged of its androcentrism. We feel that these differences are healthy and reassuring, an essential part of the project. And yet it may be that these differences are more apparent than real, that the matter of which cosmology will reign in the future of the world is already a foregone conclusion. The scientific discourse is in fact the victor of all modern cosmologies and the feminist alternatives are in reality part of the victory parade. This can be seen more clearly in the consequences (or non-consequences) of our ethical dissent. Disagreement among ourselves or with the state is unlikely to have any untoward consequences. Not for us the fear of imprisonment, deportation, exile, or impoverishment. On the contrary, it is likely that if we express ourselves with flair and articulation, our books will be published (like this one), our reputation increased, our promotion prospects enhanced. Highmindedness is both expected of us and rewarded. We have our own float on the carnival of victory, and here there is Nature as carnival queen, hiding her arbitrariness behind a mask of beauty. Her nymphs engage in a ritual duel with the devils of machismo, and then, triumphant at last, she steps forward hand in hand with her regal partner Science, now purged of androcentric error, and reveals the brave new world of reformed creation. This is the new mystery play in which the true body of God is unveiled, and we are called on to repent and revere the earth in a revived sacramentalism. The tourists and the natives applaud. The latter return to their fields, where Western science may soon claim them with a landmine, or Mother Nature fold them to her bosom through drought or famine or childbirth. Meanwhile, the tourists and the actors proceed to their air-conditioned hotel. Afterwards, on safari they may enjoy a frisson of pleasurable fear as they watch dangerous beasts at a safe distance.

But the feminist play in the pageant of science fails to tell the whole truth about our future in creation. The story of Rongelap which we began with seems to me to be more illuminating. I see it as a modern parable of the spoiling of creation. It shows up that particular yearning for earthly paradise that is a feature of the modern European psyche. It also shows how the obsession of that same society with technological solutions to its security have led to the destruction of such places of natural paradise that we have yearned for. The pursuit of this obsession has come to imperil the whole generative process on which the future of creation depends. It highlights how the presence of undeserved suffering, particularly that of children, always ensures that the question of sin will be present to each generation.

As we have seen, much feminist theology, including that of McFague, is written by those who have been reared on the myth of original innocence. Thus any suggestion of the transmission of sin is anathema. Confronted with the evidence of human sin, the ideal of human innocence must be preserved. The remedy is to overhaul once again the instruments of perfectibility — to see if the flaw can be detected and corrected in the forms of our symbolic knowledge. Thus, McFague seeks to modernize our creation stories, and present us with her organic model for both science and theology. But somehow there are problems. As Mary Grey queries in an otherwise rave review of *The Body of God*,

> Is the world the body of God or simply 'seen' as such? If all seeing is the Wittgensteinian 'seeing as', have we lost the shock of realisation that if, for example, the fishes and birds die off, God dies — and therefore the horrifying embodiment of the suffering of God?[10]

We have seen how even those imbued with organic models on their quest for restoration of spiritual harmony may soon be bogged down in an age-old conflict of political interests centring on the control of land and natural resources. We are forced to ask: is there something in our nature that means it will keep happening? And if creation is God's body, can God ever stop giving birth to all these deformed babies that are the result of our conflicts over security? Who can ever put right the genetics of sin, or that which is wrong in nature — in our nature and in creation — if God partakes in that same nature with us? Is God's body also subject to that flaw in human culture which Augustine attributed to the sin of disobedience — rather like that 'flaw' in human genes caused by the radioactivity which entered the genes of the Rongelap islanders, with the tragic consequences that we know?

Distasteful as it may be for some of us, I think we should at least consider the possibility that Augustine's thinking came out of a passion for justice and compassion for innocent suffering that was at least equal to our own. His anguish about inherited evil caused him to produce his own speculations about the 'genetics of sin' and to defend them fiercely, as when he taunts Julian, 'You see your whole heresy shipwrecked upon the misery of infants!'[11] His realization that human life is grounded in compulsion led to his refusal to share the Hellenic optimism about rational freedom that was a feature of the neo-Platonic intellectual speculation of his day. The root of this thinking recurs in the modern scientific paradigm, and generates the same optimism about rational freedom that we see, for instance, in the work of McFague, linked in her case to a particular ideal of nature.

As we have seen, the attempts to find a blueprint for our sexual and moral lives in nature have been a failure. Nature may offer us a breathtaking, compelling beauty; but long-term contemplation of nature may also fill us with a great sadness. For nature of itself is not a source for ethics. For we, like nature, are part of creation; as creatures, we cannot be taught by nature what it is to be human. As we have seen, Mother Nature is apt to be a bit careless with the lives of her children — which is why in the past and now she has been not only marvelled at but also feared by those who were and are obliged to live on intimate terms with her. Such people tend to be idealized by the ecologically minded. Yet these are the same people who are ravaged not only by nature but by the depredations of the New World Order. Those who have apparently lost this fear include many of those who profess deep environmental concern. And they have lost the fear precisely because they are victors in a centuries-old war against nature. With the aid of technology, the Western élite has secured itself against all that makes humanity vulnerable to the cruelties of amoral nature.

Since time immemorial the human race has used various forms of technology to feed and clothe and protect itself and this has been part of the human project. Yet the technology that issues from Western science has made a qualitative leap into what is essentially a search for godlike powers — the achievement of ultimate security and of penetration into the mysteries of creation in order to bring it under human control. Such an enterprise is an act of hubris, not theology, and the signs of its nemesis have begun to appear. Yet in our ignorance we proceed, and part of this quest has been to restore the wilderness of paradise, by means of technology's management of nature. But to ape the paradisal wilderness is to misunderstand our religious situation, which it was the purpose of the original story to reveal. If paradise is lost through disobedience, our efforts cannot regain it. We shall not find God in our paradise theme parks — only ourselves. And we are not, as in our self-presentation, the ethical summit of creation; rather we are like the jellyfish babies of Rongelap, morally deformed by our inheritance of sin, as they are physically deformed by their radioactivated genes. To ape the paradisal wilderness is to court futility. For the only 'true' wilderness that remains is the one we are making. As we have done with Rongelap, and the 'paradise' of the Pacific, so we are now doing to the world. The poor have been thrown out of paradise for the sake of our security and condemned to live under the debt-mountain, where they are permitted to scratch a living in the Gehenna of that smoking heap — the rotting debris of our affluence. Perhaps God's body is to be found not in the splendid parks of the New World Order but here on the stinking ash heaps where the poor have been relegated, as they were under the Old World Order — the ancient order of sin.

A fearful suspicion arises: could it be that those deformed children of Augustine's day prefigured the fate of the world — a fate that has been further unveiled for us at Rongelap, in which infants will be poisoned from the womb, and born without the semblance of humanity? The thought is so unthinkable that we must hasten to suppress it and return to the theme of our perfectibility, issuing more tracts of implicit techno-triumphalism. And yet, some of us who have begun to know that we are not moral Stakhanovites tremble at the proposal that the world's future lies in our hands, and that we are individually responsible for our success or failure in this project. The dark side of this Pelagian optimism begins to appear as the harsh impossibility of this expectation dawns upon us. McFague's body of God suddenly seems to be not only headless (as intended) but also unintentionally heartless. Perhaps we can reconsider the old stories, absurd and incredible as they might seem, and recognize them as wiser than we realized. We may find in them, as Augustine did, the pointer to another sort of bodiliness — of both God and ourselves — that is not only more divine but also ultimately more humane.

Notes

1 Rosemary Ruether, quoted in Elizabeth Green and Mary Grey (eds), *Ecofeminism and Theology: Yearbook of the Society of Women in Theological Research* (Kampen, Netherlands: Kok Pharos, 1994), p. 51.
2 See Julian Evans, 'Letters from an invented Eden', *Guardian*, 26 Sept. 1992.

3 Information from Greenham Archives kept by Lynette Edwell.
4 Sallie McFague, *The Body of God: An Ecological Theology* (London: SCM, 1993).
5 McFague, p. 220.
6 McFague, p. 159.
7 Sandra Harding, *The Science Question in Feminism* (Milton Keynes: Open University Press, 1986). See Charlotte Methuen's review of this in Elizabeth Green and Mary Grey (eds), *Ecofeminism and Theology: Yearbook of the European Society of Women in Theological Research* (Kampen, Netherlands: Kok Pharos, 1994), p. 124.
8 Catharina J. M. Halkes, *New Creation: Christian Feminism and the Renewal of the Earth* (London: SPCK, 1991), p. 159
9 See Simon Tisdall, 'Californication of a wilderness', *Guardian*, 15 Sept. 1992.
10 Mary Grey's review of McFague, *The Body of God*, in Green and Grey, p. 114
11 Augustine, *Opus Imperfectum*, 3.109.

15 *Divine bodies and the idols of despair*

Behind McFague's optimism about her theological model of the world as God's body, one can occasionally detect a less confident note — an anxiety that planetary responsibility is too much for us.[1] What if the decay of the planet is inevitable, and there's little or nothing we can do about it? As she says, 'One has to get up in the morning and look in the mirror. It may come to nothing more than that.' It is a mood that is sometimes echoed in other contemporary theologians. Carter Heyward in her book *Touching Our Strength* says:

> I am writing between sadness and hope. My faith in you, in myself, in our sacred source seems irrepressible though why I cannot tell in this moment for around me there is much despair. I'm afraid it will not be long before we know we are not exaggerating when we speak of fascism here at home. We are destroying ourselves, our flesh and blood. It is not 'those people' who are shooting up with dirty needles; not 'those others' taking their lives in shame and terror; not 'them' battered to within an inch of their lives; unless we know at the core of our integrity that we are they, neither this book nor any resources on love will make much sense to us now.[2]

This 'sacred source' that she refers to has various embodiments in ecotheology, whether it is the world as God's body, the earth as our mother, the Goddess, or the cosmic body of Christ. It can become rather confusing. As Mary Grey asks, when reviewing McFague's *The Body of God*, 'Are there just too many bodies?'[3] Perhaps the problem of this plethora of godly bodies can be clarified by uncovering the polemic that underlies all of them. For they would no doubt all agree that whatever God's body is or is not, it cannot be identified with that of the Mediterranean carpenter who lived and died two thousand years ago. These stories are substitutes for the unacceptable Christian story of the incarnation. They are apparently anti-traditional. But at another level, oddly enough, they are actually very traditional. The trouble with the Christian story was that it spoke of God not only as the creator of the whole cosmos, but dared to suggest that God had once become the body of one particular human being. This made God distinctly unGodlike — sharing all the limitations, physical, cultural and racial, of being a particular human being, and subject to mortality. In his case, it was a disgustingly painful mortality, the consequence of political defeat and religious rejection. No wonder educated people of the time treated the idea as a bad joke. Educated people of our own time continue to see it as problematic if not preposterous.

And there is another aspect to the problem. Apart from the affront to feminist sensibilities caused by this male naming of God, there is the affront represented by the institution of the church, those who claim that their presence through the centuries and in the present age represents in some sense the body of this 'son' of God. For the church is an institution much like other human institutions — subject to decay, corruption and moral sclerosis. No wonder people like Sallie McFague feel the deity deserves something better, the divine word requires a more fit embodiment. God must be rescued from the scandalous narrowness of the Christian story and Christian institutions.

Nevertheless, true to her more inclusive approach, she is anxious to give credit where credit is due, and make sure that all the 'usable' bits of Christian tradition are duly recycled in the new creation of her own model. Thus we have the pick'n'mix approach: the incarnation she rejects because it is 'offensive to other religions' but the resurrection gets through because it is affirmative of bodiliness. Likewise the sacramental tradition, though she considers it a bit primitive, receives a qualified approval because it has preserved an appreciation of nature within Christianity. The doctrine of redemption, on the other hand, is much too narrow for her vision, and salvation is to be re-visioned as healing. God is no longer the Lord of creation, the one who created the world from nothing, because the cosmos, as understood by Western scientific theory, is now the body of God. Our belonging to this body, unlike that of the body of Christ, gives us no obligations to the institutional church or to the teachings of historical Christianity. The mystical body must be demystified and made available for sensible people. We are free to take what suits our individual preferences and dump the rest in the trash can of history.

McFague in company with many other contemporary theologians believes in the plural principle and this implies that respect for differences is fundamental. In looking at other faiths, that of native Americans for example, she would no doubt agree that there is something important about the integrity of the belief system, its 'bodiliness'. But in relation to Christian faith this principle apparently does not apply. One could well argue that Christian faith has its own bodiliness, that it is an organism whose integrity is contained in its distinctive type of speech and teachings, however much these are adapted and interpreted according to the particular cultural circumstances. To subject it to the pick'n'mix treatment as McFague does is not to interpret the tradition for modern hearers but in fact to dismember it; not much evidence here of respect for bodiliness, rather more like a serious case of GBH (grievous bodily harm). The effect of her efforts is to destroy the original and replace it with a substitute.

That this is precisely the effect of 'the feminist theological revolution' is the contention of the editors and contributors to a collection edited by Alvin F. Kimel Jr., *Speaking the Christian God: The Holy Trinity and the Challenge of Feminism.*[4] Its aim is to examine the 'revolution that is taking place in the worship and discourse of English-speaking Christianity',[5] the revolution produced by feminist theology, which, as he says, presents a powerful critique of traditional theology and faith as well as offering an attractive and, for many, compelling substitute in the name of Christ. The contributors to the book are drawn from several ecclesiastical traditions including Anglican, Reformed, Lutheran, Catholic, Orthodox, Methodist and Evangelical. According to the editor, 'If being a feminist means being convinced of the absolute equality ... of man and woman as created in the image of God, then each contributor to this volume is a feminist.'[6] But theological feminism, he suggests, has moved far beyond this position towards a comprehensive critique and revision of orthodox belief, where fundamental doctrines of Christian belief, such as God, Trinity and Christ, must be rethought and reconceptualized in service to contemporary liberation. To provide a serious theological response to these far-reaching reconstructions is what the contributors are aiming to do.

The problem with all the attempts to reconceptualize God, as one of the contributors, Leslie Ziegler points out,[7] is that we end up by hearing only that which in the final analysis we have determined we are capable of hearing. The method takes control and acts as a kind of sieve for God's address. For the method presupposes the Cartesian self-understanding with its stress on the autonomous 'I'. Our theological productions are in fact reproductions of the Western notion of the transcendent self with its rational and autonomous consciousness. Thus, what is common to these new models of the divine whether they are based on existential or ontological analysis, process theology or phenomenology or on feminist ecological 'sensibility of our time' is that they tend to give rise to the mood of despair noted earlier. This is because in each case there is something which we have not been able to incorporate in our model of the divine. Since we are in control of what addresses us, God no longer has a voice. We have closed off the possibilities of hearing any word from God that could relieve our despair.

Thus, David Scott in his essay 'Creation as Christ' comments on the passage from Carter Heyward that I quoted earlier. Although, he says, this 'witnesses commendably to a heart sensitive to the pain of the world', her despair also flows logically from identifying our efforts at mutual relationships as the place where 'god' happens.[8]

Since the majority of contributors to this volume are male, it is not difficult to imagine that some feminist theologians will dismiss their critique as representatives of the male church making a comeback with some more subtle attempts to preserve their ascendancy under the cloak of a defence of doctrine. If this is so, I have no doubt that in due course the weakness of their defence and self-deception will be exposed. But I suggest that not all defence of traditional doctrines proceeds from these motives, and that sometimes it may be the doctrines that we have casually discarded that have the power to rescue us from the impasse and incoherence that our own substitute doctrines have led us to. Thus, Elizabeth E. Green, herself a feminist theologian, suggests that ecofeminist theology finds itself caught in a contradiction.

Its commitment to the liberation of women means it stresses the notion of women as *imago dei*, but its commitment to ecological integrity means that it seeks to avoid that anthropocentrism which the *imago dei* has traditionally grounded.[9]

This unresolved tension, she suggests, comes to the fore in the eschatology of ecofeminism. Here the many — humans, animals, plants — are absorbed into the one God-world which knows no end. The consequence of this is that human beings are deprived of their grounding in the future of God.

Bodiliness, an exceptionally important category for ecofeminist theology, actually has no future. The potentialities released by our death go into a sort of giant lucky dip from which the world now takes its pick.[10]

She concludes that by cosmologizing the resurrection in this way, ecofeminist theology is inadequate to 'women's basic longings for a reconciled corporeity, true selfhood and a just community'. She calls for an ecofeminist reading of the resurrection, because otherwise the choices we make concerning our fellow-creatures do not ultimately count, and the human and non-human victims of ecological destruction never experience ultimate vindication.[11]

Although McFague claims to accept the resurrection, she has jettisoned so much of the rest of the faith that it is difficult to know what meaning it has in the new context she creates. Her attitude and that of many of her colleagues to the 'body' of faith is, I suggest, comparable to the Western technological mind in its attitude to economic resources; it seeks to rationally extract the 'usable essence' from natural resources in a way that ignores and disturbs the balance of nature of which they form part. Thus, trying to abstract the ethical essence from the body of a historically outdated faith may not be as useful or as simple as it seems. McFague rejects the incarnation because in terms of the new science it is irrational, in terms of her own vision, ethically distasteful. Yet here we should recall that McFague's perspective is not somehow neutral and objective. It also emerges from within a mythological framework, one that is unacknowledged by the author, and the genesis of which took place in reaction to the faith she now dissects. If we follow back the genealogy of her thought we find it is part of a sustained polemic, rooted in the myth of original innocence.

The effects of this allegiance are apparent in every aspect of her thought. One of the consequences of her rejection of the incarnation is her ignorance of the particularity of bodies. She focuses on the universal body of the Cosmos, of God and on the uniqueness of the individual, or the individual life form. But she doesn't have much time for what you might call intermediate bodies — the institutional bodies that shape and inculturate human life in manifold ways. In her focus on the unique individual and the universal body, she obscures from us her own location in the dominant individualist ideology of the particular society that she emerges from. It is evident that she shares with many of her feminist predecessors, as well as with other liberal or radical writers, what I will call the doctrine of Institutional Sin. This holds that the origins of sin are to be found not first and foremost in the individual, but in corrupt and authoritarian institutions. It is these that condition and constrain the rightful desires and instincts of the natural person. Thus, to be free from sin is to seek liberation from the corrupt power of these institutional and impersonal structures and to re-locate oneself in the original harmony of the human person and the cosmos, in the return to Eden. Thus, there is a sense in which our horror of the body has been transferred to the body politic which we regard as a source of corruption rather as gnostics and platonists regarded the physical body.

I suggested earlier that feminists were strongly opposed to the notion of the transmission of sin. But this is not strictly true. The doctrine of institutional sin can be understood as a direct response to what has been understood as the doctrine of Original Sin. It claims implicitly that the individual is not the site of the sin of our origins; the individual is a 'free' place of pure potentiality, and the hope for new beginnings. It is institutions that are the source of danger, the place in which human sin is transmitted, passed on, and all that limits the human spirit is stunted and constrained. This doctrine of sin was implicit in much of the earlier feminist theology and was responsible for the culture of hostility towards 'structures' that were characteristic of the women's movement in those days. Feminists whose formation was in the radical feminism of the 1970s and 1980s were thus unlikely to engage in long-term non-confrontational building up of institutions to protect and advance the position of non-feminist women in a low socio-economic position, since this would risk compromise through involvement with 'structures'. This meant in effect that the 'advancement' of women was only likely to take place on an individual basis. For despite the rhetoric of solidarity, this was an almost inevitable consequence of a movement that evinced such a fierce distrust of structures and regarded institutions as being embodiments of male sin and corruption. But institutions do not merely constrain us to corruption — they also provide people with protection, a protection which they need and desire even when, or perhaps especially when, it protects them from being on an equal level with other people of the same sort. Institutions are also bodies — they resist attack, attempt to preserve their inheritance, are subject to decay and also sometimes give birth. The feminist revulsion from setting up institutions and structures concealed from ourselves the ethnic and class nature of our enterprise. As I observed before, this hostility to structures on the part of women in the CR groups concealed an unwillingness to put sisterly co-operation to the test by challenging the authority of their traditional male protectors. The CR groups had little appeal for black women who were not primarily interested in intrapsychic self-examination and who, as one of them observed, were 'more likely to start a feeding program for the neighbourhood'.[12]

Thus, much of the radical separatist rhetoric concealed a fine adjustment to the protectorate status of Western women, which was well served by the ideology of structurelessness. And although McFague has attempted to bring feminist theology out of the ghetto by addressing the ecological crisis in the mainstream discourse of post-modern science, the effect is largely to move it into the wider class captivity of which the ghetto was always part. This is evident in the fundamental texture of her work. For despite the changes and significant re-locations there is a kind of recurrent uniformity about feminist theology of this type. It is what you might call the turkey-after-Christmas syndrome. After a while, no matter how ingenious the recipe, one begins to be able to detect the same old texture and taste as the turkey keeps coming back.

The turkey, I suggest, is a certain kind of theological flaw which, because we have not properly identified it, keeps on repeating itself. McFague reproduces the by-now classical feminist reaction to what she sees as the dualist, anti-materialist approach of theologians like Augustine. Yet her own thought is permeated by a particular brand of Cartesian construct that relies on abstraction to a high degree — an abstract ideal of the body that is grounded in the well-protected bodies of the Western élite. Her approach is based on the attempt to extract the kernel of truth from the garbage of particularity. Yet ironically, as we shall see, in the very nature of this approach she reveals her own particularity.

Unlike the post-Christians she does not regard the church as any sort of threat. She can belong to the church on her own terms, dictating what she will accept and what she considers unacceptable. She writes about it as if it were a stage too small for her operations, too narrow for her all-embracing vision of a cosmological ethics that will lift her above the compromising political realities of her nation and the parochial perspectives of her church. But it is these very same abstractions which locate her as precisely as DNA links particular cells to a particular body. For language is the means by which our cultural codes are passed on, and our theological errors are passed on through our linguistic genes.

Leslie Ziegler in his essay 'Christianity or Feminism?' refers to a study published by Peter Berger in 1961 called *The Noise of Solemn Assemblies*[13] in which he suggested that American Protestant Christianity had become a cultural religion serving to legitimate the American way of life. Twenty-five years later, Berger updated the study and found that important changes had occurred in American society, notably the rise of

a new middle class, based on the production and distribution of symbolic knowledge, whose members are the increasingly large number of people occupied with education, the media of mass communication, therapy in all its forms, the advocacy and administration of well-being, social justice and personal lifestyles.[14]

But one kind of change had not occurred — that between church and society. The one still served to legitimate the other. The Protestant churches drew their membership from both old and new middle class, but their younger clergy, denominational officials and intellectuals have strongly identified with the political agenda of the new middle class, for whom feminism is the prevailing orthodoxy.

Thus McFague's abstract universalism is quite as scandalously particular in its conceptualizing of God as the Christian version — but in a rather different way. The fact is that there is no concept that is outside the mythological body, as the genealogy of her thinking reveals. As we have seen, her own thinking is situated within the Cartesian 'antibody' to Christian thought, and its understanding of the human self is based on abstraction performed by the rational intellect. It has no room for the role of the Holy Spirit, or the body of God in the historical community of the church. But the self of Christian tradition in its non-Cartesian form is constituted by its relation to God, and not the other way round. The Holy Spirit creates its hearers and our identity is determined by God who addresses us and who incorporates us into that history to which the scriptures bear witness. Here it is the process of discernment that is the true alternative to abstraction, that enables us to proceed amid the corruption of structures, and that has the possibility of the renewal of ourselves and our tradition under the guidance of the Spirit.

The response of ecofeminist theologians like McFague to the problem of corruption witnessed in the ecological crisis is to abstract a vision of the good. But these abstractions will always return us to the captivity of our class confinement. This is because they urgently maintain the fiction of our unfettered will, and sin that is located not in any deformity of the soul but in the constraints of corrupt institutions. Thus, our ideal godly bodies of ecotheology hold up as long as we are in good health, and the social boundaries protect us from mental or physical destitution. But if by some chance or process, we are exposed to the terrifying realization that we are at one with the raw flesh of human wretchedness, then suddenly our bright shiny divinities may begin to buckle under the weight of our despair. Something of this sort seems to be happening to Carter Heyward in the passage quoted at the beginning of this chapter. In these circumstances, we are perhaps like the character in Isaiah, who makes a god for himself — out of impeccably natural resources, the same wood that provides him with fuel in fact. To this God he bows down and worships and prays: 'Save me; you are my God' (Isa 44.17). But as Elizabeth Green says, 'To put it bluntly, sacramentalism only "works" when nature is not considered divine.'[15] And as Isaiah says, even more bluntly, 'Shall I bow down to a block of wood?'

Our idols these days are more sophisticated — not images fashioned out of wood but concepts crafted at the keyboard, requiring constant update in line with the latest model of cultural perceptions or scientific knowledge. Yet it seems they are no more effective in saving us from despair than the block of wood. This mood of radical despair, as we have seen, can surface even within a comfortable co-existence of church and society. And this is not surprising, because the logic of despair must always lead to an accommodation with the status quo. If God is simply 'in us' then the 'works of men' are all we can know of reality and there is nowhere else to turn, no basis of hope from knowledge of a different source. There is no longer any 'other' God who has the power to call us out of our class, ethnic and gender captivity. Our brave new bodies of God are merely these idols reconstituted and re-mystified. To rest our faith in these is, according to Elisabeth Achtemeier, 'the ultimate idolatry, in which the Trinity is destroyed, the holy otherness of God from creation is lost, and human beings have usurped the place of their Creator'.[16] But those who are touched with radical despair also have another option — that is to explore a more daring story of the body of God; to re-consider perhaps that story of God, where God shows us to ourselves, not as we would be but as we are, eating the flesh of the victim. Yet this God claims to be present in that victim, calling us to eat his own flesh and drink his blood. What kind of unspeakable sacrament is this? There are certain stories — and this is one of them — that can only be heard from within the body, as it were. They cannot be heard if we have first dismembered the body in order to get at its ethical core. We must enter the body in order to remember a particular death, to discern a very particular body. Thus the meaning of the incarnation suggests that we should seek God not in some idealized virgin Mother Nature, but in the body of God in Christ, even in its flawed institutional form. To participate in the particular pattern of remembering which is the life of the church is to enter the body of tradition that speaks to us of sin and redemption and of God's final judgement and God's grace. It is this that is the basis of any truly radical theology and not the many varieties of self-worship and class containment that underlie such theologies as McFague's. Paradoxically it is the realization that we are not God, that we are subject to sin and cannot be the final judge of ourselves, that has the power to liberate us from the paralysis of guilt and to regenerate hope.

Notes

1 Sallie McFague, *The Body of God: An Ecological Theology* (London: SCM, 1993), pp. 207–8.
2 Carter Heyward, *Touching Our Strength: The Erotic as Power and the Love of God* (San Francisco: Harper and Row, 1989), p. 88.
3 Elizabeth Green and Mary Grey (eds), *Ecofeminism and Theology: Yearbook of the European Society of Women in Theological Research* (Kampen, Netherlands: Kok Pharos, 1994), p. 114.
4 Alvin F. Kimel, Jr. (ed.), *Speaking the Christian God: The Holy Trinity and the Challenge of Feminism* (Leominster: Gracewing, 1992).
5 Kimel, p. ix.
6 Kimel, p. x.
7 Leslie Ziegler, 'Christianity or feminism?', in Kimel, p. 318.
8 David A. Scott, 'Creation as Christ: a problematic theme in some feminist theology', in Kimel, pp. 255–6.
9 Elizabeth E. Green, 'The transmutation of theology', in Green and Grey, p. 55.
10 Green in Green and Grey, p. 55.
11 Green in Green and Grey, p. 56.
12 Susan Brooks Thistlethwaite, *Sex, Race, and God: Christian Feminism in Black and White* (London: Geoffrey Chapman, 1990), p. 21.
13 Peter Berger, *The Noise of Solemn Assemblies: Christian Commitment and the American Religious Establishment* (Garden City, N.Y.: Doubleday, 1961), quoted by Leslie Ziegler in Kimel, p. 315.
14 Peter Berger, 'Reflections of an ecclesiastical expatriate', quoted by Ziegler in Kimel, p. 316.
15 Green in Green and Grey, p. 54.
16 Elisabeth Achtemeier, 'The impossible possibility: evaluating the feminist approach to Bible and theology', quoted by Ziegler in Kimel, p. 329.

16 The Last Judgement as liberation

If the kinds of creation theologies developed by McFague and others are not a basis for a radical theology and politics but a form of illusion tied to the fatal idolatries of the Western world, where then shall we ground our hope for justice? I suggest that we must look towards the work of those feminist theologians and others who demonstrate the capacity to use the resources of scripture and tradition more faithfully and with less hubris. It is only with the aid of these resources that we have the hope of breaking out of the prison of the Western discourse of self, and its idealized rhetoric of liberation.

In this connection then, we should consider the thesis of Kari Børresen, a Norwegian patristics scholar and feminist theologian, who aims to produce a theology based on 'sana doctrina' (healthy/sane teaching), which incorporates the Catholic understanding of a coherence between scripture and tradition as parts of an ongoing revelation.[1] In this she follows the line of the reforming Cardinal Nicolaus Cusanus who understood revelation to be the unfolding in history of God's eternal unfolding. Her concept of ongoing revelation is centred on the incarnation of Christ, but incarnation which must be realized in a manner understandable for human beings. It presupposes that creation is not wholly alienated from God as a result of the Fall, and that redemption is fulfilled by divine and human interaction, by the Holy Spirit acting in human history.

But living at the end of the twentieth century as we do, to place any hope at all in the workings of human history seems intensely problematical. As the mists of post-cold war euphoria clear away, new clouds of a resurgent fascism in Europe have appeared on the horizon, and reawaken terrible images still present in living memory that our century has produced. For in the twentieth century, though we have dispensed with the Last Judgement of God, we have provided ourselves with the detailed imagery of hell, in the form of the holocaust, prepared by those who were given over to the totalizing myths of modernity. And it is from these myths of modernity, myths in which feminism has had a share, that we need to be liberated. I am suggesting that we can only take on human history without resort to these myths if we first understand how, in the last analysis, the judgement of God is the only source of liberation — for women and for men.

I have already demonstrated how the feminist ideals that were supposed to liberate us from guilt in fact did exactly the opposite — redoubled the burden of guilt so that in some cases we were subject to guilt from two sources — the old ideal of the feminine Woman and the new ideal of feminist sister. Those of us who were unable to put on instant sisterliness became vulnerable to self-reproach when we discovered in ourselves feelings of anger, resentment or envy towards our sisters. We believed that the oppression of women committed us to judging the world by our own ideals and were unaware of how this would plunge us into moral contradiction. For assuming the role of judge in relation to corruptible and self-interested men, we rapidly came to fear that our own seething and fearful emotions would betray us as equally corruptible and self-seeking. Hence the necessary myth of women's innocence and the temptation to hypocrisy in the interests of the idealized self.

But the ikon of the idealized self is by no means exclusive to feminism. It is the form of the fundamental idolatry of the society of which we are part, and all forms of it bring with them the inescapable burden of guilt. For as we seek to find an image of our selves reflected in the mirror of our ideals, we are confronted time and again with our stubborn unloveliness. We seek our lost loveliness in the face of the earth — but here again we are too often reminded of the ghastly ugliness we have created. We are determined to re-possess the Garden of Eden as of right. But we watch with horror as we are forced to acknowledge ourselves as the abuser, like the one who seeks in the child his own lost lovableness and innocence, and in so doing destroys her. And we recoil as we show up on the screen of our desires as both the abuser and the abused. For while our ideals proclaim and commend the autonomous self, exercising its power of choice, our desires tell a different story. It is the story of the self that is suffocated by an autonomy that denies its helplessness, and seeks to reclaim itself as a dependent being, weak with desire and vulnerable to pain. Ironically these manifestations of our desire may tell us more about the condition of our souls than our idealistic fantasies of the self can ever do.

For the mirror refuses to show us the acceptable face we dream of. Here there are only shadows and inconsequential fragments and ugly distortions. The mirror tells what we would rather was left untold — it is unforgiving. We are tempted to smash it, to accept the mirror of ideology which tells us a more flattering story, in which we appear in our true loveliness and the Other bears all the ugly marks of sin.

And thus we have that strange paradox of a modern society: we have enshrined the principle of the autonomy of the individual and cast aside with contempt the belief that we are subject to the judgement of God in all our doings. Yet we are perpetually subject to a yearning for crisis (*krisis* is Greek for judgement), for the judgement of God that would free us from the terrible burden of self-judgement that is the product of our unforgiving idealism. It is crisis in the form of war that most frequently has satisfied this desperate modern hunger and this helps to explain the peculiar thrill that war generates for many of those caught up in it. Despite its horrors and deprivations, many people have testified to that sense of enhanced living that war has the capacity to create. Many of those who flocked to enlist on the eve of the first world war sensed in it the possibility of a cleansing from the weight of inherited iniquity. But this 'war to end all wars' soon reduced them to rotting flesh in the trenches. With a terrifying inevitability it seems, the satisfaction of this hunger for 'cleansing' is only achieved by a washing in blood.

This yearning for a solution to our perpetual and recurrent guilt is shaped in European history by the particular form of our Christian inheritance. The image of the Last Judgement is one that has conditioned the European popular religious imagination for centuries. In the last two of these centuries, we seem to have dispensed with it. Yet it now seems that it has not been so much discarded as recycled. Repressed from sophisticated and civilized consciousness, it has regained power in the unconscious of our imagination and surfaced in a fearful political real-ization. Those who brought us 'The Final Solution' could be said to be working on the model of 'The Last Judgement'. They were the prototype of the post-Christians for whom God is definitively dead, and therefore God's traditional functions, such as the Last Judgement, needed to be taken over and re-designed in the image of Man. But although we have officially rejected the Final Solution as Last Judgement, there is a sense in which the Final Solution which was pioneered and established by Hitler is still being applied to millions of our fellow inhabitants of the world. For despite the defeat of the Third Reich, there is a real sense in which we are the daughters and sons of Hitler. We, the sophisticated post-Christians of the post-war world, cannot credit the reality of God as Judge of the world. The Last Judgement, it seems, has been such an intimate part of the European soul that after its suppression we have had to re-invent it. For the vision of God's judgement, as we find it in our scriptural heritage, is a threat to the New World Order as it was to the previous world order. The suspicion that we may be judged on our treat-ment of the poor and wretched is unlikely to be popular in a society like ours that has reduced two-thirds of the world to a desperate destitution. Thus,

we have used all our scientific and technical ingenuity to find a 'final solution' to the threat of God's justice. For in the Twentieth Century we know ourselves to be image-makers on a grand scale: The whole world has become a theatre for our cosmic dramas and their special effects. At the press of a button whole populations can vanish… Why then should we wait on God — who by all accounts is notoriously unreliable — to act in such an important matter as the final judgement when we have all the means available to do it ourselves? [2]

With the extermination camps and the Gulag, we perfected the construction of hell; now in the post-war period we have come up with a designer paradise for the consumer elect.

Yet feminist theology has consistently attempted to expose the political and theological arrogance of our current world designers and resist their claims at every level. It has drawn our attention to those who are the victims of the post-war world order and to the fact that they are a female majority. The problem about this endeavour is that it has led us too into the role of designers of the 'final' judgement. For much of feminist theology, as we have observed, has been a matter of contesting the 'first judgement' of Paradise Lost — as far as woman is concerned. According to a common feminist motif, Eve never really did anything to merit being thrown out of Eden and therefore can be considered to have the right of return there at any time she wishes to make use of it. And if God can't be trusted to get it right at the beginning of time, there's obviously no sense in leaving it to the final judgement for Him to establish the true worth of women.

But as I have suggested in my examination of McFague's theology all such attempts to 'reverse' the judgement and relocate salvation back in the innocent garden of Nature's paradise will lock us firmly into the idealist trap. We are part of a society whose huge technological competence in this century has conquered Nature. And it is not really Nature that we honour and idolize in these creation theologies but the image of human competence and autonomy — our capacity to make blueprints of the future and carry them out. A recent TV documentary entitled *Blueprints for Hell* examined the case of newly recovered documents that showed conclusively the complicity of the architects and engineers in designing the crematoria of Auschwitz. We already know of the complicity in the holocaust of a whole range of professions from railway officials to theologians. So is there any particular significance about the corruption of a large section of professional people? Only that it reminds us of the Faustian dilemma which all our professional competence and scientific knowledge exposes us to. It is not simply that there are good blueprints and evil ones; it is rather that every blueprint, including our theological blueprints, which is not subject to the judgement of God has an evil tendency. The blueprints for the crematoria of Auschwitz only make explicit the hubris that is implicit in all blueprints that issue from the exercise of human autonomy and human competence.

But this is a conclusion that we are likely to resist for it appears to strip us naked. How can we act for justice if our blueprints for justice will not serve us? It is at this point that Børresen's understanding of revelation unfolding in history can take on meaning for us. But rather than examine it as a concept at this point, I would prefer to test it against a particular piece of history to see what it shows up. Thus, I want to look at the case of those, particularly those women, who resisted the perpetration of the holocaust.

The picture of women's reaction to the Third Reich, as presented by Claudia Koonz, shows that she has little sympathy for the idea that the relative political powerlessness of women has absolved them from responsibility for the period of history which perfected the technological arts of genocide. Her account shows[3] that whatever private doubts and reservations some women had, the majority of German women, like their male counterparts, gave their assent to Nazi rule and obeyed its directives. Many women were only too happy to retreat into a 'women's sphere', safely away from the realm of male politics, while others, like the infamous Scholtz-Klinke, had an eye to the main chance, and competed to be able to organize this sphere for Hitler. For Hitler needed women to convey an illusion of clean-cut decency to mask a murderous state.[4] His female organizers were often aided in their task by Christian women and their organizations. Together they created the ideal of a women's world and marketed its feminine image. In particular, Hitler was able to make use of the 'family of Western nostalgia' for his own murderous purposes.

But Koonz also shows how it was this same structure of the family that proved so manipulable for fascist purposes, that at the same time was the crucible for resistance to the total allegiance that Hitler was demanding.[5] For those who eventually came to resist those claims, it was very often family bonds that gave them alternative values to the values of Hitler's state. The bonds of family could be used to resist the dehumanizing logic of the Third Reich, whose meaning was finally demystified for its victims in the concentration camps where the system of brutal polarization of the sexes reached its climax, and all family connections were cut off, and women and children were segregated from men. In the camps, the first stage of resistance was often marked by a refusal to submit to the dehumanization of gender separation — as people re-created non-biological ties to replace those that had been severed. And in the world of resistance outside the camps, opponents tended to guard their humanity in an integrated society of people from varied backgrounds and both sexes. Victims and resisters used the model of the family as a basis for secret preserves of decency, love and trust, a reassuring vision of strength and steadfastness.

But as Koonz shows, the sex-stereotype roles of culture and the family also underwent changes in the particular situation of the resistance.[6] Most of the resistance was non-violent and didn't depend on military skills normally attributed to men. So opponents were forced to apply skills that culture normally considers feminine — such as deception, analysing the enemy's personality, manipulating the weaknesses of the most powerful, and cultivating an innocent appearance. Thus, although victims and opponents often played out stereotypical roles for pragmatic reasons as well as because of unconscious assumptions, it seems that life underground or in the camps often helped to dissolve some of these assumptions.

Memoirs ... abound in stories about how men learned the skills that most women learn as children — nurturing, caring, cleansing, and sharing; and women discovered unknown strengths when they had to run dangerous missions in places where any man of draftable age would have been arrested on the spot.[7]

In short, those who resisted Nazi rule knew that sporadic acts of defiance produced only martyrs. Resistance meant long-term collaborative deviousness — pitting wit not physical power against the enemy. And though, as Koonz points out, this is a 'quintessentially feminine strategy' it was not by that token widely adopted by the majority of women in the Third Reich. Those who opted for resistance, both women and men, did so at great personal risk, but most women chose to employ their feminine strategies in less risky areas.

In her book, *When the Light Pierced the Darkness*,[8] Nechama Tec made a study of Christian rescue of Jews in Nazi-occupied Poland to see what, if any, special characteristics there were among those who were willing to risk their lives and offer safety — a chance of salvation — to those others whose lives were under sentence from Nazism. She found it very difficult to identify any special set of characteristics which they shared. There were examples of help extended by the least likely individuals, and denied by those who promised it, or who because of a special relation of love and friendship were expected to provide it. There were even cases of known anti-Semites who risked their lives for Jews. Nevertheless, as a result of her research, she was in the end able to make some observations about those who showed themselves willing to engage in life-threatening behaviour for the sake of those who had no other claim on them except that they were a fellow human being in dire need. She found they came from different walks of life and related differently to politics and religion, and they only rarely confined their aid to friends. They tended to be people who were independent in their personal convictions, and who had a broad and long-lasting commitment to standing up for the helpless and needy. They tended to perceive their aid to Jews in a matter-of-fact unassuming sort of way, denying its heroic or extraordinary quality. Their aid to Jews often had unpremeditated or unplanned beginnings, which could have happened gradually, suddenly or even impulsively. They apparently had the ability to disregard the attributes of those they saved except those that expressed extreme suffering or need. Thus, in some cases they were able to save those for whom they had no liking or respect.[9]

Koonz' study of resistance among women in the Third Reich confirms some of these findings.[10] She found that people who made the greatest choices of all felt that, in some sense, they had no choice — even though they frequently had to endanger their own nearest and dearest in order not to betray others with whom they did not have those sorts of ties. Yet it is interesting that many of those whose resistance was most profound did not apparently undergo agonies of moral doubt, but saw it simply as a duty which they had to respond to. Koonz quotes the case of a German woman who protected a Jewish family and who hardly understood the question when a historian asked her to explain why she had taken the risk:

Basically, that's just how it was. I say to myself simply, 'This is a fellow human being in trouble and I can stand by him. Well, that's just my damned duty.' God, or maybe it was just life, gave the orders. I am no heroine.[11]

Koonz noticed that in interviews, whereas ex- (and not so ex-) Nazis routinely justified their participation in the Third Reich in terms of 'higher ideals' like patriotism and admiration for Hitler's authoritarianism, the resisters minimized the decision-making process altogether stating simply that they saw no alternative. Recalling their choices, they did so in terms which are personal and moral, not ideological. Their memoirs do not include many references to their ideological principles and abstract ideals (quite common in the memoirs of those on the other side) but instead recall events in daily life — friends and neighbours in trouble — which led them to resist. The stories seem to suggest that the ability to make 'saving' moral choices is based on a capacity for response that is, unlike ideological choices, careless of personal security, even moral security. Thus resisters sometimes made options that might well have been hard to justify even on the best moral principles — like the endangering of dependants and those closest to them. To have the capacity for such a choice, though it may be made suddenly, almost impulsively, would seem to be a result of a life pattern of little choices and habitual response to human need — a slow education of feeling and action that in a crisis knows, as if by instinct, what it is to choose human — and not inhuman — being.

The testimony of these resisters suggests to me the way in which history in conjunction with our scriptural heritage can be a source of revelation for us. For we can see at a distance against the canvas of history what it means for someone to act humanly. But in our own times the issue is clouded by our interested involvement in the present. We may subscribe to ideologies that speak of justice and yet be unaware of how the very language that we use to speak of justice somehow veils the injustice that is rooted in our history. The point about the resisters is that they are able by their concrete actions and response to tear aside this veil. Such is the essence of revelation. By their response to the historical circumstances they find themselves in, they are able to discern the judgement of God and demonstrate both the nature and the cost of obedience to it. Thus in their actions, liberation is released from its rhetorical bondage and given a new meaning in costly historical and personal reality.

Perhaps it is here then, in the discernment of the final judgement of God, that we may find release from the burden of guilt and self-righteousness and the temptations of spiritual pride. Our terror in giving up our right to be right is that we shall in so doing surrender our freedom, that which we have been taught to believe is the sacred part of the self. To lose it may feel like losing our selves. Yet what if the losing of the self is the key to gaining the freedom we have longed for? We inherit a tradition that speaks in these paradoxical terms — of losing one's life in order to gain it. Could it be that we are not — as we been accustomed to suppose — the authors of justice, but rather witnesses in the court of justice who do not know exactly when they will be called?

Notes

1 Kari E. Børresen (ed.), *Image of God and Gender Models* (Oslo: Solum Forlag, 1991). See her 'Introduction: Imago Dei as inculturated doctrine', pp. 9–10.

2 Angela West, 'Why Remember the Dead?', in Alastair Redfern (ed.), *Beyond Contradiction: Essays for Peace and Justice in Memory of Paul Baker 1954–1989* (Bristol: Paul Baker Estate, 1992), p. 36.

3 Claudia Koonz, *Mothers in the Fatherland: Women, the Family and Nazi Politics* (London: Cape, 1987), p. 388.

4 Koonz, p. 389.

5 Koonz, p. 407.

6 Koonz, p. 310, and p. 408.

7 Koonz, p. 408.
8 Nechama Tec, *When the Light Pierced the Darkness: Christian Rescue of Jews in Nazi-Occupied Poland* (New York: Oxford University Press, 1986).
9 Tec, pp. 188–9.
10 Koonz, p. 343.
11 Koonz, p. 342.

17 *Discerning the body*

The idea that the judgement of God is the ultimate source of our liberation from guilt and of justice for women is likely to cause scandalized astonishment to those nurtured by liberal theologies. According to these, it was fear of judgement that is the source of unhealthy anxiety and guilt, and thus theologies were designed in which forgiveness is preserved but judgement, the unwholesome element, is played down or removed altogether. For such as these, the suggestion that the judgement of God is a healthy teaching (*sana doctrina*) and the only one that can make sense of our struggles for justice is hardly to be believed.

But in a world where two-thirds live under the sentence of the most terrible judgement of our inhumanity, these liberal theologies, including much feminist theology, betray their limits — their vision of liberty is limited to the few and the fortunate. Without judgement, the concept of forgiveness becomes a nonsense. For without the knowledge of good and evil, and an understanding of the precise way we are implicated in the latter, there can be no forgiveness. And if we do not know what is truly good, as opposed to good for us, then we cannot have any experience of how the mercy of God is the flip side of the judgement of God. The point about those who resisted the holocaust is that they were able to draw aside the veil that occurs in our perception of a situation when our interests are involved. If revelation can be understood in this way, they offer us a model of the Christian vocation, as the drawing aside of the veil over truth as it presents itself in our historical circumstances, and a coming forward as witnesses to God's judgement.

But in response to this, it will be pointed out that not all resisters were Christians; and that a majority of Christians were guilty of the great betrayal which made the holocaust possible in the first place. Nevertheless, that this is so should not prevent us from seeking to identify the precise significance of those witnesses. For if Christian faith can instruct us in what it means to be fully human, then it seems appropriate that we should take as our models those witnesses, both Christian and non-Christian, who in the 'krisis' did not betray either their faith or their humanity. In a curious way, it seems to me they can throw light on the mind-set of our spiritual forebears, including those saints like Julian and Hildegard whom we admire though we do not share their understanding of the spiritual necessity for orthodoxy.[1] They were deeply conscious of the burden of discernment, the necessity to 'discern the body' in St Paul's phrase (1 Cor 11.29), to find the narrow way to the life-giving body and avoid the plurality of routes to spiritual death. We, on the other hand, coming from a different place, are apt to proclaim the plural routes with approbation. Accustomed to a multiplicity of consumer choices of ultimate insignificance, we have lost the sense of what it might mean to make 'mortal' choices that bear a final meaning. Perhaps we have also lost that sense which our Christian ancestors possessed of the arduousness of the struggle for a self-knowledge that can free us from the prison of the self.

If we accept the obligation to 'discern the body' and take these witnesses as our model, we shall become aware that the initiative for justice does not lie entirely with us. If we can do justice at all, it is only on God's terms and in God's time. Thus, it is only in very special circumstances, at a particular kairos, that the opportunity is given to individuals to make judgements that are visibly 'saving' for other human beings. And such occasions are, in any case, as much to be feared as desired since most of us, like me, are very uncertain that in the time of 'krisis' (judgement) we shall be capable of acting in the manner of those who risked their lives to oppose Hitler's Final Solution. We are aware that most of our day to day judgements are much more ambivalent in their import. Nevertheless, in many of these daily choices and decisions we do in fact exercise power in relation to other people — a power which our liberal theology causes us to minimize. For we have come to associate the exercise of power, the consequential decision, as itself a source of corruption. This I think is partly what lies behind the fear of institutional sin that I examined earlier — the fear that we shall lose our innocence and be corrupted by the weight of institutional iniquity. And from this comes the dangerous passion for purity, the desire to take refuge in the myth of the innocent individual who is justified by virtue of the victimization of her gender. But such virtue is fake virtue and such innocence is deadly. For it prevents us from achieving a true autonomy, and using whatever skill and competence is ours, whether professional or maternal or whatever, to act and judge humanly — but with fear and trembling, knowing that we do so in the sight of God. It also prevents us from developing the 'true virtue' which the resisters displayed — that slow education of feeling and action through a pattern of little choices and habitual response to human need that prepares us for a great-hearted response in the time of crisis. The story of the resisters also shows that certain fundamental institutions, like the family and church, though they are indeed subject to corruption, are simultaneously the matrix of that which makes possible the resistance to corruption. It suggests that women's role in the family, whose reactionary and oppressive potential has been justifiably exposed by feminist critics, can also be the basis for a radical resistance to the oppressive rule of idolatry.

The submission to the judgement of God is precisely not a return to the endless burden of guilt that women assume as part of their social inheritance. It is, on the contrary, that which offers a way out of all these false guilts as from false innocence. Though it will certainly undermine the spiritual pride present in some feminist theologies (as in their predecessors) this undermining can, if we are willing to allow it, become a liberation. To know oneself as a sinner is to be freed from the crushing burden of self-righteousness, from the burden of having to judge oneself by the ideals one has adopted. It is liberation from the vulnerability to guilt manipulation by one's fellow idealists, or the compulsion to engage in projection and scapegoating oneself.

Thus, we are in a better position to understand why Augustine thought the route to liberation lay through the seemingly perverse method of identification of our sins rather than pursuing our ideals. Having identified — 'confessed' — his sins, his strategy was to place all reliance on the grace of God, whose mercy he believed is greater than our own self-judgement. Augustine, in his rejection of the doctrines of Pelagianism, refused to accept the pessimistic and uncompassionate idealism which held each individual personally responsible for all their moral failures. His own teaching about Original Sin, whatever its imperfections, was far less individualistic for it portrayed our sinful nature as something corporate and inherited, thus making it in some sense a collective human responsibility rather than the cause of despair for the solitary individual sinner.

Let us at this point return to Børresen's understanding of 'sane teaching' as that which is based on ongoing revelation, centred on the incarnation of Christ. We may see in the action of the resisters a discernment in history of God's eternal unfolding; a testimony perhaps that truth in the last analysis is not an analysis, but a revelation of God's judgement, to which we are called to witness. Nevertheless, this leads on to further questions — questions about how and why the judgement of God is revealed in the incarnation of Christ. But before we can deal with that we must observe that these questions inevitably involve us in the process of theological analysis. For analysis is surely part of the business, the proper task of a theologian. So how is it possible to be a theologian and still be a witness, one who in their work must strive to 'discern the body'?

It seems to me that theological writers are basically of two types: those who use their terms and forms of speech and formulations without serious qualms, to present their version of the truth; and those who do not have this peace of mind: who behave as if there had been a bombshell within the language, a holocaust of meaning. All they can offer us is a few clues, twisted fragments from an enigmatic tale. Despite his frightful prolixity, it seems to me that Augustine belongs in the second category. He is aware that communicating faith raises a literary problem. In his *Confessions*, as I understand it, he intended to write a 'how not to' narrative of this life so as better to display the triumph of God. But unfortunately, it has frequently been co-opted by the church into a triumphalist narrative of a quite different sort.

As theologians then, we need to regain his sense that faith is something that has to be 'confessed', that, in the last analysis, can only be confessed. For our sins are the record of our failure to capture truth in our lives (or our literary productions). But viewed from the other side, so to speak, they also testify to our faith that we are not completed by our own efforts. God is that which shines through the holes we have been willing to acknowledge.

Kierkegaard's strange antics with peculiar authorial devices[2] (like manuscripts discovered in secret drawers and what not) seem to signal to readers that he felt himself to be a witness to and not author of some part of the truth that he perceived. Yet it is also possible to achieve this same effect by less contorted means. The foundational doctrines of the church, as I understand it, are the 'common speech' of those within the body of the tradition; it is speech that is not privately possessed or authored by an individual, but belongs to those who inherit within that body, who confess its particular story and hand it on through the generations. Thus, the doctrine of the church is that speech which is proper to it, and it is part of the familiar bodiliness of God, with which, through carol or carving, sacred text and solemn rite the story is told of how we have been released from the bondage of guilt that signifies our sin. And however enigmatic, obtuse or downright offensive this 'common speech' seems to us, it is necessary to submit to the discipline of learning it if we wish to enter the body that is life-giving — even when, for some, the loyalty to this speech leads directly to their death.

Those who are appointed, or appoint themselves, to decode the deep structure of this story and what it tells of God assume a special responsibility. They are neither proprietors nor authors — but guardians. And failure to fulfil this function is to betray the story and to risk condemnation. The Christian story has been many times betrayed in the history of the church — in fact it is a story of betrayal right from the beginning.

And we as feminist theologians, or as liberal theologians, are at least in part a product of this betrayal. It is, I suggest, because of the failure of the church of our times to represent to us the judgement and mercy of God in a manner 'understandable for human beings'³ that many moderns, including feminists, have turned away and produced their own versions of these mysteries unaided by the doctrines of the faith.

But it is to this doctrine that we must return if we do not wish our desperate ignorance to trip us into a lethal hubris. For within this body, those who take up the task of teaching or expounding the truth about God, risk (according to the New Testament — Matt 18.6) being worthy of the fate of drowning by millstone if they fail in their commission. Not a nice thought for a theologian! Is it perhaps the 'millstone' of our own publications and authorial productions that can drown us? Feminists in the past have frequently evinced a distaste for doctrine, and been anxious instead to extract what they see as the 'ethical essence' from the traditional body. This is the delicacy they desire. Or to vary the metaphor somewhat, they have treated the work of theological predecessors as a great rummage sale in which they hope to pick up a valuable antique with which to furnish their own apartment.

But although discernment is indeed a matter of selection and rejection, it is that which must be accomplished with the aid of the Spirit. We are not only the ones who choose — but we are the ones who have been chosen. It is this condition of 'being chosen' that enables us to discern the body. The body is the bearer of the story — a story which can only be understood from within this body. That is why it is an incarnation — word made flesh and become a human body. And the food we are offered to eat in this body is far richer and more nourishing than the delicacies we have desired. We are invited (to our horror) to eat the flesh and drink the blood of this body; and in so doing, to know all our elaborated idealisms for the spiritual junk food which they are.

But at this stage we may perceive no mystery and be simply mystified. Whose is this body that we must discern? And why should the story of it release us from our guilt and free us from the condemnation that we fear? In order to answer this, we must go more deeply into the question of redemption and of what meaning this story, this doctrine, holds for us.

Notes

1   See Kenneth Leech, *Soul Friend: A Study of Spirituality* (London: Sheldon Press, 1977) p. 154.
2   See Kierkegaard, *Either/Or: A Fragment of Life* (London: Penguin, 1992).
3   Kari E. Børresen (ed.), *Image of God and Gender Models* (Oslo: Solum Forlag, 1991), p. 10.

18 Julian's story of the remedy for sin

The classic Christian story of redemption is one that is both all too familiar and desperately alien to us at the same time. Perhaps now is the moment to adopt our new policy with regard to tradition and approach it with the aid of a Christian woman whose experience of God was mediated through the language of an age very different from our own. Julian of Norwich is already familiar to feminists, many of whom have been charmed by her vision of a motherly God, which seems to strike a chord with our attempts to re-envision God in a womanly way. She has also been claimed by the representatives of the creation spirituality as one who testifies to the real truth of the Christian scriptures, rather than the pernicious Augustinian distortion that would have us believe that it is a story about Fall and Redemption.

But on closer inspection, it seems that she is not simply a purveyor of sweetness and light, all motherliness and the celebration of nature. It was she who wrote: 'This place is prison, this life is penance, and he wants us to rejoice in the remedy.'[1] Far from contradicting the Fall/Redemption pattern of Christian thought, the whole of Julian's writings can be understood as an attempt to elucidate precisely this doctrine of the church. She devoted a lifetime to trying to understand how it is possible that we are redeemed from the bondage of sin by the death of Christ, and what is the meaning of God's judgement on us and for us.

But what is strange for us who are accustomed to the feminist gospel of freedom and equality, is that Julian, who is deeply perplexed by the question of sin, apparently never gives a thought to the discrepancy in status and power between men and women, nor does she seem to be oppressed by it. Yet she lived at a time when women enjoyed hardly a fraction of the kind of freedom, physical, mental or social, that is available to the likes of us. Her world was marked at every turn by sharp distinctions between the 'honour' of individuals according to their different and usually fairly fixed status. It is fundamental to the imagery she uses to talk about God, especially in the lord-and-servant parable, which is given to her as one of her 'showings'. She apprehends this parable as the answer to her agonized petition, that she be granted a clearer understanding of the impossible dilemma that she perceives: the necessity, according to revelation (that she fully accepts) of God's judgement on our sinful nature; and her equal certainty that in God there is no wrath, and 'the sweet eye of pity is never turned away from us, and the operation of mercy does not cease'.[2]

The lack of status and freedom of women in her situation is in our eyes a major stumbling block. But for Julian it is not the gulf of gender that troubles her, but the seemingly unbridgeable gulf between the infinitely courteous Lord who is God, and the weak, woeful and foolish flesh of Adam that we are, both women and men. The specific sins of men towards women seem to be nowhere in her view. How could she be so untouched by them, and yet remain apparently so confident? For despite our own grand claims and even grander condemnations, there is a kind of audacity about her writings and revelations that is lacking in our own. Her vision is of a man who is, as she understands it, also God, who before her eyes is tortured to death, and yet who says to her:

Are you well satisfied that I suffered for you? If you are satisfied, I am satisfied. It is a joy, a bliss, an endless delight to me that I ever suffered my Passion for you; and if I could suffer more, I should suffer more.[3]

Julian envisions God suffering torments for her sake and asking her if she is satisfied. It is a strange kind of lovers' talk that is difficult for us to understand. We become aware that she does not appear to crave freedom in the sense that we know it. Her response to the revelation of her divine lover is to submit herself to a lifetime of penance and devotion in the role of an anchorite. But Julian does not respond in this way because she is crippled with low self-esteem. On the contrary, she is rich enough in self-worth to be able to afford a profound humility and self-gift. She is untroubled by the scandal of a male saviour; for in her eyes, the gulf of inequality between God and the human soul is infinitely more immense than that between male and female. Yet it is only after twenty years of persistence in prayer that Julian is able to know the meaning of her parable, and to see that even the immense inequality represented by God and humans can be brought into relation by love and the mystery of redemption.

But perhaps we cannot take on board this story of redemption before we have explored how it is that Julian can be so oblivious to that which matters profoundly to us. How can distinctions of status and worth between women and men matter so little to her? And how can she be content with the narrowness of the existence that she opted for?

It may have something to do with the question of the soul which for Julian and people of her day was a vivid and universally accepted reality. People believed in the potential of the soul to be saved or mortally endangered. The soul was the ultimate site of worth in the individual — not the status achieved by the self in this life. The deeds done by the soul while in the body would be open to judgement on the Last Day — which meant that potentially all achievement of honour and status by the self in this life might be reduced to dust if the soul had been compromised.

But for us, in Western culture of the twentieth century, the fear of judgement in the life to come is something we feel we have been liberated from. The soul is hardly a reality to us. It is the self that we are concerned with, and what the self can achieve here and now. And instead of the fear of judgement, we have assumed instead the burden on the self to achieve equal honour, and deem it freedom rather than slavery. We do not share her perception of humanity sunk in helpless sinfulness, nor believe ourselves to be in need of a saviour — especially a male one. Our mental boundaries are far beyond the narrow confines of Julian's cell. For we have been invited on a Cook's tour of the cosmos, where with the help of Stephen Hawking and his ilk we may follow up the ultimate triumph of human reason and be able, through discovery of the secrets of the universe, to 'know the mind of God'. And sin, as Julian knew it, has all but disappeared. For if there is to be no judgement by God, what reality has sin? How can it be known? What counts as sin now, according to Saul Bellow, is to 'violate the orderly processes of thought as prescribed by the higher rationality'.[4] To be unscientific, in our time, he observes, is a grave mental offence. For we are children of the century in which humankind came of age — an extra-moral age, when as Nietzsche saw it, we could no longer rely on God, but only on ourselves to construct a morality, a sense of the sacred, a knowledge of Good and Evil.[5]

If all this is true, can there be any conversation with Julian possible in any meaningful sense? Or are we just too radically different, as Hampson would no doubt conclude? For we live in an age of strange configurations of morality that Julian in her cell did not have to confront in her meditations on sin. She was in some sense innocent of much that we, who are so obsessed with innocence, are obliged to know in our spiritual researches. Not for her to have read Freud or Althusser, or Foucault, to understand the construction and deconstruction of the self through multiple discourses. For Julian it was relatively simple — our self consisted of our substance and our sensuality. With the insight of her visions and what she knew of the doctrines of the faith she was content to make the journey towards the 'mind of God' from within the narrowness of her cell.

So are we forced to conclude that Julian's vision of redemption by a male saviour in first-century Palestine cannot really be much help to us? It may be that we shall indeed reach that conclusion; but before we clinch the matter, we should perhaps attempt to understand how our own reaction to this story is part of an argument that has been going on now for several centuries since Julian lived and died.

Notes

1   Julian of Norwich, *Showings*, translated and edited by E. Colledge and J. Walsh (New York: Paulist Press, 1978), p. 331.
2   Julian of Norwich, p. 262. See also p. 267 and editors' introduction, pp. 70ff.
3   Julian of Norwich, p. 216.
4   Saul Bellow, 'Saul Bellow on Mozart', *Guardian*, 2 April 1992.
5   Friedrich Nietzsche, *The Will to Power*, edited and translated by Walter Kaufman and R. J. Hollingdale (London: Weidenfeld and Nicolson, 1967). See also Alasdair MacIntyre, *After Virtue: A Study in Moral Theory* (London: Duckworth, 1981) pp. 238–41.

19 Why sisterhood is no substitute for redemption

The classic Christian narrative of redemption, as Julian knew it, is a story about release from the bondage of slavery. This is what redemption literally means; the redeemer (Latin: *redemptor*) is one who 'buys back' those who have been sold into slavery. The slavery is understood by Christians to be the slavery of sin. But with the coming of the Enlightenment, a new story gained acceptance about the nature of our bondage and the means by which we could seek to be liberated from it. Thus, slavery was redefined as the slavery of oppression, and sin was now to be found mainly on the side of the oppressors. Those who were the victims of this oppression were deemed to be innocent, an innocence that was to be expressed by rising in revolt against the oppressors. Only by failure to claim their birthright of freedom in this manner would the oppressed be guilty — of the sin of servility and a failed selfhood.

Thus, it becomes clear that the roots of the modernist mythology that we have already encountered, with its presumption of original innocence, are to be found here. The etymology of emancipation is also connected to slavery, and we can see that it is, in fact, a countermythology to that of redemption — a polemic against a form of liberation from slavery that requires a redeemer. Emancipation, on the other hand, requires that the enslaved take their destiny into their own hands and win back their freedom by their own courage. Christian dependence on a redeemer is presented as little better than an alternative slavery.

This story, of course, raises questions about power. How does the slave have power to liberate herself or himself? The answer is that the slave must use her intelligence to transform bondage into bonding with fellow slaves. This alone will provide the basis for a successful revolt against the power of the oppressors. The watchwords of the narrative of emancipation are familiar to us; they are those of the French Revolution — liberty, equality, and fraternity — that is, solidarity among the oppressed. In the modern period, the tradition of the myth of eman-cipation that stemmed from the Enlightenment has released enormous energies to overthrow the corrupt structures of the *ancien régime*. Begin-ning with the French Revolution, it continued its momentum in the Com-munist societies of the twentieth century and is echoed in the rhetoric of other radical movements including feminism. At their height, and in their best aspects, these offspring of the Enlightenment produced a movement of the human spirit that was both radical and humanitarian.

But now, at the end of the twentieth century, we are witnessing a faltering of the whole modernist trajectory. And since as feminists we are intimately implicated in its fate, it is necessary to understand where we are coming from, and how we have appropriated the particular mythol-ogy of this tradition.

In the early days of new-wave feminism, sisterhood was the key term of reference both at the political and the theological level. The feminist critique of androcentric theology sought to expose its real concern as the desire to establish and defend male status and identity rather than the knowing or naming of God. Thus, the *ancien régime* of theology dis-guised a claim for male honour, not the honour of the divine. Feminists took it on themselves to depose this divinity made in the male image, and proposed a God who could be known in the image of woman too, and found in women's experience and women's lives. Under this new dispensation, salvation by a male saviour was no longer appropriate and it was replaced by sisterhood as a locus for the new feminist soteriology. The pre-existent myth of emancipation governed the interpretation of this concept. Thus, it was essential that sisterhood should be understood as all-embracing. No distinctions of class or race between sisters should be stressed, no projects of personal honour or hierarchies of status should have any part, for these were the mark of the oppressors. For salvation to be accomplished, it was vital to show signs of belonging to the class of the victims for it was only these who were destined for life, for the future. To belong to the oppressors in habit or behaviour was to be fit only for the dustbin of history.

But twenty years on from the heyday of sisterhood, it seems that all is not well, and what was once a blank cheque seems now more like an overdrawn account. Underlying this perhaps is the realization that sisterhood has not had the all-conquering appeal for other women that we once assumed. And among ourselves, it seems, sisterhood is not quite as powerful as we made each other believe. As Annette C. Baier observes in her article 'Whom Can Women Trust?':

Many of us vacillate between making sisterhood powerful and turning on our sisters in displays of petty infighting, squabbles for ascendancy and secret leagues with the supposed enemies ... Most of us have no good reason to

trust ourselves to be trustworthy custodians of the welfare of women and
of children.[1]

Sisterhood, we may have discovered, is powerful — but only rarely. It is
more often fragile and vulnerable to the pitfalls of female rivalry, both
ancient and modern. It is not that this rivalry is something exclusive to
women, but rather that envy — that deadly disease of the soul — is
endemic to the human race. Nevertheless, the way in which we have
conspicuously ignored its presence in our sisterly relations is indicative
of the specific social roots of the mythology that we have adopted.

If we say that the female competitiveness that flourished in the
kitchens, convents and salons of the pre-modern period is still alive and
well among women in the kitchens, convents and university depart-
ments of today, this is not to make a claim for some timeless and
unchanging version of reality. In fact there have been some fairly fundamental changes. One of these is the development of a new model of
women's honour — one that is strongly connected to the fortunes of
feminism, but not entirely coterminous with it. Thus, under the terms of
the old gender hierarchy, women's honour was complementary to male
honour and there was no opportunity for competing with men on equal
terms. And whereas the terms of women's honour were highly restric-
tive as feminists have pointed out, they must also have been acceptable
to a majority of women at some level, since it was women who took on
the role of internally policing their gender stereotype in matters of
sexual morals, or intellectual self-restriction, political participation or
social leadership.

Yet with the coming of the bourgeois revolution, liberalism introduced
the concept of the individual, and under this guise women of the appropriate class began to be able to mount a challenge to the restraints of the
gender hierarchy. But the myth of emancipation also insisted on the
rhetoric of solidarity; and in feminism this has given rise to some interesting contradictions and resulted in some curious ironies. Thus, in
the early days as we saw, feminism dedicated itself, under the banner of
sisterhood, to a highly promotional version of women's history and
relationships — herstory and all that. But at the same time feminists
were using the language of women's liberation to forge a ladder of
escape for themselves as individuals from the constraints of 'women's
culture' which, at another level, they were eagerly romanticizing. This
allowed them to climb out into the sunlight of the male terrain for the
first time, and use their intelligence to compete with men and not just for
them. I suspect that some of the exhilaration of those early days was due
to precisely this — the sense of having escaped — at least temporarily —
from the female ghetto in which women kept each other strictly in line.

The temporary nature of this sense of triumph became evident when radical feminism gained the ascendancy and re-instated, from a very different angle, the deep-seated female inhibition of challenging men on their own ground. The notion of 'women's sphere' and women's special nature re-gained currency. Because feminist theology was born at this moment in the history of feminism, there is a sense in which it remains coloured by the circumstances of its birth. Thus, while some secular feminism has been ready to surrender the myth of women's innocence, and move on, those engaged in feminist theology are more likely to retain some version of it. Thus, a certain type of feminist theology shows signs of becoming a kind of conservation area for some of the earlier preoccupations of the movement. But there is a flip side to this too. For while feminism's children, outgrowing sisterhood, are pressing on with their search for equal honour in terms of fair shares of fun, freedom, success and power with their male colleagues, feminist theology tends to preserve the memory of an equality that once meant a commitment to those women who are fundamentally dishonoured by the system. But unfortunately much of it also retains the myth of original innocence, which, as I have suggested, may not be ultimately compatible with the desire to challenge the system that establishes injustice for a majority of women.

Redemption, in this genre of theology, is replaced by an account of salvation that involves the struggle to vindicate the honour of women, throughout history and especially in the history of religion. To expose the dishonouring of women and to challenge whatever contributes to their continuing servility is undoubtedly a vital project. Yet, I suggest that those of us who originally embraced it may need to identify, in retrospect, some rather serious errors of perception that were not apparent to us at the time. It seems we overestimated the desire for equality on the part of many women, as we tended to make the rather naive assumption that those in the lower echelons of a hierarchy have no interest in its continuation. But women, like people in general, aren't on the whole interested in abstract equality; they wish to be equal to what is perceived as good, or to those who represent it. The hierarchies of value are the means by which we ascertain what is best — and how we may conform to this. Those who are lower in the hierarchy mainly do not wish to abolish it, but to have a better place in it. And if, with shifting paradigms, the old hierarchies of value are declared false, it is certain that new ones will immediately appear. To condemn all hierarchies as such is about as useful as cursing the weather.

Our other error, as we have seen, was to vastly underestimate the fear that women have of each other. Conditioned for centuries to compete with each other for men, it was perhaps unlikely that we would learn instant solidarity. Women who regarded the feminist project as dangerous no doubt feared losing the degree of relative protection they had achieved in a dangerous male-dominated world. But women who embraced feminism were equally subject to this fear — the fear of being replaced. For if we are indeed equal (i.e. equivalent) to another woman, then we are equally replaceable by her. The one who is most like us, our sister, is the one who is best placed to replace us, the greatest threat. Envy among women has a characteristic face, whether among feminists or non-feminists. For due to our fragile self-esteem and poverty of self-worth we often seem to be shaken to the core by another woman's achievements, threatened with annihilation in the depths of our being.

Yet, against this and in spite of this it can be pointed out that much solidarity among feminists was indeed achieved. Nor should I or anyone want to devalue the triumph of sisterly affection and female friendship where and when it has occurred. But at the risk of seeming motivated by ill-will, I suggest that we must dare to scrutinize some of those achievements, and check out some of the assumptions they rested on — notably the assumption that as feminists we were representing (to the male world) the cause of oppressed women. The text of our manifesto addressed all women, and our own faith rested on the universality of its appeal. But just as the language of advertising appears to address everyone without discrimination, yet many have good reasons for knowing that they are not included, so something similar may have been at work in our case. For though feminist texts claimed implicitly or explicitly to speak on behalf of women as a whole they were very often written in such a way as to address only a very specific minority of women (or of men, for that matter). As Mary Midgley has commented: 'Much feminist literature is sunk in the kind of unreadable Victorian Germanic language through which only the acclimatized faithful can keep awake.'[2] Thus, to outsiders feminism may have appeared to display some of the characteristics of a cult. It has had not only its own distinctive speech but also its own body language — the latter being read by more people than the former. Thus feminists could be seen as women who read certain books, name certain names and tend to dress and talk in certain ways. They are usually women who are confident in their ability to order the world through language — and abstract reasoning. Hence, they are more likely to be found among middle-class professionals, especially those associated with the academy, the church, or the 'new church' of the media rather than in other trades and professions, like shop assistants or hairdressers, dinner ladies, pharmacists, home helps, dental receptionists, women caring for elderly dependent relatives and the like. These on the whole do not tend to hear themselves addressed by the speech or the 'body language' of feminism.

Thus there is a problem when feminism claims to speak in the name of all women. For in what sense could we be representing those who see us

as representing only ourselves? Feminist literature has tended to emphasize inclusiveness but not accountability. This, I suggest, has put us in a
position of considerable spiritual danger which many feminist writers
have begun to be aware of and is responsible for a far greater modesty
of style. Yet in some places, especially the academy, something of this
dilemma remains. For while we are not accountable to those for whom
we sometimes claim to speak, nor have we in some cases accepted full
accountability within the structures of the hitherto male-only world that
we have now penetrated. For as feminists we have sought, often with
good reason, to keep ourselves aloof from the codes of conduct and criteria of worth of the patriarchal world. We may regard with suspicion
those men who might question us or our thinking from a traditional
perspective, whether academic or religious, deeming them to represent
merely self-interested privilege or reactionary folly. Men of a liberal
persuasion, however, are inhibited from questioning us for a different
reason. For any critique of our contradictions could very easily lead on
to an exposé of their own position, since this rests on a variant of the
same mythology.

Thus, it is possible to see how those who set out to champion the lost
honour and dignity of dispossessed women can all too easily end up as a
small pressure group of bourgeois women, whose claims to speak for all
women merely disguise a preoccupation with matters concerning their
own honour and dignity. In the UK, as in the USA, many of those who
write on theology and spirituality, or form part of its networks
or newsletters, still seem to operate out of the 'injured innocents'
mode. This may be because whether Christian or post-Christian they
have been infected by that chronic form of spiritual idealism that the
church has so often succumbed to, with its instinctive need to repress
disturbing contradictions. Fortunately, there are a number of women in
the theological field in Britain whose work avoids this tendency.[3] These
writers have preserved more of the self-questioning habit that to
my mind is one of more useful bequests of the Enlightenment heritage
and also, together with prayer, an absolute necessity for a discerning
Christian life. In some ways, the specific contradictions of feminism
have been more thoroughly examined by secular critics. Thus, in her
recent work *Our Treacherous Hearts* Rosalind Coward focuses on some
of the dilemmas faced by feminists, or women who have adopted the
new model of female honour and challenged the assumptions of the old
gender hierarchy. She shows that when women move beyond
the traditional domestic realm and become highly successful in the
competitive world of work, they often feel alienated and uncomfortable
in situations where they are continually obliged to compete with both
men and women.[4] She documents many instances of women in such
situations reverting abruptly to a much more traditional division of

labour with their husbands and partners where they assume the major responsibility for care of the children. She suggests that it is insufficient to explain it simply in terms of the strength of maternal instinct. It is at least as much an attempt to create a space exempt from the ruthlessness of individual competition in the modern workplace, and establish some sort of viable co-operation necessary for the bringing up of children, even if this means accepting restraint on her own struggles for autonomy and fulfilment. Perhaps such women, in flight from the ruthless self-promotion of the market-place society, have dimly sensed that the division of labour in the traditional family was in the nature of a damage limitation exercise. And for all its constraints, it was partly effective in preventing endemic human rivalry from invading the relations of the couple, therefore permitting a necessary co-operation between them for responding to the needs of the next generation.

As we have already seen, women in modern European society, while enthusiastically embracing their new freedoms, have from time to time been vulnerable to bouts of nostalgia for the certainties of the traditional family. For the possession of a fixed status, though it limits the potential of the individual, also serves to guarantee some sort of protection against instant replaceability. One consequence of the struggle for equality or the competition for equal honour is that there is no longer any real honour in difference. There are only those who have achieved 'equal' honour — and those who have failed.

Against this background, it is not hard to see why women are sometimes tempted to revert to the old paradigm of women's honour, and to fall back on the dignity of motherhood. Yet as Coward shows, women seeking shelter in the family from the cold wind of competition in the workplace may find only a temporary respite from the ravages of rivalry. For the erosion of the old bonds has meant that the taboo on heterosexual competition has been irrevocably removed. Thus, heterosexual partnerships are exposed to the prospect of each partner fighting off the terrible threat to self-esteem in the person of the other. Moreover, taking refuge in the domestic realm has never been a sanctuary for women against competition with other women. For the woman returning from the intellectual highlands, or life with the lads, to the world of mothers is likely to find that some of those who never left it will take every opportunity to remind her in one or other of a million small ways that she is no better than she ought to be, and certainly no better than them. Such women might be among those who would indignantly refute my claim that envy is a native in women's world, and counter claim that it is they and their ilk who represent the womanly virtues of care and co-operation, which aspiring businesswomen, academics and female priests have abandoned. Yet who among them, as well as among these latter, can truly claim that she is a stranger to the ancient art of the put-down? Of course she will acknowledge that she has often been a victim of its offensive import; but as to being a practitioner, she will concede only that she has sometimes found it necessary to defend her own threatened self-esteem.

Thus, women are as ready now to defend their honour as they ever were. The difference is that there is now more than one model to appeal to. On the one hand this gives women a lot more scope. On the other, it also serves as a rich source of conflict and confusion. We should of course recall that the radical feminist analysis did not ignore the presence of female rivalries, but attributed it to the oppressive structure of heterosexual relations which limited women's autonomy and thwarted her potential. Their answer was to offer the model of lesbian sisterhood — an ideal of self-chosen intimate female friendship as an alternative to coercive bondage of the heterosexist family system, in which women were enslaved by the imbalance of power between men and women. But there were several problems with this ideal of political lesbianism. For although this feminist analysis had accurately exposed the cruel and pathetic reality that often lay behind the romantic ideology of marriage and family, the ideal it proposed was in its own way equally romantic and equally exclusive. The function of this idealization of a specific form of female relations could be seen as a kind of status claim, marking out the distinction between those women who showed themselves 'fit for freedom' and those who remained wedded to servility.

The extent to which it was in fact an option for freedom can be questioned. For if it is true, as Ros Coward suggests, that the main impetus behind feminism was not primarily women's relations with men, nor even with their sisters, but with their mothers, then it seems unlikely that this agenda could be entirely absent from female intimacy. And if that was the case, then it was also unlikely these female relations would be an area of freedom unmarked by issues of power and pain, rivalry and betrayal.

But the problem with this and other ideals of sisterhood was the inherent weakness of the particular doctrine of election that the celebration of 'women's choices' implied. For the extent that it is possible for some women to opt out of the traditional burdens of womanhood is more likely to be an index of their relative economic security rather than their merit or grace-full response. It suggests a doctrine of election to grace on the basis of 'the power of choice' which is a fundamental tenet of the market society, and which functions to mystify those freedoms which belong to some of us by virtue of our class and race. This is not at all to say that there is no role for 'difference' and differing roles among women, but it is to suggest that our present model of bodiliness is inadequate to envisage this except in ways that lead us back to the privileges of our birth in the aristocracy of world womanhood.

Family structures of some kind or other are the ground of human bodiliness, and family metaphors feature in all our attempts to envisage human solidarity and bonding — including sisterhood. But just as the family of Western nostalgia is often in reality an exclusive, ethnocentric institution, so sisterhood, as understood by feminists in the seventies and eighties, was sociologically speaking a narrow social form. In retrospect it is possible to appreciate that the feminism of those days was a play suitable for a minority audience. But as long as our mothers were in the audience, it seems we could delude ourselves that all the world was watching. But as we in our turn become the mothers' generation, as daughters or nieces or partners' daughters walk out in derision or indifference, off to the big screen where 'woman as individual' is showing, only then do we fully understand that our version of bodiliness was not quite as all-inclusive as we once believed. For that which is born out of reaction presupposes that which it protests. Only the offspring of revelation have the capacity to manifest an original freedom.

Thus in our naivety, we have frequently failed to understand how sisterhood could be perceived as less than good news by many of our sex. In our option for the artificial solidarity of gender, we tended to repress and deny the facts of our existing cultural bodiliness. Our preference for more equal and informal relations has made us insensitive to the fact that the less we are protected by traditional separation and social distances, the greater is the possibility for rivalries to invade and predominate. Our option for the abstraction of freedom has made us ignorant of the nuances of true freedom and its ambiguity. It has allowed our vision of equality to become confused with that 'equality' that a capitalist society requires of each of us — that equal availability for exploitation and for the pursuits of consumption which makes each individual the competitor of the other.

It is time to recognize ourselves as the descendants of those who spearheaded the bourgeois revolution with the aid of the printing press, and elaborated the 'black legend' to discredit their opponents whose power they wished, consciously or unconsciously, to replace. We should purge our theo-babble of women's capacity for connectedness by acknowledging the class connection which ensures that our theology is to a large extent a class discourse. Our concern to establish the equality of women in theological matters can be seen as an attempt to establish our credentials, to lay claim to a status that entitles us to the same privileges as Western males. Perhaps this is partly necessary, if women are to respond to the fullness of their calling. But we should be aware that in some cases it has not so much redressed the balance in favour of God, as remade God in woman's image — or rather in the image of the Western bourgeois woman of the mid twentieth century.

And the effect of this discourse has been, as it has been in other neo-liberal areas, to promote an individualism that weakens the radical potential of the bodily bond as it occurs in family or in religious and civil institutions. The ultimate beneficiary of this weakening is the state. And last but not least, it also threatens to break for ever our dialogue with the dead. For as theologians like Daphne Hampson have observed, feminist theology is fundamentally secular in character.[5] For if our equal status in this world has become the ultimate measure of our worth — we must commit everything we have to achieving the highest possible value before we die. To fail in this is a kind of eternal death for post-Christians, or even for feminist Christians who have 'translated' God. And if such value is the only value that counts, then those who were ultimately devalued in their lives, like those who have died in concentration camps, or in poverty or oppression, remain ultimately devalued. By denying the resurrection, we deny their existence, their possibility of ultimate justification. They merit nothing but our pity and have no part in our future. Our dialogue with dead sisters, the communion of saints as it used to be known, falls into silent oblivion.

In our enlightened wisdom, we rejected the Christian myth because it failed to single out the oppressors and distinguish them from the oppressed. We, on the other hand, were anxious to know the sheep from the goats. The Christian scriptures have traditionally instructed us to reserve such judgement, and leave it to God, pointing out that the attempt to pull up the weeds at this stage will result in damage to the crop. But we have cast away such caution, and deemed ourselves capable of making the 'final judgement' in this life and without reference to God. We have committed ourselves to an alternative myth, which bids us affirm the universal solidarity of the oppressed against the wickedness of the oppressors. This myth celebrates the power of human autonomy and human reason, and lays upon the believers the duty to identify the oppressor and free themselves from his yoke. But in the unfolding revelation that is the history of the late twentieth century, the seal on the outcome of the narrative of emancipation has been broken. We have looked into the abyss, and witnessed how what was to be the true narrative of liberation has been enlisted in the most fearful project of human enslavement that the world has ever seen.

Against the background of the holocaust, and the ongoing holocaust of the New World Order, perhaps we may look again at the original tale of redemption. From it we learn that though we are far from equal as victims, yet we are nevertheless all considered slaves to the rule of sin. None by their own judgement may claim exemption; but equally, none by our judgement may be deemed beyond redemption. Perhaps, on second thoughts, this story of a divine redeemer may turn out to be a more human option than we once thought.

Notes

1   Annette C. Baier, 'Whom can women trust?', in Claudia Card (ed.), *Feminist Ethics* (Kansas: University of Kansas Press, 1991), p. 242.
2   Mary Midgley and Judith Hughes, *Women's Choices: Philosophical Problems Facing Feminism* (London: Weidenfeld and Nicolson, 1983), p. 13.
3   See especially work by Janet Martin Soskice, Jane Williams, Janet Morley, Susan Dowell and Sara Maitland.
4   Rosalind Coward, *Our Treacherous Hearts: Why Women Let Men Get Their Way* (London: Faber and Faber, 1992), p. 13.
5   Daphne Hampson, *Theology and Feminism* (Oxford: Blackwell, 1990), p. 170.

20 The excavation of our religious repressions

Every mythology has its own pattern of light and shade, of affirmation and repression. While the myth is in the ascendant, the repressions hold; but as the generations change, aspects of the story that could not be told come to light. Feminist critique exposed the shady bits of androcentric assumptions in many areas, but in due course, its own enlightenment got under way, and some of its own assumptions needed to be hidden from view. The myth of emancipation required many middle-class feminists to repress consciousness of their class inheritance in the interests of sisterhood conceived as solidarity of the oppressed. But in retrospect, it becomes evident that this myth rested on a class cohesion that was inherent in the structures of our particular use of language. Effectively it included only those who had been initiated into these.

The truths we once clung to as the seal of our identity now begin to seem — to some of us at least — like half-truths; and those who never shared our presumptions, especially those of a different race or culture, have sometimes been more than willing to point out our errors. In this chapter, I want to look briefly at this process of the moderation of feminist identity. The uncovering of our repressions is never likely to be a painless affair, but I suggest that this work of mythological excavation is nevertheless a fruitful one that can eventually lead us to a more mature perception of our religious and cultural identity, as well as our feminist one.

Many feminist investigations of scripture have been carried out with a sense of single minded mission — to establish and vindicate women's honour. At times this betrayed a tendency to treat every woman in scripture as either an unsung saint or an unrecognized martyr in the face of androcentric ignorance or neglect. The problem with this approach, however, is illustrated by the question of Sarah and Hagar. For a while, we were content to reclaim Sarah in relation to her male counterpart

Abraham. But it soon became evident, with the help of scripture scholars like Phyllis Trible,[1] that the story of Sarah was also the story of Hagar. It was no longer a simple story of reclaiming the forgotten deeds and qualities of the woman that had been overshadowed by the celebrated doings of her mate. It also raised the uncomfortable question of the relations between the free woman and the slave woman. For Sarah's behaviour simply could not be represented as a model of sisterly solidarity. And just as the idealizing tendency of our mythology in reading scripture ran aground on the story of Sarah and Hagar, so too its inherent contradictions were exposed in our politics also by the relations between the daughters of freewomen and the daughters of the slaves.

Our mythology prescribed that the oppressed would unite to throw off the yoke of the oppressors: or to put it in religious terms, since the oppressed were those destined to be saved, the status of victim came to be an important one since it was the badge of election. The myth of emancipation required us to condemn all existing hierarchies of status. And yet, from the very beginning, as we have observed, a new hierarchy appeared — that of virtuous victimhood. Those who had been oppressed, i.e. women, were seen as justified (in the biblical sense of made righteous) by virtue of their suffering. But if eligibility for salvation was to be measured according to the degree and extent of oppression endured, then clearly some women were in line for claiming a higher status than others. In the US, black women were not slow to realize that on this basis they should be in line to become the new elect.

Thus, as we have seen, black women confronted white women with their failure to take into account the differences between them. According to Maria Lugones[2] white women had not considered the differences important because they had never really *noticed* those who were different from them. Yet when the differences were pointed out, the makers of feminist theory could not afford to ignore or dismiss these criticisms as they might have done if they had been made by men. For according to their own liberation theory, black women were highly deserving of respect on the ladder of virtuous victimhood.

The acknowledgement of differences among women ran counter to the mythology of emancipation that required unity among the oppressed gender. Nevertheless, for the reasons I have mentioned it had to be accommodated. And so in the reformed feminist consciousness of the nineties, to be eligible for salvation one needs to claim 'difference' — to be not merely a woman but a member or descendant of an oppressed ethnic group — black, Jewish or some such. Those who can only trace their ancestry to WASP Americans or imperial Brits must either reinvent their family tree or settle for a lower order of merit.

Yet the repair to the theory was not able to solve the problem of the unending spiral of guilt that the challenge from black women set in motion. At Greenham, as we saw, the whole enterprise of the women's peace camp eventually foundered as a result of the introduction of the issue of racial guilt. Somehow white feminist theory had managed to re-create exactly the same situation that it had sought to escape from in the first place — low status and chronic guilt. This may help to explain the emergence of the creation theologies. Those who had briefly turned the tables on men's dominance found themselves displaced by a further twist in the reversal of values they had instituted. Anglo feminists were obliged to try a new tack and hence the new claim that we all (and particularly we women) are children of victimized Mother Earth and by this means eligible for salvation.

But as we have seen, there are some serious flaws in the assumptions of the creation theologians. The real escape from the contradictions of salvation by victimhood is not to produce another version of it but to question some of its underlying premises. We need to consider that, as products of Western education, even those who are black or Jewish are intimately implicated in its discourses, and cannot pull rank on the basis that they are the most victimized members of the gender. Those who are truly in this category are not in the business of making claims at all. It is this claim-making aspect that we most need to re-evaluate.

Some of the recent feminist theology continues to keep alive the image of the battered or violated woman.[3] The authors would no doubt argue that exposing the crimes against women past and present and alerting the world to female degradation wherever it occurs has always been, and must continue to be the vital task of feminism. To this I can only say amen. And yet, I suggest that a certain painful self-scrutiny is in order even here. For although we are rightly outraged by these images of victimized women, there is also a sense in which we have an interest in them, for they justify our claim against a male-dominated society, and so perversely they become the basis of the equal status we are seeking to achieve. It is noticeable that we are not so given to contemplating those other causes of female suffering like old age, sickness, childlessness, poverty and loneliness (unless these are male-induced). Such images terrify us and do not empower us. We shudder at the possibility of what we might become. For it is not unadulterated compassion that moves us to consider the sufferings of our sisters; they also have a role in the pursuit of what is our due.

For similar reasons, I suggest we should regard with suspicion the claim of the politics of political correctness to serve as a redress to the racist and androcentric values of our society. For it purports to promote the interests of the marginalized, yet the logic of its thinking, far from being radical, is politically naive in its undertaking and reactionary in its effect. It is likely to reduce issues of justice to a level which makes them a subject of ridicule — as, for example, when champions of PC insisted that an old-fashioned British band, the Black Dyke Mills Band, should change its name, since 'it offends sensitive minorities like blacks and gays',[4] or when the editors of a new American version of Hans Andersen's stories took exception to the 'white' arms of the little mermaid. This attempt to 'clean up' language, allegedly in favour of the oppressed, fails to notice that we have redesigned them (the oppressed) in this conceptual scheme without seriously attempting to change underlying political realities. It is a politics of decoy that serves to distract us from the real political tasks that face us. For this change in language is actually in favour of the PC designers, not in the favour of those groups for whose welfare they profess concern. For it allows them to adopt a position of moral superiority, of moral whiteness, while seeming to champion the rights of the non-white, non-straight. It avoids the option of serious political engagement that might dirty their hands, or reveal their own position as morally ambiguous. And thus it leaves the fundamental realities of racism, poverty and prejudice untouched. A politics of this sort shows a fundamental ignorance of the institution of language, by holding up an ideal of redeeming ourselves by pure or correct language. It repeats that fertile gnostic error — the error of believing it is possible to disassociate ourselves from what we deplore simply by superior knowledge, by correct political or theological thought.

But in its worst aspects, PC is not merely a result of error but a product of the manipulation of meanings. Thus it is characteristic of the new brand of management-speak that is invading all the institutions of society, where the talk is of empowerment and participation in the workplace, while the reality is de-skilling, redundancies, exploitation and obsessive control from on top. It is a fraudulent discourse that masks the machinations of the market society. Far from being inclusive of those races and classes who have been excluded from power, the whole debate about political correctness is in reality an American domestic argument between old and new élites competing for status and power. It has little or nothing to do with the utter otherness of the mass of the world's oppressed. But the nation with most global power has the power to impose its language, including the language of its domestic disputes, on its client societies — of which we in Britain are one. And the fact that by means of PC rhetoric, some women, some blacks, some gays — and even some European feminist theologians — are admitted to the charmed life of the American élite, and therefore gain a personal interest in this sort of rhetoric, does not mean that the existing hierarchies of power in the world are undergoing a conversion. It only means that, with the aid of these mascots of pluralism, they are now slightly better placed to claim improved credibility in relation to the minorities and majorities that they exploit.

If then, as I seem to be saying, all our political aspirations and ideals, all our scriptural and theological efforts, amount to little more than an expression of our class or racial interests, what outcome can there be except cynicism? If we remain at a certain level of thought, then this is indeed the logic of it. But this is also a turning point — the point where we have the choice to go deeper into the matter; to realize that the formulations which at one level mask our class and racial interests, at another level express some of our most profound religious yearnings. But we live in a society that has lost its theological bearings, and is in bondage to idolatry, the concrete historical form of the universal rule of sin. Because of this our religious yearnings are perverted or distorted but they are none the less recognizable. Underlying the movement for political correctness, one can discern the hunger for a sound doctrine as to how the just life may be lived. And underlying our struggle for equality, there is a fundamental religious intuition of our equality before God. Kari Børresen's work shows how the knowledge of equality belongs to a Christian inheritance that pre-dates our Enlightenment conceptions and she traces the 'unfolding revelation' of it in the patristic era.[5] She shows that traditional Christian anthropology rested on two tenets that were in tension with each other. First, the doctrine of humanity in creation, where traditional exegesis established an androcentric gender hierarchy, and female subordination was seen as part of God's creational order. But the tradition also contained a doctrine of human equivalence in the sense of woman's parity with men that is realized through redemption achieved by Christ. This contradiction was seen as a problem by some of the church Fathers, notably Clement and Augustine, who tried to include women in human godlikeness already from creation by means of an incorporeal and sexless *'imago dei'*. The split in theological anthropology was upheld until this century, because women's subordinate status in *imago dei* had survived in early medieval exegesis by being falsely attributed to Ambrose and Augustine, and thus became incorporated in canon law. While scholastic anthropology respected Augustine's gender-free *imago dei*, pseudo-Augustinian male precedence remained influential in arguments against women's ordination to the priesthood.

The post-Enlightenment world of Europe and North America has assumed the definition of *imago dei* which holds both men and women as created godlike. In doing so it has built upon equality strategies of biblical interpretation inherited from patristic exegesis — strategies which affirm that both men and women are saved in Jesus Christ through baptism in order to be restored in the resurrection. All feminist theology, whether Christian or post-Christian, assumes these conclusions of female godlikeness. We are thus building on foundations laid by those whose contribution at times we have often been anxious to dismantle. It is interesting — and a little ironical — to note the earnestness with which feminists have felt the need to emphasize that women are made in the image of God. Yet Julian, living in an age when women's rights were hardly recognized as such, apparently felt so certain of this that she never attempted to prove it.

Now that the Enlightenment foundation of our commitment to equality is being shaken, this intellectual archaeology of our thought, such as Børresen achieves, may help us with the task of disentangling our vision of equality from that version of it that characterizes the New World Order, and which in many ways parodies that equality we have before God. If we can thus re-ground our equality before God within this tradition, we can afford to recognize the defects of our account of salvation through sisterhood of the victimized, where the religious and political were conflated in such a way as to serve the detriment of both.

On the political level, the it's-not-fair mentality threatens to trap us in a politics of the terminally immature. It prevents us from engaging in a realistic collaborative action to improve the economic and social position of women not just in our class. At the same time, it may hinder our attainment of our true stature as women. A woman's dignity in the long run cannot be advanced solely on the basis of how she and her sex have been wronged. Her dignity is in her calling whatever it may be, how she makes her profession; not on how she claims her debts but on how she pays her dues to the community that she belongs to. Thus, it ought to be possible to judge a true feminist not by the purity of her theory but by her fruits of sisterly compassion, loyalty and co-operation. The phoney virtue through victimhood is a continuation by other means of that attitude which feminism has so consistently and rightly deplored — that women can be seen as less than full moral agents — that they are to be somehow excepted from the moral standards we use to judge other human beings.

Nevertheless, the excavation reveals that our preoccupation with the victim is at the same time an authentic one. We may discover that our religious roots, whether we accept or reject religion, are more deep-seated even than our race or class instincts. Perhaps at this point, we can take it further by going back to Julian. Could it be that the plot of the Fall-Redemption drama which she wrestled with is, in fact, not so strange to us after all? Could we have re-worked this fundamental paradigm of our culture and come up with another version of it? In order to perceive it, we shall need to listen to ourselves in a different mode: not just to our self-presentation in the text, but as if with an anthropologist's ear.

In Britain, unlike the US, there has not been a significant proportion of black women engaged in the making of feminist theory and feminist theology. I remember noticing, some years ago, that at almost every feminist gathering there was heard what I may call 'the ritual lament'.

This acknowledged with public regret the unfortunate fact that so few of our black sisters, or Third World sisters, had been able to be present with us at our meeting. The assumption was that, because of their double burden of sexist and racist oppression, they had been prevented from joining us; but that if — as we hoped — this burden could be lightened for them they would, of course, be anxious to be present and sharing in the sacred task of liberating women. These latter assumptions were not usually made explicit, but I never heard a voice raised to question any of them. And I never quite had the courage to suggest that some (at least) of our black sisters were not there because they had better things to do; or that a feminist theology conference (for instance) was perhaps not their idea of a night out.

The ritual lament, it seems to me, reveals something about the ground of our theology at that time. It appeared to take the form of a hope that has been disappointed. But was it also concealed relief that a fear had (temporarily) not been fulfilled? For if our black sisters had turned up in strength their presence might have been painful for us. They might have confronted us with our double standards — the fact that we assumed that they would want to be included in our universal visions but we did not expect them to include us in theirs. We were not hammering on the door of black churches or Third World liberation movements, for we accepted that these should be ethnic, and separatist and particular in their concerns. We would, of course, have loved them to come and share these concerns with us; but perhaps we did not intend that they would come en masse and take over the platform, redefine the world from their angle, and the terms on which we would be included or excluded. This is more akin to what happened in the US, an outcome that was, as we saw, difficult for white feminists. Perhaps, in short, their real presence was not what we desired; for we were much better served by our symbolic remembrance of them.

But what has all this got to do with Julian? I suggest that we, like Julian, but rather less consciously, have evolved a drama in which sin has to be accounted for and redemption is necessary. For to admit to the reality of sin lays us open to facing the terrifying prospect of a world inescapably dominated by it from which there is no prospect of escape. But we, unlike Julian, have been unable to accept the idea that God in the form of a male saviour can save women. Yet we have somehow preserved a hidden mythology in which innocent victims still have the power to 'save' others who are linked to them by gender. Thus women, who have been the innocent victims of patriarchal oppression, are deemed to be 'justified' by what they have suffered on behalf of womankind; and other women, like ourselves, may vicariously partici- pate in this justification of their gender achieved by the suffering of women as a whole. A very neat scheme which has the benefit of being both novel and familiar — novel because it has never been expressed in precisely this form before, but familiar because it makes use of the basic Christian soteriology which Westerners have had several centuries to get used to.

If this is what underlies the account of salvation by sisterhood it helps to explain how sin is paid for, and women are justified (made innocent). It would also clarify the 'hierarchy of victimhood' which recognizes that some categories of women have suffered more — black women, poor women, women of the Third World — and thus paid an excess, as it were, for sin, far and beyond what they might need for their own sins. Thus with their surplus, they have contributed to the salvation, the redemption of womankind and particularly of the likes of us, whose existence — though we do not stress it — has been relatively comfortable.

So when in the ritual lament we expressed our need for the presence of black women, etc., there was also something genuine about this. It is not that we simply wished secretly to exclude them so that we could continue in our privilege. It was also more fundamental than that. We needed them because they were necessary to our salvation, they collectively were our saviour and redeemer. What higher honour could we pay them?

From this it is clear to me that we do in fact inherit more from our religious tradition than we have sometimes been prepared to admit. This adapted version of redemption present in feminist soteriology can be found in slightly different form in other sorts of liberation theology. It has the merit of being deeply incarnational. In fact there is a sense in which it has a scriptural warrant. Nevertheless, I think there is an important and no doubt obvious reason why it does not work and this I hope to explore in the following chapter.

Notes

1   Phyllis Trible, *Texts of Terror: Literary-Feminist Readings of Biblical Narratives* (Philadelphia: Fortress Press, 1989), pp. 9ff.
2   Maria C. Lugones, 'On the logic of pluralist feminism', in Claudia Card (ed.), *Feminist Ethics* (Kansas : University of Kansas Press, 1991), pp. 40–1.
3   See E. Schüssler Fiorenza and Shawn Copeland (eds), *Violence Against Women* (London: SCM Press, 1994).
4   Reported in the *Guardian*, 9 Oct. 1993.
5   Kari E. Børresen, 'God's image, man's image? Patristic interpretation of Genesis 1.27 and 1 Corinthians 11.7', in Kari E. Børresen (ed.), *Image of God and Gender Models* (Oslo: Solum Forlag, 1991), p. 188.

21 *Debt and redemption*

The other day, I saw a programme about a Thai prostitute made by an Australian film-maker, Denis O'Rourke. In the film, he told how, disillusioned after a broken marriage, he went to Bangkok in search of professional and sexual adventure, and made contact with one of the night club girls in the traditional manner — through the services of a pimp. Back in the hotel bedroom he persuaded her to tell her story for his film.[1]

The title of the film was *The Good Woman of Bangkok*. It was a painfully poignant story and the film-maker described it as 'an ironic parable of living a good life in an imperfect world, and about prostitution as a metaphor for capitalism and for all relations between men and women' (*Guardian* preview). The young woman, Aoi, came from a landless peasant family and she was partially sighted, being blind in one eye. Since she was a child, she had been accustomed to hard work in the paddy fields, helping to pay off or at least prevent the increase of the family burden of debt. At some stage she had fallen in love with a young man and married him. But within a few months he had cast her off, and she was forced to return to her family, by now two months pregnant. After her son was born, she left for the city and here she got the only job available to her — work in a night club. After the death of her father, and the outlay on his funeral which she organized, the family situation worsened still further, and her earnings — gleaned almost entirely from tips — were all that stood between them and starvation.

In the film, she spoke about her job — the things she was forced to do for survival, her bitterness towards the men who lied and cheated and used her cruelly, her brokenheartedness after the rejection by her husband; her unexpected tenderness towards her feckless and demoralized father; and her humility towards the gods whom she hoped would pardon her for the shameful life she was forced to lead. She dreamed of being able to own her own rice farm — so that she could support her mother and little son whose welfare was now her chief concern.

The film-maker also interviewed some of those who knew her or worked with her — a sympathetic neighbour, an older woman from the village who had known her since childhood; and in the city, some of the other girls who worked in the night club — and some of the clients — well-off men from all over the world — who frequented the clubs and paid the pimps for the services of the girls.

Aoi told her story in a low voice, sometimes in broken English she had learned in the bars, sometimes in her own language. It was the kind of story that could hardly fail to move those who heard it — and indeed, it seems that the journalist she told it to was so moved that he began to get involved in the story he had set up for this film. He became not just the producer of the film but an actor in it — albeit only one who was briefly glimpsed through Aoi's response to him in her narrative and comments, and in the editorial comment in which he recounts, sparsely, the course of events. In order to save her from the slavery and almost certain death resulting from her present employment, and as a reward for co-operation with his film, he bought her the rice farm of her dreams. A year later, he returned to Thailand to find her — but she was not on the farm. He found her eventually, in a sleazy massage parlour in another city. He asked her, 'Why this?' and she replied, 'It is my fate.'

I have recounted this story in some detail for several reasons. Its effect on me at the time was very powerful. It remained with me for several days like a physical presence; the figure of Aoi, in all its heart-rending pathos, seemed to haunt me with her sad voice, her broken English and slightly disfigured eye — and her terrible tale of abuse and indignities suffered as a result of poverty and betrayal. Perhaps part of its appeal was that at one level it perfectly encapsulated the feminist vision that gripped us in the seventies and eighties. Wasn't this the classic story of woman's fate in a man's world? The true story of Aoi showed how the suffering and silenced woman is exploited endlessly by men for their pleasure and their profit. Yet behind the exploited body of woman is a self — one who retains her dreams, her own vision and version of reality. And it is these dreams, these unfulfilled dreams of our sisters, that we were committed to fulfilling. These were the dreams that were blazoned on our banners and fuelled our rage for justice.

The truth even of true stories is usually a many-layered thing; and the more I pondered on this one the more I became aware of some of its layers. I perceived that it was a story about redemption — the attempt to buy back someone from slavery. O'Rourke feels such compassion for Aoi that he tries to retrieve her from the slavery of her means of existence by buying her a rice farm. But his attempt to purchase her freedom does not succeed. A year later he finds her back in her old life. Some of the sisters would have said but of course...How did he think he could get her out of slavery when he is an agent of that same system of slavery that exploits and degrades her? He was not averse to making use of her services in one way or another, and an over generous payment to her for co-operation in his film could not be expected to free her from the ruin that men's exploitation had brought her to. Aoi herself in the film reflects at one point that there is something in her which is no longer available to 'give' to a man. Her freedom has been lost. From our viewpoint, we can see that it is folly on the film-maker's part to think that he can somehow give it back to her.

But if a male film-maker cannot offer Aoi her freedom, what is it that Western feminist sisters can offer her? According to our original story it is the shared basis of experience, woman's experience that provides a true basis for compassion, solidarity and for liberation.

But there is, as we have already begun to realize, something a little amiss with this construction of the situation. I do not share Aoi's particular experience as a woman, never having had to labour in the paddy fields to support my family in the hopeless struggle against debt or been reduced to selling my body so that my family can survive. Despite the fact that I am a woman, my experience is actually a lot closer to that of the male film-maker who, while not being an initiator of the exploitative system which he personally deplores, is nevertheless at certain points a beneficiary of it. Of course, as some sisters would no doubt point out, we are not the ones who go to Bangkok and order up the services of a prostitute, nor are we (mostly) in a position to bribe her to make a film about her life by offering to buy her the fulfilment of her dreams. Nevertheless, we share with O'Rourke the desire to redeem Aoi from the slavery of poverty. What we would have offered her was not a crude material bribe but the opportunity to claim a precious spiritual inheritance, her freedom, freedom for all women under patriarchy. But as we have become aware, the particular language of freedom we speak is a result of our Western education, in the course of which we have imbibed the myth of emancipation. It is this that we would have offered Aoi so that she might enjoy the same freedom as we now have and not be merely the plaything of a cruel fate.

The trouble is that these feminist ideals might have been just as useless to Aoi as O'Rourke's gift of a farm was in restoring her to freedom. We believed that our ideals of freedom are free — all you had to do is to believe in them. For us they have been 'free'. But actually they are expensive — they have been paid for — but not by us. And to offer these liberating ideals to women whose situation is not ours, is a bit like modelling expensive clothes — ones which they might love to wear, and we might dearly love them to wear — but which unfortunately they can't afford.

Of course they have been paid for, we might exclaim, more than paid for. This is where we reveal our secret belief in redemption. All women's dreams of freedom have been amply paid for by the vast weight of women's suffering throughout history and throughout the world. Whatever men have paid for their sins against women is nothing by comparison. As far as sin is concerned, the great debit of women's sufferings means that all women are morally in credit.

But have the sufferings of women like Aoi in some sense 'paid for' the sins, errors or complicity of women like me? What kind of sharing is this? Is it not rather along the lines of the present world economic system whereby the poorest nations, by means of interest and debt repayment, help to pay for the pleasures and freedom of the richer nations? If one were to put this notion to someone like Aoi, I wonder what sense she would make of it. Would she not find it a little strange, the idea that because of the sufferings of women like her, we Western women are somehow justified, innocent of the depredations of Western society in a way that men are not? Might she not be inclined to say that what she has suffered she has done so for herself, or at least on behalf of her family or her people? Her sufferings do not somehow 'pay for' the innocence of women on the other side of the world. And to regard them in this light is to be in danger of colonizing them — as we have colonized so much else that belongs to people of societies like hers.

But our sense that the suffering of our Third World sisters has 'paid for' our sins is an unacknowledged claim rather than an explicit one. Our relation to them is not, in fact, simple and clear cut. It is ambiguous — in the same sort of way that the relation of the film-maker to his subject Aoi is also ambiguous — marked with contradiction. Like him, we are moved by compassion for her and would dearly like to liberate her. But as he discovers, he does not have the power to give the one who is enslaved her freedom. He cannot effect her redemption any more than we can with our ideals. Our gifts are not really ours to give. They reveal us to be part of the same system of slavery that oppresses her. We are indeed, as we have sometimes suggested, her fellow slaves. And because we are the latter, we cannot buy her back from slavery. A slave does not have the power to redeem a fellow slave. A slave may labour for all she is worth and never have the power to buy back her freedom or that of another slave.

But these conclusions may take us a bit further than we wish to go. Although we might have rhetorically pictured ourselves as fellow slaves with Aoi we do not believe it. Feminism taught us to see ourselves as the ones who are emancipated, who can spread the liberation to others. We are reluctant to see that we live in a world where everything has been sold up — a world in which one belongs either to those who have the power to buy, or else to those who have been sold up and bought out.

We too, as women, are part of the possessor culture, which disinherits Aoi and her sisters and brothers from their share of the Earth's benefits. The recognition of this may induce in us guilt — and the desire to do good to the poor, to respond to their neediness. But this widespread need of ours — not confined to feminists — to give to the needy may prevent us from facing the fact that it is the poor who are the ones who are doing most of the giving.

During 1985, for instance, the year of the first terrible African famine, the hungriest countries gave us in the West twice as much money as we gave them — all in interest repayments. In 1991, Red Nose Day raised £12 million — enough to cover one day of interest repayments for 44 of the poorest countries. Against this stark background, it should be fairly clear that no amount of sisterly sentiment on our part is going to free Aoi from the appalling burden that is carried by the likes of her in these societies ruined by indebtedness to the West.

As a feminist, one might suggest that it is principally men who have the power to change this state of affairs. But let us try to be honest. Would all the women in the West be eager to give up their cheap mortgages, their cheap food? Would feminists be willing? Wouldn't we be quick to argue that really women (i.e. us) shouldn't have to shoulder the burden? The fact is that we do not really want to count, let alone to pay, the cost of redeeming Aoi and her kin from the terrifying, crushing burden of debt that is ruining their lives; we want to keep at bay the realization that it is the poor who are paying for our pleasures, our needs, our sins; the thought that it is we who are incurring an impossible debt that we can never hope to repay. Such a realization — of our chronic indebtedness — is not in keeping with the vision of ourselves as emancipated, as those who are on the threshold of taking charge of their destinies. We desperately need to hold on to the much more manageable notion of ourselves as actual or potential benefactors of the poor.

But perhaps, if we are to make any progress with understanding the mystery of redemption, it is precisely this sense of hopeless indebtedness that we need to hold on to. In an environmental context, it is not difficult to understand that the earth has been damaged and abused, and that to put right the damage that has been done, and to limit further damage, is costly. The issue as to who pays for this has become a major issue between the West and the Third World. The latter maintains that the West should pay for its profligate consumerism. The US maintains that 'consumer freedom is not negotiable'. As radicals, we probably recognize the justice of the claim that Third World countries should be able to charge the West for the privilege of making use of the biodiversity of the forests, though we may have misgivings about them exercising the right to pursue a lifestyle of sophisticated consumerism that we enjoy.

But when we come to the matter of the economy of salvation there may be a good many reasons why feminists and spiritual radicals of all sorts profess to find the idea of redemption a distasteful one — even though, as I have suggested, we also operate it on one level. Why should it be necessary for sin to be paid for, we ask? Isn't God supposed to be almighty and all loving? Why shouldn't God forgive us our sins without any 'payment' — especially as in our case, being women, our sins are of a lesser order than men's? And anyway, what about God's mercy? God's mercy is supposed to be endlessly available. This doesn't really square up with God allowing God's son to be crucified for our sins. It's a barbaric medieval idea which in our enlightened times we really don't need.

But could it be that the reasons we feel we don't need redemption go rather deeper than we suspect? It comes down again to the question of who we are, the question of self-knowledge. Could it be that part of what we are, as middle-class women, is the spoiled and petulant children of the Western protectorate? We think it rather mean-minded to count the cost of things that are spoiled and broken by us, because basically we are so used to the idea that father, who loves us, will of course pay up. After all he has lots of money and lots of power and it won't make much difference to him.

And of course, being children we are 'innocent' and need not enquire too closely into the complexities of how the real cost of our breakages might be borne elsewhere. Ours is not a situation where some petty thieving might involve us in being put on the next transport to Auschwitz, or where the innocent are daily sentenced to starvation and terror not even for small crimes but for no crimes at all. Yet we have in the past been fervent on the subject of our innocence and the necessity for our freedom to be continued and extended. We are not concerned with who really foots the bill for this 'innocence', so sure are we in our confidence in the ever-giving and forgiving God. Thus have all the liberal theologies tended to edit out the God of Judgement whose presence is unmistakable in the New Testament as well as in the Hebrew scriptures. For we, the liberal enlightened people of the twentieth century, cannot be doing with the barbarous images of a bygone age.

But perhaps we have mistaken the deal with God. The New Testament which introduces us to the God who is the father of Jesus Christ is rather specific as to what is required of us if we wish to enter into relationship with this God. When Christ teaches his disciples to pray, the prayer includes these words: 'Forgive us our debts as we also have forgiven our debtors' (Matt 6.12). But we have not forgiven our debtors. We have condemned them to a death-in-life. We do not like the image of God as judge, but this does not prevent us from passing a terrible judgement on our fellow humans. Of course, many of us have merciful sentiments towards them — as judges often do. But we are constrained by the system. Indeed, we cannot, we do not know how to begin to forgive our debtors the crippling burden of debt that is ruining their lives — and indeed ours too; for we are also enslaved to the system not as its victims but as its beneficiaries; and we are frequently trapped into the illusion that we may somehow buy ourselves out by good works. But that with which we seek to do our good works is that which has already been stolen from the poor. They have already paid for it, as indeed they have already paid, against their will, for all our good works as well as our bad ones — our sins.

But because the poor have been obliged to 'pay for' our sins, does this mean that we have thereby been 'justified'? For the poor, our suffering sisters (and brothers) are not simply pure, innocent victims whose suffering has the power to 'take away' our sins. Though some of them, like children, are in a sense innocent, they are, as a whole, just ordinary people, sinners like ourselves. We have rightly perceived that the oppression and exploitation of the poor in society is a 'judgement' on that society, as the abuse of women in Christian tradition is a 'judgement' on male Christians. The poor are always a judgement on the rich. But this is different from saying that individually the poor are licensed to become judges of the rich — that they are in possession of some special virtue or wisdom because of their oppression. For poverty and degradation, as I have already suggested, is more likely to impoverish and degrade than it is to ennoble. Their poverty is not of itself likely to fit the poor to be wise, any more than women's oppression makes them into saints. Thus the poor cannot be our redeemers. To image them in this way is an illusion, unhelpful to them and harmful to us. And we cannot be their redeemers either. Of course, it is true that some of our sisters have found some use for the feminism that we have offered, though they have adapted it and discarded those features that did not appeal to them. Unlike Aoi, they seem to suggest that there is something we can offer that is a remedy for their desperate plight. Surely this is a cause for rejoicing? And indeed we should rejoice that these sisters who may be our friends, our colleagues, our students, even members of our family, have been able to escape from the ruination of their bodies and destruction of their hopes through unmitigated childbearing and sickness and poverty and debt. Yes, we cannot help but be happy with them and for them, as we would be for ourselves. And yet, by the same token we may also be required to weep with them — weep that there are only the few who have been able to scramble aboard the boat of the international bourgeoisie, or swim alongside; weep as perhaps they do also, that the vast majority of their kin are still drowning in that terrible sea of poverty, as the ruination of their societies inexorably proceeds. And in the weeping we may be aware that this 'saving' is not the 'saving' of God — salvation; for it is arbitrary and inadequate — and tomorrow it could be reversed. We or they may even have fallen among those who are drowning.

So if there is this arbitrariness, how then can we understand the meaning of this terrible burden of suffering? We do not believe that it is God's judgement upon the poor, because we are aware that it is a 'judgement' that has mainly been imposed by us. We have condemned the poor to a brutal and almost inescapable poverty. But it may indeed be that the suffering of the poor is God's judgement on us, that by which we are condemned because we have failed to forgive them their debts. And if this is the case, then we shall be desperate to know how we may escape this condemnation. Is there any hope — any possibility of redemption? And here at last we may find ourselves ready to look again at the mystery of our redemption in Christ. For perhaps this time our options do not look so healthy and it is all we have left.

Note

1   *The Good Woman of Bangkok*, Channel Four, 12 May 1992.

22 Christ and the problem of difference

In the 1990s, feminist faith has found itself in the middle of the horror movie of post-modernism, as the universalizing ideals of the Enlightenment are subjected to a new scepticism. It began, as we saw, with black feminists pointing out firmly to white colleagues the fact of their differences. From then on, the affirmation of difference became the correct perspective on race, class and gender. Gender generalizations were no longer acceptable.[1] The language of rights was recognized as being far from 'natural' or instituted by God — but rather the ideological superstructure of a particular construct of masculinity.

It seemed at first that we had been able to weather the storm and adapt to the new state of affairs. The hierarchy of victim status, though it ran contrary to the unity requirements of the myth of emancipation, had somehow managed to accommodate this affirmation of difference. We may now suspect that it drew its strength from a secret re-instatement of the Christian drama of redemption in a new form – as we discovered by analysing our response to the story of Aoi. But it may now turn out that the problem is far worse than we expected, that the damage is structural and our solution can only be temporary as it is highly unstable. The feminist concern has been with the marginalization of women, and a determination that their particular stories should be told. But what are we to make of the post-modern view that there are anyway only particular stories; that there are no margins because there is no centre, no central court where rational standards can arbitrate between differences?[2] There is only us with our particular tribal stories and rituals and them with theirs. A world-wide vision of justice for women is an illusion — just a particular group of women trying to write large our own tribal mythology. But now it seems that this our writing has become the writing on the wall for us. The fall of the Berlin Wall was in many ways the outward and visible sign of this crumbling of the myth of emancipation. It represented the deep dualism in our society which as radicals we all loved to hate. But it was a dualism that ran through us too, and our myths; with their neat separation of the oppressors and the oppressed we held God's judgement at bay and deflected its possibility away from ourselves. The Wall thus kept us all safe and sane. Now that it is down we are threatened with the slide into chaos and insanity. And even our insurance policy, our own little radical drama of redemption, which we had encoded in our narrative and in which the innocent suffering of the wretched (women) of the Third World mysteriously paid for our sins, even this can now be seen to be invalid.

So what is to be done? In this great collapse of the grand narratives, is there any narrative that can withstand this terrible holocaust of meaning? Perhaps this is the moment to review our relation to Christian faith and see if there is anything that can be salvaged there.

'Can a male saviour save women?' was for a long time accepted as the question that expressed the feminist problem about Christian faith.[3] But the more closely I look at this question the stranger it begins to seem. One could also ask, 'Can a Jewish saviour save Gentiles?' (In fact, in the first century they did raise a question along these lines.) But then why Gentiles? What about respecting differences among Gentiles like, say, Roman and Greeks, blacks and whites, Germans and British — no sorry, Irish, English, Scottish and Welsh? And would female Gentiles of each sort require their own saviour? Clearly mixed-race people and transsexuals will present special problems. If sameness in race and gender is a qualification for being a saviour, we are going to need rather a lot of them. It is not difficult to see why theologians like Hampson and McFague and Daly have concluded that a Jewish male saviour who lived in the first century can't really save anyone at all.

But looking back at the work of Nechama Tec, in a situation where the issue of 'saving' people was a very real one, it is clear that it was possible for people of one race and gender to save those from another. In a situation where Jews were fatally threatened, Gentiles could and occasionally did save Jews — people who differed from them in many fundamental respects. Difference, it seems, is possible in this sort of life saving. Why then have feminists declared it to be inadmissible in the matter of theology, especially now that we have discovered the affirmation of difference?

For some feminists the problem may be one of recognizing the problem. The view from the cliff may sometimes not include the realization that the ground beneath us is about to slide into the sea. Feminists, they may claim, are well aware of otherness and difference; for it was the foundation of our discourse to discover Woman as the archetypal Other, and from there to reverse the whole dualism and hierarchy of the phallo-logocentric scheme in favour of the Other, woman, and all who histori-cally have been made to share her Otherness and suffer for it. Feminist theology exposed men for making God in their own image and not noticing the difference. We, on the other hand, have recognized difference and put it at the centre of our whole scheme.

And yet, as we saw, there is evidence that black women in the US feel that their differences are not being taken seriously by white feminists. Maria Lugones says that when the differences were pointed out to the white theorists, they were rather more concerned about rescuing their *theory* from these pitfalls that would render it false, weak and trivial than in acknowledging the existence of those who had challenged them.[4]

This testimony gives one a slight sense of *déjà entendu*. In the early days, feminists detected that men had frequently made women the scapegoats for their own unease with their bodies. And feminist theology revealed how this male psychological manoeuvre was often disguised under theological and philosophical theorizing. Could it be that feminist theologians have assumed the mantle of their male predecessors and in defending a challenge to their theory, find that more than the theory was at stake? For as it became clear in our reflection on the story of Aoi, the real perception of difference can be radically unsettling to the identity of our knowing selves.

The strength of feminist theology at its best was its capacity to present a genuine incarnational critique of a faith that appeared to have lost touch with what is most fundamental to it — its gospel of good news for the dispossessed. This had been captured by a certain class of males and recast as an idolatry of the image of God as male. Feminist theology directed us to consider the actual suffering of real victims and question fundamentally a piety directed towards an iconized male saviour, the mode of whose brutal death has been metamorphosed into a stylized object of religious devotion. It was an insight that is firmly marked out in the gospel itself, that the 'saviour' appears to us in the form of the victim, someone in desperate need. See Matt 25.31–46: 'Lord, when did we see you hungry or thirsty or a stranger or needing clothes or sick or in prison and did not help you?'

But unfortunately, in the same moment that we uncovered the incarnational truth of the Christian gospel, we also rediscovered the original offence of its particularity. Why this particular man, why this particular period in history, we asked. It appears to be so arbitrary and thereby to us, women of the twentieth century, irrelevant. Our concern was how women like ourselves can be liberated into the universal having been so long confined by our particularity. Thus, through our re-definition of the universal to centre upon the concept of women, we re-joined an ancient quest — the flight from the particular. We defined the patriarchal world as alien, and ourselves as souls who must nurture the vestige of womanly divinity that exists in each of us, and by such means pursue enlightenment. Thus we hoped to be able to release ourselves eventually from imprisonment in the pseudo-history of patriarchal tradition. Under this scheme, we had no use for a male saviour from first-century Palestine.

Hence, despite the radical nature of our beginnings, our religious concerns have come to centre not on the incarnation but on a form of gnosis, knowledge as power, the manipulation of words and ideas that will enable us to find a safe path through the cosmic maze of omnipresent androcentric reality. Our goal is a form of re-birth, a re-possession of the psyche. And whatever nice things we say about the body, our understanding of our basic spiritual nature is intellectual not bodily. We preserve the fiction of ourselves as bodily, but in fact the body confines us to the particular and the historical and it is this which we have come to disdain and from which we yearn to escape. The body that we love is the fit and able body of our ideals, an ideal which our situation gives us a reasonable expectation of possessing. As for the diseased, dying, defeated body that is the lot of the majority of our sisters and brothers, we are naturally full of pity, and of a righteous indignation; but it is an indignation that conceals our secret revulsion and terror.

The real failure to respect difference is achieved by the mystifications of liberal pluralism, which is confident that it can take on board the 'difference' of the Other and enrich its own theories with this difference. But this is the mentality of the imperialists who admired the cultural and religious treasures of those they conquered and took them home as booty to their own museums and art houses. This sort of 'understanding' of other faiths and cultures, understands only what it thinks it can possess. Since post-Christian feminism, and some sorts of 'Christian' feminism have discarded as without value the sources of their own religious tradition, they are fated to become spiritual tourists who are now dependent on the technocratic society and not on the hospitality of hosts. So they are no longer guests with gifts of their own to offer to their hosts, and receive gifts from them also. Instead they will become spiritual trinket hunters in an alien land, relating to its inhabitants only through the market — or worse.

Thus, pluralism is not just the altruistic discourse we deem it to be but the objectification of culture of the Other and the appropriation of it to our Western selves. The temptation to become cultural booty-takers exists for those of us who are educated by the hegemonic culture, whatever our ethnic origins; and those who have been educated in the academies of the Enlightenment cannot unproblematically represent subordinated cultures from which they may have emerged. Feminism, which arose in response to the disadvantages and handicaps that women face within the hegemonic culture, at first sight gave a promise of a new order of justice in the face of ancient corruption. But as feminists attempted to process the claims of the latest claimants, the system began to fracture into a host of competing claims between the different groups of sisters it was supposed to unite. Thus it was revealed not as a new order of justice but a system of claims for what is due to women under the old one. And as the radical rhetoric dissolves in this disorder of competing claims, the lie is given to the unifying ambitions of the pluralist myth.

So we have the irony of a feminist theory and theology that loudly proclaims its respect for difference, yet is carried forward on precisely that form of rhetoric which threatens genuine cultural difference with extinction. It serves like a Trojan horse for a 'post-cultural' imperialism that devours all remnants of true cultural uniqueness in its consuming maw, reducing everything to the tasteless uniformity of the ubiquitous burger. It may be shocking to suggest that feminism's gospel about the liberation of women is as firmly inculturated in the spread of the New World Order as was the missionaries' preaching of the gospel in the empire of nineteenth-century colonialism, but in fact they are not unconnected. We inherit the cultural genes of the missionaries. And our gospel has become linked to the myth of pluralism, because it is part of the identity which we impose on the Other, to cope with the terror of their Otherness. We, who inherit the capacious mantle of liberalism, believe that we have banished this fear of difference that is so common to most peoples in the world. The trouble is that we have not so much banished it, as failed to confront it in a way that the universalizing power of our language enables us to do. But the terror remains, waiting in the wings to seize us by the throat. What I mean here is well illustrated in E. M. Forster's *A Passage to India* where the liberal-minded young woman, fresh from England, suddenly comes up against the reality of India that she has fantasized. The terror of an alien culture grips her, and she re-enacts the nightmare of the colonial society.

In the 1970s and 1980s we rejected the Christian story of a Jewish male redeemer, for we considered this to be irrelevant to our concerns for justice. But now that we find ourselves in the painful impasse of postmodernist challenge, we are forced to re-evaluate our self-identity of those times. Perhaps in retrospect we can acknowledge that we signed up for the movement in those days because we wanted a piece of the pie, a slice of the action. We wanted to play on our own ground in our own team colours and to show men that we could play the game too and beat them at it, exposing for ever the basis of their monopoly of privileged access. Of course we wanted to represent all those women players who never quite qualified to get on the pitch with us, for we believed that through our gender we represented them. So in our mind's eye, they were cheering us from the stalls as we fought our mutual opponents with all the skill and resources and teamwork that we could command. But unfortunately, it didn't quite work out as planned. These days there aren't so many people cheering from the terraces — and they are as likely to be hurling bottles and shouting abuse. And we are no longer — if we ever were — a multi-coloured team. Black women have gone off to play their own game elsewhere. And worst of all our opponents, whom we counted on to fight back, are deserting us. Although we frequently berated them for foul play, we never expected them to withdraw and re- write the rules of the game. But the philosophers who have announced the collapse of the 'grand narratives' are walking out of the courts of the Enlightenment. Suddenly, we are aware of 'the vulnerability of the feminist project to being disarmed both theoretically and practically by the impulses of postmodernism and postmodernity as they bear on the unity of women's experience of reality'.[5] Or as Mary Grey says, 'If every- one has the right to make truth claims, what means do we now have of deciding between rival and conflicting ontological claims?'[6]

It is difficult to resist the conclusion that feminists in the court of the academy have been outwitted by their male peers in the Western philo- sophical tradition, who were never really comfortable with women joining the club; that is, if we assume, as Esther Reed suggests, that 'post-modernism is a predominantly male response to aspects of a modern philosophy which was itself predominantly male'.[7] One can see why some women, determined not to be thus outwitted by men in the search for intellectual honour, have been willing to abandon the whole system of women's claim for justice and opt for post-feminist gender studies which no longer define women in terms of their oppression. Yet others, like Mary Grey, are equally determined not to abandon the claim for justice. For to do so would be to deny any responsibility for the vast system of slavery that we have created, such as enslaves Aoi and her kin. To surrender the field to post-modernism is to allow unchallenged the latest version of the classic opt-out that all the privileged beneficiaries of such systems will tend to favour.

But equally we cannot simply ignore the question of difference that post-modernism has raised. And perhaps it is precisely this crisis that may force us to consider whether a new understanding of the classic Christian doctrine of the incarnation and redemption might have more to offer us as women than anything which has been dreamed up by the Western philosophical academy in the last six hundred years. The prob- lem with our own version of Christian soteriology was that our reversal of the system of 'male' values actually reinstated it; its outcome meant that black women were entitled to put in a massive claim for damages against us as well as white men. If on the other hand we conclude that others' suffering does not justify us or anyone else, we must then con- clude that each suffers for and is responsible for her own sins — that bleak vision which Augustine did his best to counteract.

If we now return to the question, 'Can a male saviour save women?', we may be better placed to appreciate that it was never really a theological question. In fact, it was not really even a question. Rather it was a claim about the honour of women (a certain class of women) and the necessity for this to be acknowledged by men. Nevertheless, we can in a sense answer it and say no, a male saviour cannot save women, but neither could a female saviour simply by virtue of being more 'like' us. The heavenly city of God is not a representative democracy. And if we can be saved at all it is only by God, and by virtue of the fact that God is not 'like' us but utterly and fundamentally Other. God does not belong to the political community in which we have a system of claims against each other, debts which, if we are lucky as we are in the West, are paid to us in the form of our rights. But with God we have no rights, no claims that God must recognize. God has no debts to us, but we have a share in the vast impossible debt of sin. In that respect we are sisters of Aoi, we are like her.

And yet 'likeness' is also part of the story of redemption. As the New Testament tells it, we have been released from this debt by one who was both like us and yet radically different; 'like us in all things but sin'. The narrative of faith requires us to believe that this debt was paid once and for all by a Jewish male who was tortured to death in the first century — in one sense a victim so ordinary it could have been anyone. Yet this obscure individual was raised from death by God and 'will come again in glory'. This then was that 'remedy for sin' that Julian understood in her 'showings'. This is the scarcely believable promise of the gospel which requires from us the 'obedience of faith'.

This faith has seemed to feminists and other sophisticated moderns to be irrational, exclusive and arbitrary, and we have sought to replace it with something altogether more reasonable. But the trouble with much of our gender theology is that it preached a salvation that is unobtainable to those, like Aoi, who are condemned to dishonour. For faith is the only possession to which the poor have equal if not greater access than us — they may be richer than we are in faith. Like us, the poor have a choice about faith. Unlike us, they do not have the choice of the false innocence of idealism because the cruelty of their situation makes this option impossible. Faith is the only possession that we can truly share with them — the faith that this world has been redeemed. For, as I see it, this question of redemption becomes the only real question for us and for them. All our smart spiritualities are useless if they do not take this question into account; and all our resolves and exhortations about working for justice are futile if we are not redeemed. For the scale of the outrage by humanity and against humanity is so vast, our ability to repair or restore or compensate so negligible, that all our little busy-ness for justice is just so much froth on the ocean by comparison. If we are not redeemed, then we are wholly abandoned, truly lost.

Thus, I suggest that for those of us who stand within the Christian cultural inheritance, sisterhood can more truthfully be expressed through a faith based on 'sane doctrine', and on a more orthodox reading of the scriptures. For this tradition itself deals with the question of what is due to different categories of people who form part of our world. There are our enemies and those who persecute us; our neighbours and those in the same household — our sisters and brothers; there is the stranger who is within our walls and depends on our protection; and there are those to whom we owe debts (of loyalty as well as material debts) and those who owe debts to us. It is an extremely rich tradition and what we need is a new discerning of it for our times and our places, not a new ideology of pluralism. We need not fear that it licenses oppression of the Other for it is this faith, rightly interpreted, that frees us to act justly towards the Other, to offer them justice and protection, and the acknowledgement of their humanity, not merely to treat them as the stimulus for the revising of our theories.

This faith has the Other at the very centre of its life, and recognizes that in all our search to express the divine, we are vulnerable to the desire to domesticate God. This is why in Christian tradition God comes in person — in the person of the Other. And for each generation the issue is recognition of this incarnation. God in Christ is not a person like us — as feminists have already recognized. This was somebody not from our time, different gender, different race, not speaking our language or endorsing our ideals. This God is certainly not in our image. And that is the point. The task of Christian preaching is to remind whoever is tempted to forget it that God cannot be made in our own image. So as God is to us twentieth-century women so God is to all men and all women. God is not of our gender, nor of the opposite gender. For God does not personify maleness either and undermines the claims of arrogant men, including men in the church, as well as women who seek a share in their power. But God is the God of those without defences, either practical or theoretical, in a patriarchal society.

And here there is also a paradox. For we must acknowledge that the doctrines of the Christian community are a kind of defence. But they are not exactly a defence of a theory of explanation, for a mystery by definition cannot be explained. The function of a doctrine like the incarnation is to safeguard the narrative that it contains *in its proper bodiliness*, to preserve it from the covetous conceptualizing that would abstract it into the self-divinizing narratives of idolatry. The narrative must remain in its incarnational context, so that those who approach it learn the humility to cope with the uncouthness of scripture — and the even more intractably unprepossessing body of the church.

Thus, we may say that the doctrines of the church are the 'familiar speech' of those who are members of the body of Christ — the speech by which they may be recognized and recognize each other. But these doctrines do not guarantee us possession of the meaning of God. This, as we know from the testimony of holy souls like Julian and Teresa, can only be found by waiting on God. For Julian, anguished by the weight of human sin and suffering, longed to understand the import of her revelations but did not seek to soothe the pain of seeing with instant theory. If twenty years is what it took for the meaning to become clear to her, then she was willing to encompass the waiting. In faith she held that this human being she saw was also God, God revealed in the victim. And, like St Teresa, she felt a deep pity for this man suffering the dishonour of paying dearly for sins he didn't commit. Thus she was able to look on suffering of this victim not as a potential claim for damages but as an act of reparation voluntarily endured. And perhaps it is thus, through pity for God in Christ, that we are drawn into the mystery of the incarnation. For it reveals a gracious kind of dealing, unlike that in our world of claim and counter claim: and if we are willing, it evokes the capacity in us to receive from God that which is unearned and undeserved, and to offer to each other that which is not owed and cannot be claimed.

Notes

1   Christine Pierce, 'Postmodernism and other skepticisms', in Claudia Card, *Feminist Ethics* (Kansas: University of Kansas Press, 1991), p. 65.
2   Pierce in Card, p. 63.
3   Rosemary Radford Ruether, 'Christology and feminism: can a male savior save women?', in Rosemary Radford Ruether, *To Change the World: Christology and Cultural Criticism* (New York: Crossroad, 1981), p. 53.
4   Maria Lugones, 'On the logic of pluralist feminism', in Card, p. 41.
5   Esther D. Reed, 'Whither postmodernism and feminist theology?', *Feminist Theology*, no. 6 (May 1994), p. 15.
6   Mary Grey, 'Method in feminist theology', *Feminist Theology*, no. 6 (May 1994), p. 91.
7   Reed, p. 15.

23 *Amazing grace*

The question I would probably want to ask the author if I had just read the chapters I have written is this: But how do you *know*? For what I have written seems to presuppose that I 'know something' about God. But how can I know anything about God? This question is not merely rhetorical. I mean it very seriously. And in the next three chapters, I want to explore it rather more personally, because I have the sense that this is necessary if I am to come further with the mystery of how it is we can have any knowledge of God.

One might say that my knowing of God is determined by the shape of the Catholic faith that I have adopted, and that is certainly true. But still there is something unaccounted for. Since I did not start at this point, how did I arrive there? In terms of background there is not much to indicate that this would be a destination. From the same starting point an abundance of other options would have been as possible, and I can see an even greater abundance of obstacles to becoming what I have become.

I began this book by looking at the thesis of the feminism that I encountered in the 1980s; that women may best do theology by basing it on their personal experience. It proposed that we make ourselves by our own choices, that we are in a sense our own creation. And in this lies the unique and special quality of our personal experience, its suitability as a basis for knowing God. But the burden of my text so far has been my increasing conviction that I do not make myself — I am already made — and rather precisely determined — by those forces of class, culture, race and gender that have shaped me into the particular person that I am. I began to see that I am not preciously unique in the manner we had assumed but in fact I am terribly common.

As this growing sense of my own commonness dawned on me, I began to be aware that there was a similarly common aspect to much of the work of feminist theology that I was reading at the time. While there was a strong affirmation of the universality of women's experience, there was also a certain resistance to recognizing the assumptions we — its creators — had in common. Since then, as we have seen, belief in the universality of women's experience has given way to a strong recognition of their difference. But at times this has been treated as almost the same thing. Thus, the universality of our differences has been read as the charter of our own uniqueness. But actually it is not the same thing. And there is still a resistance to acknowledging that the differences are not determined by us. There is a deep, I might say archetypal fear of seeing ourselves as creatures — creatures of our past, and of those habits of body and mind that our past has structured in us. For this is a nightmare vision that allows us no freedom — no freedom to become anything at all except that which we have already become. If I cannot truly choose who I am, how can I choose to know God? For any knowledge I have will be pre-determined by the limits of my 'personal experience' whose limitedness I have begun to perceive.

And yet, a very common sense tells me that we cannot abandon personal experience because it is what we have, what we are given. And here it seems to me is the clue — in the what-we-are-given. I have never understood very well the theological concept of grace. Yet recently, I had an inkling about it — a suspicion that it could be of some use in exploring precisely the problem that engaged me. I saw that it was, as it were, the small lamp with which I could embark on the task of excavating personal experience. For this, I think, is what we have to do with it — to excavate it to a certain depth, and in such a way that those forces of class, culture and gender that have made us into the very particular product that we are, are laid bare. For we must know how we are determined before we can know in what way, if any, we are free. The notion of grace, I suddenly suspected, could be the clue to this quest.

So how do we understand grace? Is grace an obscure theological doctrine that the majority of us don't understand? Or is there a kind of grace that is familiar to everybody, even if they do not call it by this name? I suspect that the answer is both but it is the latter that I want to start with — a kind of secular notion of grace. Most people, I think, recognize a quality of specialness that belongs to certain people, a charismatic quality (charisma is the Greek for grace); and also a specialness about certain times in our lives. And this secular grace is sometimes there for certain people at certain times. Thus, there may be times in history that seem to have this special quality about them. It's a time perhaps of clarity, creativity, potentiality — a time when certain things are possible which later are no longer possible.

For many people, childhood and youth exemplify their experience of the time of grace — a time when one has not yet learned to reject what is given in favour of something else. Later on, we may hark back to this period and imbue it with a specialness. It may be this specialness that forms the basis of our inklings about grace.

So perhaps I can test the hypothesis on myself. Was childhood a time of grace for me? I'm not so sure. I recall myself as a 14-year-old at boarding school wrestling uncomfortably with a double burden — that of the onset of puberty and of the question of God's existence. Not a combination that with hindsight I would recommend. One of these problems solved itself in the course of time. The other became life-long — a state of permanent struggle. However, I do remember a sort of moment of truce when, in exasperation and despair, I realized that one could not ultimately think oneself through this problem. God wasn't going to turn up and settle the matter. Faith, as far as I could see, was not a leap, but a crawl — blindfold through a low door. Thinking could bring one only so far. And then thinking had to take off its cap and submit to the indignity of going the rest of the way in this manner. I was doubtful at the time and my doubts continued. Supposing I accepted faith on these dubious terms, what would it entail? I was afraid that God might send me to Africa as a missionary, or demand life-long celibacy or something equally dreadful. So I stalled, I played for time. I let God know that this wasn't quite what I had in mind. I wanted a proper personal revelation — something one could be quite sure about...

But looking back on it now, I suddenly see that I missed the point. It was in a sense a revelation, but I wouldn't accept it. Even at that age, I clearly had my own ideas about what was or wasn't a revelation. Though I didn't realize it, I had decided that God had to do it my way.

Childhood is not of course, for many children, that sweet time that adults sometimes dream up in their later ideals. But it is a time when we start off with the capacity to receive trustfully. But as the unacceptable gifts come with the acceptable ones we become more selective. And being in a position to choose begins to matter most. In my own case, my 'choosing' of God was tempered by the fact that I had already learned something of this 'choosiness' about how God should behave. My own childhood had not taught me to be unduly trustful. My acceptance of God was hedged around by reservations. And it was also dictated by needs and fears. So despite my grave doubts about Him (as He undoubtedly was in those days) I continued to call on Him from time to time to express my dissatisfaction. God, so we had been told, gives his children bread — not a stone. So I used to turn up after some fresh outrage either personal or global and say, 'Well, what do you call this then, God?' Here were stones from the stony God.

As I continued to wrestle with this question of faith at various stages in my life, I noticed that somehow I always seemed to get back to the same place. The level of sophistication changed of course, but the place was the same. But I wasn't too keen on the idea of a single choice —

I had a range of choices that I wanted to explore, such as the privilege of my class and race entitled me to. Though at times I was semi-meek and half trusting, I opted to pursue my quarrel with God, which was marked by much self-pity and frequent fits of despair.

Thus, I entered upon my youth in a critical frame of mind and what I saw around me did not encourage me to change it. I saw a society that excelled in ugliness, that was bereft of all beauty whether cultural, physical, moral or spiritual. I felt myself to be orphaned in a wasteland of the spirit. Emerging from a sheltered middle-class background, I became a student in the period of the sixties, which was perhaps one of those historical periods of grace. It may have been as Richard Gott, writing in the nineties, suggests 'the last occasion in world history when people and movements — on the largest possible scale — had the audacity to believe that it was possible to change the world for the better'.[1] And thus I filtered into a stream of young people who shared my dissatisfaction with the world they had inherited. Our response to the great absences we perceived was to adopt a desperate idealism, little knowing then how grossly this would betray us. For we had been touched by righteous rage, the rage for justice, and believed it to be a sacred force, one that was necessary for the causes that we had espoused. And in a sense, so it was — the first and necessary step towards the hunger for justice. But we were also ignorant about anger and did not recognize it as one of the deadly passions that is capable of harassing the soul and undermining its endeavours.

But hand in hand with the rage for justice that was a particular feature of the Western youth of the sixties, there was also the search for Otherness. In my own case, this seeking the Other took me to Africa. Africa's fabled darkness seemed to me the antidote to the fake brightness of the Western world which everywhere revealed ugliness and devastation and decadence. I wanted contact with a society that knew something of a sense of community which was absent from the alienated and individualized pattern of Western culture. I wanted to see a young society that had hope for the future and which, so I thought, was not knee-deep in the guilt and bloodshed of the past.

All this I projected on to the Africa of my dreams. But the Other, as I was forced to learn, is not and cannot be the vehicle for all our yearnings and desires. The Other is not Other to itself. In Africa I was treated as a European, with all the historical weight of African assumptions about how Europeans behave. And although I resented this — for I felt myself to be 'myself' and not 'a European' — it also perhaps stimulated my curiosity. Was I in fact a European? Was being a European some part of myself that I had not yet met?

Thus I experienced how the pursuit of the Other in its early stages leads back to the self and its own origins. My preoccupation with the meaning of community led me next to Europe and to a particular experiment in educational community in Denmark run by an eccentric Dane. It was populated mainly by a number of restless Americans, who perhaps like me were in search of their European origins. Here I met a Californian Jew, a student of philosophy, who introduced me to Plato and the Socratic dialogues. Thus, in life's paradoxical fashion, it was an American Jew who initiated me into the leading intellectual traditions of Gentile Europe. It was he who acquainted me with that passionate pursuit of intellectual truth by the individual that is fundamental to the model of education in Western culture. And by a further paradox, it was this same Jewish philosopher who introduced me to the Danish Protestant philosopher Kierkegaard. It was from Kierkegaard that I began to receive a first inkling of the significance of the incarnation — a teaching which had hitherto made no sense to me at all. For God I had already encountered — after a fashion. But Christ seemed nothing more than an unnecessary complication.

It was while I was in Denmark that I gradually began to realize that escape was not possible in the terms that I had hitherto conceived it. There could be no escape as long as I was carrying my prison around with me and re-erecting it at each fresh location. Neither Africa nor Denmark could ultimately liberate me from myself. Sooner or later I saw that I would return from where I had come, since in symbolic terms this was the origin of the problem. But before this happened, something else took place which set the conditions for my eventual return.

It happened by means of one of those odd little epiphanies that one's life presents from time to time. In the course of an informal seminar where much of my learning was taking place, my Jewish teacher made a somewhat sexist remark. This caused me to leave the group in protest, though actually I could not have applied the label sexist at the time, for I was innocent of feminism in those days. But this did not stop me from feeling justified in my disapproval — nor did I cease to feel this way after I had returned a few days later. But in the meantime, I had made a discovery. I had understood that the unfettered pursuit of individual truth is not simply the highest calling, but at a certain point turns into its own opposite and becomes a kind of cul-de-sac, for it leads away from that which has been its generative context, the ground of its knowing. And it also became clear to me that community, authority, and the acknowledgement of one's own imperfection were intimately and mysteriously connected. My immediate response to these perceptions was to return to the seminar and grit my teeth over the loss of face that this involved. But my longer-term response to these thoroughly insignificant events was to become a Catholic.

How strange it seems in retrospect to have decided to become a Catholic in Denmark. For Denmark is a most unCatholic country and

Kierkegaard is a most Protestant philosopher. I remember Denmark with its tidy brown fields in spring as the gulls wheel after the seed-sowing tractor and its austere little white churches with the ship hanging from the roof. I recall its flat but (to me) beautiful landscape divided by the shining stretch of the fjord and illuminated by that special quality of light that characterizes those parts. This Denmark was for me a most illuminating experience. The Danish soil had produced that wise and humane educator of adults, Grundtvig, founder of the Danish folk high school movement, who understood that people need first to be 'enlivened' before one can seek to enlighten them with learning. My time in Denmark was both enlivening and enlightening in a way that still seems to me strangely mysterious. For there were — as far as I know — no Catholics for miles around, and I was reading no Catholic literature at the time, except a newsletter from Taizé (not precisely Catholic) and later, when the direction had begun to take root, a copy of Pascal's *Pensées* on the boat home to England.

Looking back on this decision, I note with curiosity that my reasons, which at the time were adequately coherent, have greatly improved with the passage of time. Twenty years ago I did not understand much that is now clear to me about my reasons; and yet, in a sense, these latter reasons do seem somehow to belong with that decision. Thus, I see that I have in a sense enacted what I first learned about when I was 14, but which I did not really understand or fully accept at the time, and which even now I can only grasp with the greatest difficulty. And seeing this, it occurs to me that God is not put off by our spiritual illiteracy, our half-hearted choosing. Grace, through the agency of the Spirit, is very determined. Perhaps this is why the hymn-writer dubbed her amazing...

Yet this apparent point of arrival was in reality only the first point of departure. Conversions are all very well — but would it all come out in the wash?

Note

1   Richard Gott, 'We had a dream', *Guardian 2*, 18 July 1994, p. 2.

24 The impossible possibility of faith

When I returned to England in the early seventies I soon encountered the emergence of new-wave feminism. Because of my previous baptism in the radicalism of the sixties, it was perhaps a foregone conclusion this wave would sweep me in its progress. But in the meantime I had become a Catholic and so I was once again in a rather paradoxical situation. For a feminist of those times to profess any kind of allegiance to the authority of a male-dominated church was a rather uncomfortable contradiction. As a child of the Enlightenment, I felt that some of my freethinking ancestors would be tugging at my sleeve, Alice Walker-style, and reminding me of their own robust rejection of religion, how they saw through the whole edifice of sickly piety and overblown religious sentiment that masked the cruel evils of Victorian society. And in a sense they hardly need to persuade me. For I have inherited their distrust of religion, their distaste for all forms of piety. The scepticism of the Enlightenment already runs in my veins, its questioning I have received with my genes. At one level I am baffled by godly passions and my intellectual temperament is quite agnostic. And perhaps for this reason, to be a feminist as well as a Catholic was in some sense necessary for me — a tension that was difficult to live with but which was even more difficult to live without. And in retrospect I can see that it was strangely fruitful for me. It was the particular course through which I was to discover (and find the language to express) how the process of conversion is a very lengthy one that is never quite completed.

And so it turned out that at the same time that I embraced feminism, I began to study theology in a Catholic (and Dominican) context and more particularly to study scripture. My new teacher had a great love and understanding for the scriptures and was himself a convert. With his help, I entered the world of the scriptures, and began to see them as the life story of a suffering and persecuted people, who worship a God of justice, yet are intimately preoccupied with the terrible unfairness of God, and wrestle with the scandal of a God who seems unable to protect the innocent.

At the same time, I embraced a feminism that was also intimately preoccupied with matters of justice and unfairness. Feminist theology addressed itself to the issue of women's low status in the life of the church and their exclusion from the image of God in Christian tradition. Christian feminists re-interpreted the New Testament as a revelation of the Sophia God, focusing on Sophia as a means to reclaim the female in the divine, as a means to reconcile ourselves with a Christian tradition from which, because of our doctrine of the equality of women, we felt excluded.

The interaction of these two halves of my conversion was richly productive of new insight for me. But on both sides, as it were, it raised some stubbornly awkward questions. Thus, as my acquaintance with scripture deepened I came to doubt — like, but totally unlike Daphne Hampson — that this faith which the Jewish and Christian scriptures bear witness to was something that could be 'cleaned up' in order to make it suitable for feminist requirements. I began to suspect that it might be us who would need to clean up our thinking before the faith which these scriptures testify to can make any real sense to us. For perhaps Sophia was not quite as we had fashioned her — and she too had her scandalous particularity. Scripture makes clear that she does not give herself to all those who profess a love of wisdom, but only those who follow her along particular paths. In our justifiable excitement about Sophia, and our desire to reclaim her, we seemed to have forgotten to reclaim her opposite number — Dame Folly (Prov 9.13–18). We were apt to assume that women have had no part in the folly and sin that is part of Christian tradition, that had rendered it 'exclusive'. We defined in advance what we considered to be an acceptable presence of women in scripture. Either we must see them wielding power and having a particular measure of approval and status; or we must see them in the role of innocent and sinless victims who contend with Christ for the role of sacrificial victim and by implication also the role of redeemer.

But Sophia, speaking through the scriptures, tells us that those who are 'wise in their own eyes' will not be able to find her. It seems she has ordained that those women or men who approach her with their own neat schemes for how justice is to be done on earth will not find her. And this hidden or secret nature of the wisdom of God seems to require of those who would learn the speech of Sophia a special kind of reserve, of modesty, which on the whole we did not practise in our feminist theological endeavours.

Thus, it was not exclusively the 'exclusive' language of Christian tradition that cut off feminists from faith. I began to see that the appro-

priation of God through a particular ideology of justice can also undermine the possibility of faith. Our exclusive focus on the female aspect of
the Sophia tradition may have meant that we missed the most important
lesson that Sophia has to teach us. The New Testament as a historical
document marks a parting of the ways in the Sophia tradition. In
Christianity, Sophia makes her dwelling in the Christos, the Word made
flesh, the victim made by God into the redeemer. But in the Jewish tradition, Sophia has pitched her tent in the sacred Torah, the law of God, the
source of holiness. In both cases, these new stories of Sophia replaced
worship and sacrifice in the Temple that had been destroyed. Both these
rival heirs to Sophia gave up or transmuted the religious tradition of
animal sacrifice. The scriptures from which both emerged contained
stories of how a younger brother outmanoeuvres and gains the advantage over an elder brother — Jacob cheats Esau out of his inheritance.

And so, you might say, it has come to pass between Judaism and
Christianity. As I began to study scripture and the history of Christian
tradition, I came across some fearful skeletons in the cupboard — those
of the Jewish millions who had become sacrificial victims for the sins of
Christian Europe. I learned that it is possible to see Christianity as preparing the ground for the unspeakable event of the holocaust from the
earliest formation of its scriptures to the latest forms of their interpretation. For Christians, it seems, interpreted their 'good news' in such a
way as to render Jewish faith religiously redundant. Jews were cast in
the role of those who failed to recognize the true Messiah, the saviour.
Jews, according to the Christian story, are those who put to death the
incarnate God.

It was a feminist theologian, Rosemary Ruether, who was among the
first to explore this fatal racial dualism that has grown up at the heart of
Christian faith.[1] And this, in a sense, is no accident. For feminism has
celebrated and upheld women's right to a personal autonomy, the right
to challenge the forces of the old corruption, the right not to submit un-
questioningly but to question that which sorely needs to be questioned.
This is the strength of feminist tradition. But this same strength raises
serious problems for the acceptance of a traditional faith. How could it
be right for a woman who is a feminist to submit herself to that which by
requiring 'faith' seems to require that she set aside the function of the
critical intellect, that she suppress the knowledge of its discoveries —
like the knowledge that Christianity is not an innocent but a blood-
stained discourse, deeply oppressive to all those, like women and Jews,
who have been cast in the role of the Other?

At this point, it might seem that I had placed myself in a logic that
would deliver me to a post-Christian position. For the post-Christians
would declare that this violence stems directly from the continuing belief in the Christian God — a God of punishment and violent judgement.

God the Father is now seen as the ultimate child abuser who tortures his son for his own perverse pleasure, and as 'payment' for the sins of humanity. Is it surprising that his followers should behave in similarly brutal ways? The Christian God must be supplanted by something much more rational and humane — a gospel of liberation for women through rights, rationality and mutual respect.

But ironically, the post-Christians are here following an example already set by Christians. For Christians saw themselves as 'post-Jews' believing that the Jews worshipped a primitive, punitive and legalistic God, while they had discovered the God of love and forgiveness. Thus the Jews and their God became a superseded religion, and a redundant people. And two thousand years after the origin of Christianity, a post-Christian government took this perception to its 'logical' conclusion, sending six million Jews to the gas chambers, while most Christians stood by as dumb witnesses of this sacrificial procession. For although the scriptures, both Hebrew and Christian, testify to a God who wants mercy not sacrifice, it seems we are incapable of believing ourselves freed from sin. Post-Christians, no less than Christians, cannot do without the scapegoat, the sacrificial victim. And so we hasten again and again to wash ourselves in blood as the only remedy for our impurity.

Thus I understood that the claim of spiritual supersession is an inherently dangerous doctrine, dangerous to us either as feminists or Christians. It seemed to me that if we were to remain loyal to the calling of Sophia, we should eschew as spiritually perilous this kind of replacement theology, whose function is our personal or ethnic or gender self-justification. I observed how it often goes together with an espousal of victimhood as a kind of sanctifying grace. Thus, feminists have at times claimed that the killing and the bloodletting is all the work of men, whereas women are numbered among the sacrificial victims. But the scriptures, Jewish and Christian, do not confirm this picture of the sinlessness of women. Certainly the bible presents us with examples of women who are abused. But it also shows us jealous and scheming sisters, treacherous lovers, murderous and power-hungry queens. We may remember how Sarah, our ancestor in faith, used her maid as a means of gaining offspring for herself and then when she conceived, grew jealous and threw her maid and her son out into the desert to die of hunger, thirst, or from the wild beasts. Have there not been a few Sarahs among us over the centuries since Christ, who have been willing to throw their sisters into the desert to starve and thirst, and be torn apart by the beasts of human cruelty? Were there not a few Sarahs around in the period of the Third Reich — and not a few since then?

And yet, it is in the Hebrew scriptures also that we meet that beautiful story of a rare and tender devotion, solidarity between women of a different race and generation — the story of Ruth and Naomi. I began to realize that my criteria for theological truth were partly literary. I had begun to perceive that the underlying narrative of much of the feminist theology I read was that of the new ideal woman. Yet scripture stories combined a vision of God with realism about female (and male) relations that was often lacking in the feminism I knew at that time. In the elegant designs for God's embodiment that feminist theology proposed, I began to see that what we sought was not God but a concept to hold the Other at a manageable and unthreatening distance. The terror and unknowability of God receded. And as God slipped away, the excitement of our theology also departed. I began to notice its increasing predictability — no surprises, no illuminations, no difficulties that couldn't be solved by the formula. All our inclusiveness, it seemed, had somehow failed to include God. We had reacted against a church that had made scripture into a series of feeble fables for gentlefolk and their servants. But we in our turn had re-moralized it with our own message, and edited out all the outrage, the enigma and the challenge of scripture's unmoral stories. At the end of the day — after seeking wisdom in the depths of our own little pool — one could be sure of looking down and seeing again the reassuring image of one's own reflection.

But from this the idealized image of self, I turned away to seek the face of the truly Other. I began to see that the question of woman made in the image of God was one that was rich in mystery and significance which we had not fully fathomed. Our version of this question did not open up the mystery but confined it within our preconceived limits. I realized that it may be necessary to surrender all our own designs for God's embodiment, for it seems God has already chosen a body — a body that is offensively particular. Yet I found that it was precisely this Otherness of God that I yearned for. And it was only there, amid some of the ancient and traditional formulations of faith, that I could find any recognition of that terror without which, as I now suspected, there was no going forward towards the God who is Other. Only this language seemed to speak of that necessary modesty without which we cannot progress beyond the narrow limits of our inculturated selves.

And so, despite my doubts, despite my revulsion from piety, I embraced and held on to that faith that rests upon the scriptures. Though the female image of Sophia is precious, yet it seemed to me that we would have to surrender the notion that Sophia embodies an exclusively female wisdom. For the real children of Sophia will recognize that women are quite as capable of being caught up in the mystifications of ideology as men are; that women — even the children of the oppressed — can be adept manipulators and children of Folly. And men — even white middle-class ones — can occasionally possess the milk of human kindness.

But this conclusion began to raise for me the question: was there anything left of our feminist claim for liberation of all women — or was it only the self-justifying puff of those of a particular gender, race and class? A young Dominican nun once told me that she thought feminist theology was about 95 per cent rubbish and 5 per cent pure gold. So what was the golden bit? Are we daughters of Sophia because we have apprehended, albeit dimly at times, the mystery of an incarnational faith where it is in relation to the victimized that God is revealed? We have balked at the full implications of this mystery, because we feared the image of the manipulative male God who wants to keep us in the dark, and his male agents who have a vested interest in keeping us ignorant. It is a very genuine fear. For it is one thing to make the submission of faith and quite another to hand oneself over to the manipulators of male idolatry — those who run the household of God like company directors or mistake the vineyard of the Lord for their personal estate. And yet, it seems that the preservation of our sceptical reason has not in fact prevented us from straying down the alleyways of ideology and its mystifications.

It became clear to me that to remain within the body, and its rich nurturing, we must acknowledge that we are part of that which is subject to corruption. I saw that we are daughters of Sophia and sisters of God not through some pristine purity in ourselves but through the faith community that is founded on scripture. The implication of this is that we cannot by-pass the human institutions that this faith community has generated, however flawed we know them to be. For this is precisely what it means to be in the body — that we have to deal with the reality of the church as an institution, and all the corruption of its history.

Yet we have also to see beyond the flaws and the corruption, and to discern that which was embodied at the beginning. As I began to experience an increasing dissatisfaction with some of the more earnest and prosy attempts at liturgy among feminists, it occurred to me that the church has preserved for its daughters and sons all the motherly rituals of bathing, cleansing, feeding, clothing, comforting the dying and receiving the dead. But in its attempts to preserve them, it has often made them unavailable to many. Yet, in the end I did not find the self-conscious rituals of feminist spirituality to be an alternative: or at least, they *were* an alternative, but an alternative form of exclusion. For ironically, our brave attempts at inclusivity simply meant in practice that a different set of people were excluded: those who did not share our understanding of imagery and the self; and also those sisters among the dead who, when living, expressed their faith through the prayer of the church.

I began to see that liturgy within the Christian tradition is the work of those who 'make up' the body by recalling its proper story. A certain kind of substitution changes the story: and if the story is different, the body is not the same. The work of Janet Morley, with its capacity to appeal beyond the rather narrow confines of feminist affiliation, has helped to show me that the kind of liturgy that can 'deliver' us from ourselves is that which can resonate with the ancient speech and succour of the saints (that is the Christian dead) at the same time as it renews their vision for our own time and in our idiom.[2]

Despite the privilege of being able to share common concerns and perceptions with at least some of my sisters and brothers within the church I cannot say I have found faith in any sense an easy or reassuring option. It remains a difficult and stony path. For we live in a culture that is profoundly inhospitable to faith — a hostile and barren landscape where it seems to me that faith can only grow with the greatest of difficulty. It is a culture that shrinks and hardens the soul but does not feed it. It is necessary to understand that the church is not only in the world but the world is also in the church. And I think we cannot belong to this church and its institutions without recognizing, and being prepared to publish to our fellow Christians, that it is a church that stands under judgement.

The holocaust was not a logical outcome of Christianity, but rather the triumph of a post-Christian fascism that revealed the consequences of Christianity's betrayal. But the holocaust can be seen as a judgement on a civilization that no longer deserved to bear the name of Christ. For Christianity, by its infidelities, as well as Enlightenment humanism by its limitations, had prepared the way for this destruction and reversal of its vision by the willingness to entertain supersessionary thought. By this means were the idols afforded a foothold in the household of faith, and this ultimately led to its ruin, and to the dechristianization of Western society.

And it is those ruins we have inherited, and in which we are condemned to wander. Thus we languish in our affluence, we who are children of the spiritual slums, growing up in the vast spiritual poverty of the Western world, condemned to scavenge for spiritual food among other religious traditions, cut off from the richness of our own. We live in a century of ongoing holocausts and inherit a nuclear winter of the religious imagination. For when the transports rolled to Auschwitz we Christians did not see the Jewish face of Christ; nor did we children of the Enlightenment understand that this light was for ever darkened at that time and its darkness is with us still. Perhaps this is why I still find much expression of Christian piety intolerable for it raises the question: Can Christians have held the faith they did and yet stood by? And I ask myself: have we become an accursed culture? George Steiner has said that Europe to the Jew is a place haunted by the ghosts of the dead. But perhaps we Gentiles do not even notice the ghosts. And yet they are present in the curse of our existence. Thus, in a post-Enlightenment, post-Holocaust world there is nothing more difficult than simple faith. How can one find any simple faith in God when God's children are so abused? The very harshness of this revelation of our murderous capabilities reveals also the ludicrous absurdity of all our ideologies of personal change and individual choice. Faith becomes at one and the same time utterly necessary and utterly impossible.

Notes

1   Rosemary R. Ruether, *Faith and Fratricide: The Theological Roots of Anti-Semitism* (New York: Seabury Press, 1974).
2   See Janet Morley's work in Hannah Ward, Jennifer Wild and Janet Morley (eds), *Celebrating Women*, revised edn (London: SPCK, 1995).

25 *Epiphany in Europe*

And so my story enters the present — with the unanswerable question about how God may be known. In the summer of 1993 I attended the biennial conference of the European Society of Women in Theological Research at Leuven. And in retrospect, the reflections it stimulated have come to seem like a little epiphany of my present understandings. Here feminist researchers from all over Europe, engaged in the study of religion and theology, gathered to share their conclusions. And here, in addition to the feminism I already knew, that stems from an idealist type of American thought and politics, I encountered at first hand a more sombre and sophisticated feminism which has its origins in European history and philosophy. Rosi Braidotti, in her lecture on the 'Voicing Identity' theme,[1] spoke of how feminist identity involves more than a mere changing of the mind. Europe, she says, has suffered from a demented Hegelianism, where the concept of 'difference' has been rooted in European fascism, and requires a category of Otherness that is always negative. But despite this, we cannot afford to treat difference as a notion too dangerous to work with or take refuge in the illusory notion of a symmetry between the sexes. We must work with it from within, realizing that it is a contaminated notion and becoming accountable for the dark side of the history of difference.

But in contrast to many former feminist thinkers, Braidotti does not underestimate the pain and difficulty of this process of conversion. She is aware of the extent to which our gender identification structures our unconscious desires, and affirms with Lacan that changing one's identity — as a woman in the Western way of thinking — is about as easy as taking off one's skin. Our identity can be described as 'tattooed on our body and souls'. According to her, psychoanalysis is the only discipline that respects the pain of the process of change. As the ancient spiritual disciplines recognized long ago, the conversion of ourselves is a lengthy anguish that cannot be brought about by a 'wilful self-naming'.

I was deeply interested in the idea that the feminist struggle for a changed identity for women is intimately connected to the struggle to liberate Europe from its repeated return to a bloody fascism — fascism that corrupts its own citizens and enslaves other races especially those who are not white. Yet the question of how such change takes place remained. Under what auspices was it possible? Our conference, in a sense, was offering one sort of answer to this question. As the pluralist rites required, we welcomed black speakers from outside the boundaries of Europe, and their presence and contribution raised some of the contradictions and ironies that, as I have already observed, the pluralist solution presents. One of our speakers, Fatima Ibrahim, was a Muslim activist who had been a life-long campaigner for the rights of women in Sudan.[2] After her husband was murdered by the state, she had become a political prisoner and shared a cell with women who had murdered their own husbands (perhaps this was the practical alternative to feminist theory for those not blessed with the latter!). She taught some of them to read and write and spoke with sisterly empathy of the desperation of their plight. How different was this world from ours! Yet since she, like us, was in some degree a product of Western education she was not wholly other to us. She spoke our language, as it were, often with grace and sophistication — but we were conscious that we did not speak hers. The legacy of the colonial system was in a sense what made possible our meeting.

The other black speaker was Dr Diana Hayes, a Catholic theologian from the US.[3] In the course of her input, she suggested in passing that it may one day be the role of blacks to re-christianize the whites of Europe and North America. And who could be better placed, I thought, to re-interpret this religion of ex-slaves, this story of the redeemer who liberates us from the slavery of sin, than those who had themselves been emancipated from slavery? Yet what an irony too — that this emancipated daughter should propose a missionary Christianity to the slavetraders' daughters who have prided themselves on emancipation from all such erroneous endeavours.

Yet perhaps there was also a wistfulness about the way that some of us regarded the faith of these women, both their political and their religious faith — evidence perhaps of a desire for escape from the endless circlings of our critical intelligence, a desire to touch down on firm ground. Yet the firm ground was as ever elusive. For as European daughters of the Enlightenment we could not fail to be aware of the shaking of our own foundations. Even as we met, we were in metaphorical earshot of the guns of Yugoslavia, with their echoes from the past of genocidal passions of the holocaust era, and portents of the future where ethnic fragments in a post-modern Europe prepare to fight each other to the death. And we could not fail to notice that religion is in there fanning the flames of ethnic hatred, and faith has most frequently been an ally of all that was most backward, base and reactionary. It was enough to make us shiver and pull the tattered garments of the Enlightenment around us more closely, knowing that it is these that had made possible the civilized gathering in which we were taking part. And yet for how much longer? For as it seemed to Rian Malan expressing his forebodings about South Africa,

... the greatest ideals of the twentieth century were dying – the primordial ties of blood and tribe were powerful beyond our worst imaginings and the force of reason might be too weak to tame them.[4]

I had the sense of a time that was now going into eclipse. As a particular kairos passes into history a new seeing of its shape becomes possible. I saw that the political tasks of the 1990s would require all the generosity of our pluralist sensibilities and at the same time more than that. For as neo-fascist women gain more seats in European parliaments than were ever achieved by feminists (or women in green or social democratic parties) we may fear the restoration of the gender hierarchy and all its racial dualisms which feminists have so passionately opposed.

Braidotti represents a feminism that is responding to the particular context of the 1990s — a feminism that consciously defines itself over against the fascist form of 'sacred order' and tries to expose its pre-conditions. This, in Christian terms, is something very similar to what is required of us in discerning the nature of idolatry and exposing it in all forms, both religious and political. But perhaps for this most difficult of assignments, more than philosophical clarity or even the rage for justice is required. I was reminded of another woman of Europe who in many ways had seemed to bear the charisma for that period which now seemed to be passing. Petra Kelly was best known for her leadership of the German Green Party in the 1980s, and she epitomized the passionate involvement of European feminist women of this period in the politics of the environment and of nuclear disarmament — the same sort of con-cerns that made women in England go to Greenham. She was a woman who burned with the rage for justice, and whose fierce energy and commitment somehow made the fight against cruise missiles seem like an adventure that people wanted to join.[5] But in the autumn of 1992, Kelly and her lover Gert Bastian were found dead in their home in Bonn. Both, it seems, were deeply depressed at the course of political events in Europe, ethnic conflict in the Balkans and the resurgence of neo-fascism in Eastern Germany and elsewhere.

The death of one who had the capacity to radiate such enormous hopeful energy for the vision of justice and peace seems like a tragedy that threatens to become a victory for despair. Whatever the precise circumstances of her death, it seems that she was in some sense a victim of that savage intensity of idealism and integrity that had marked her life. The charisma that lit up her time with a burning for justice seems in the end to have consumed her. And we who are left, are left with the question: Can there be a kind of grace which tempers the flame of the rage for justice? For as the times change, and the new kairos appears, I have begun to understand that anger is like a high-octane fuel — it gets one going far and fast. But there is also a cost. For this fuel is highly toxic to the environment. And sustained anger exposes us to a kind of pollution of the spiritual environment, whose long-term effects are debilitating. Perhaps we can begin to understand why anger was regarded as one of the 'deadly' sins. Looked at in terms of spiritual ecology, we may say that anger is a disastrous fuel to run on in the long haul for justice. The indulgence of the passion of anger exposes us to a high risk that we shall crash and burn out — a phenomenon whose effect may be to leave us in a state of moral, spiritual, political and physical wreckage. In the 1960s, and again in the 1970s and 1980s, so much of our radical politics was fuelled by this righteous rage. But in the cold harsh light of the 1990s, perhaps we need to ask, can we afford it? Can we afford any more not to realize that if we do not subject our anger, it will subject us and render us incapable of pursuing precisely those political and spiritual goals on whose behalf we first embraced it? My own experience has taught me — painfully — that under the gilt of the rage for justice there was often only the base metal of ordinary bad temper and self-dissatisfaction. If we do not understand the multiple and impure sources of our own anger they are likely to trip us up into despair. Thus it is here that we have the opportunity to move to a deeper understanding of grace.

Kelly's life story and her anger echo the reactions of successive generations of youthful European idealists as they confront the oppressive and self-perpetuating structures that mark the shape of Europe's history. The consciousness of endemic pollution seems at first sight to be unique to our own generation; and yet on further examination, it becomes clear that our deep sense of the pollution of the natural environment can also be seen as the latest version of a very ancient sense of moral and spiritual pollution that recurrently holds society in its grip.

The young tend to perceive the forces of corruption as exterior to their own as yet uncorrupted bodies, and hasten to arm themselves with an idealism that promises them the power to combat the forces of ancient corruption whether manifest in poverty, or political oppression or pollution and sexual injustice. It is the special vocation of youth, it seems, to seek the re-birth of innocence. Yet the passion for purity among the young is often fearfully misguided and betrayed by its elders. On the eve of the First World War, there was a widespread sense of oppression by the weight of inherited iniquity and a yearning for purification among the young, as they flooded to sign up for war in 1914. But on this occasion the young themselves become the sacrificial victims for the sins of the elders. Amid our feminist pieties of commemoration, we should not forget this holocaust of the male youth of Europe; for the elders who betrayed them were women as well as men.

As I have tried to show, with reference to a particular feminist traject- ory, the re-birth into innocence that is undertaken by the youth is never a success. With the ageing process comes the realization that we have underestimated the forces of corruption, that they are not only external but internal. We begin to appreciate the intractability of the violence of nations, as we perceive the pattern of malign inheritance in families, and the persistence of our own defects of personality that the weakness of ageing only enhances. We feel betrayed by mortality as we know more intimately what it is to be oppressed by sin. For there is a psychological dynamic which causes us to detect guilt because we interpret suffering as punishment.

Thus, feminism took its stand on the liberation of women from the curse of guilt that was the substance of the female inheritance. If guilt could be re-allocated, then women could be free — free to claim a new female identity. Such was the good news. And thus feminism shared the hope of all post-Enlightenment ideologies from the crudest ethno- fascism to the most benign and high-minded idealism, that somehow through conversion of our minds, and the affirmation of our intrinsic goodness, we could be freed from the effects and implications of sin.

But time and the outworking of events have been a solvent of these illusions. And it is this process of ageing that, in a culture enslaved to an idol-image of its youthful self, can, in a mysterious way, serve as an agent of grace. It can begin to release us from the blinding obsessions that distort our political and spiritual vision. For in our focus on the times and people that are specially graced, we have turned away from the other times and thus rendered them times of dis-grace — times when we were not at home to grace because we were out looking for something better. The dis-graced times become times of chronic nostal- gia and despair. But if we can first acknowledge the presence of grace in the unrepeatable, and in the kairos of the special time, it may be that we can then be freed to live in a way that was hitherto impossible; to live, that is, with all our helplessness before us, with dream shards and cracked creations of our desire, and yet not to look back in nostalgia and regret, but unswervingly towards the future and towards God's time. Perhaps thus we shall be enabled to sustain the waiting that is necessary for faith without which we shall be spiritually unequipped for the grave political tasks that face us.

If grace is what makes possible our knowing of God, perhaps it is only by first looking at one's own life that one can learn to observe its operation. Throughout the special and the unspecial times, there is that which relentlessly nudges us towards the singular choice, and towards acknowledging that the multiple choice of our life is an illusion that can never bring freedom. For it is the nature of conversion that it is a life choice that has to be continually renewed and deepened, not one in which one can rest secure at any point. As I look back on twenty years of theological wrestling since those far-off days in Denmark, I am nevertheless aware that all this has been a kind of footling around in the foothills before the main journey begins. For, as I can see now, somewhere along the line there must be a discontinuity — an abandonment of the language of concept, a willingness to learn a new language and a new relation to silence. For us, daughters of the Enlightenment who are proficient in the language of conceptual thought, the prospect of having to begin again can seem like a humiliating one, threatening us with dispossession of the very thing on which, against the odds, we have grounded our self-esteem. There is every reason why a decent self-respecting feminist should eschew the descent from the PhD of knowledgeable assertion and critique to the ABC of supplication and emptiness. And yet, for some souls it may be that the quest is simply unavoidable — like the search for water in a waterless place. The seeming impossibility of the task may teach us only that we shall have to irrigate the dry and unfertile ground with the hard labour of prayer.

Grace then can be detected in that which wrestles us through all our self-defeating attempts to defeat God. Or perhaps one can understand it as a sort of thread which becomes visible at various points in one's life, a trail, a series of clues. In fact the search for God could be seen as our participation in a murder mystery. For we are the dear Watsons, whose plodding attempts to get at the truth are aided — if we can only muster the humility to consent to it — by the Sherlock Holmes of the Spirit! But ah, what a slow and life-long process it is for the stubborn, angry and fearful people that some of us are. It was a long time before I could bring myself to declare that all charges against God would be dropped. And even if I cannot quite confirm God's innocence (not being in full possession of the facts) I have begun to learn to give God the benefit of the doubt — and to understand that God gives me rather more than that.

Notes

1   Rosi Braidotti, 'Sexual difference as a nomadic political project', in *Voicing Identity: Women and Religious Traditions in Europe*, Conference Records of the 5th Biennial Conference of the European Society for Women in Theological Research at the University of Louvain/Leuven, August 1993.

2   Fatima A. Ibrahim, 'Voicing identity: women and Islam in Sudan', in ESWTR
    Conference Records, August 1993.
3   Diana L. Hayes, 'Different voices: black, womanist and Catholic', in ESWTR
    Conference Records, August 1993.
4   Rian Malan, 'Party time: finally out of the darkness', *Guardian*, 13 May 1994.
5   See David Gow *et al.*, 'The life and death of Petra Kelly', *Guardian 2*, 21 Oct.
    1992.

26 Daughters of Eve and mothers of God

It has been part of the feminist project to rescue Eve from the framing of male accusers, as it has been part of this same project to liberate us from the demoralizing ideal of the virgin mother. Seeing ourselves as the dispossessed daughters of Eve, we identified the distorted images which we believed had excluded us from our true spiritual inheritance, and denied us our spiritual equality. But in this postscript I want to suggest that we may have misconstrued the nature of our spiritual equality, and thus made unavailable to ourselves some of the resources that our faith provides.

With regard to Eve, I want to propose that it is not her innocence that can confirm our spiritual equality, but precisely her disobedience, her capacity for sin. We have come to understand the story in Genesis as the story of our origin as gendered creatures. We should bear in mind that the story as it is lodged in our collective cultural consciousness owes as much to its re-interpretation by Paul and later by Augustine as it does to its ancient Hebrew authors (Gen 2–3). The story, as we have received it, tells us that when our first mother reached out to pick that fateful piece of fruit, she brought upon herself and all succeeding generations a cascade of woes. Not only all the agony and afflictions of childbirth, not only her subjection to her husband in marriage, but all the labour of food production, the unremitting struggle for daily bread that most women are engaged in. This part was supposed to be Adam's punishment, but Eve, it seems, has been allowed to share it too. If we follow the story into the later chapters of Genesis we discover that the expulsion of the couple from the garden was followed up by the beginnings of fratricidal male violence, and this state of murder and mayhem which resulted was only 'solved' by the genocidal catastrophe of the Flood. When things started again after this it was on the basis that men and women's carnivorous tendencies were made explicit and tolerated within limits designed to restrain their homicidal ones (Gen 9.1–17). Hence the beginnings of the Law, necessitated — as Paul understood it — by sin.

If all this is the consequence of 'knowing Good and Evil', no wonder intimations of it still have the power to strike terror in us. No wonder we run to take cover in the neat schemes of ideology, in religious or irreligious moralizing, in political correctness. No wonder the patriarchal fallacy has served both men and women well in concealing the mutual complicity of their murderous inclinations. For man purports to invest his highest ideals of self-giving love in womanhood and motherhood, thus justifying his violence in defence of woman and her offspring. And woman by accepting her need for male protection confers value on the violence done in her name and for her defence.

As we have seen, some feminists have claimed that since Eve was wrongly accused, the 'innocence' of Eden can be re-constituted in each (female) individual. But this is to misunderstand the Genesis story and the level on which it works. For it is a story that 'accounts for' a condition we find in ourselves and in the world — a condition that is irreversible (by us) — like lost virginity you might say, or finding out about Father Christmas. It is precisely about something which has happened and cannot be undone.

In the story, the effect on the human pair of eating the fruit is as the serpent predicts; their eyes are opened and they are 'like God, knowing Good and Evil' (Gen 3.5). To know Good and Evil is to be put in a 'godlike' position of passing judgement on what is good and evil in our surroundings. It is a faculty that is not undeveloped in feminists, whose profession, as it were, has been to make judgements about the nature of good and evil as it affects women, to 'lay down the law' — the law, that is, of women's autonomy. It has been precisely this knowledge of Good and Evil that is at the core of our rage for justice for women.

And yet, as we have seen, this rage has a deep ambiguity about it. The burden of being 'god-like', of passing judgement on men — and many women — has been too great (which is perhaps why many women have failed to respond to the 'good news' of feminism). The form of some of our feminism suggests that we are well aware how painful it is to know good and evil, how we yearn at times not to know any more, but to be childlike again — innocent, natural, not knowing good or evil.

If we look again at Eve as she is given us in the tradition, we may observe her desire for wisdom, for beauty and for the nourishment that sustains life itself. Her action seems to stem from this desire, and the story allows us to acknowledge that what was both necessary and fundamental to human becoming was at the same time an act of disobedience — one from which flows the whole subsequent shape of human history. But what we have so far failed to note is that if so much was at stake in the matter of woman's obedience, then her role in our tradition can no longer be seen as marginal but is, in fact, central.

That Eve's initiative made us 'like God, knowing Good and Evil' is quite shattering enough in its cosmic implications. But the matter, according to Genesis, did not rest there. For God made a response to Eve's initiative. We think we already know what that is, for we have identified the punitive God who passes judgement and imposes a curse. But the story is more complex — and more enigmatic than this suggests. God, so Genesis tells us, seeing that the human pair had helped themselves to fruit from one forbidden tree, was afraid that they would move on to the tree of eternal life. This, you might say, was another of God's prerogatives, which God moved smartly to defend by expelling the culprits from paradise. But if we shift our interpretive frame just a little, we may remember that we too are now like God, knowing good and evil. We may also remember how this knowledge has wounded us and seems at times a burden that we can scarcely bear. What if we had eaten from the other tree and had to 'live for ever' with this burden? In the light of this, perhaps God's move to keep us from the tree of eternal life may appear a little differently.

Going back to the story we find that in fact life outside paradise is not life in utter darkness, nor is it life without God. God's first act, so we are told, is to clothe the human couple as they set out on the road (Gen 3.21). Thus the relationship, provided we do not give way to that most mortal of sins, despair, is not ended; it enters a new phase. And the road they travel (as we now know because we have heard the end of the story) leads on to something new, something that came about because of God's response in freedom to the freedom of God's creature, Eve.

So shall we not say, as we do of Adam in the *Exultet* that comes in the liturgy of the Easter mystery, 'O happy fault' of her who played the first act in God's unfolding drama of redemption? Is it not right to see, in Eve's initiative, that which, like Mary's fiat, has made possible this drama of salvation? For here, at the heart of this drama, is woman's freedom, despite her political powerlessness, to choose obedience or disobedience — an obedience which is precisely *not* an obedience to patriarchal law, but a freedom to choose God or to reject God. And it is an inalienable freedom. For men cannot co-opt her obedience despite their several attempts to do so; and whatever the obligation of the strong to protect the weak, this freedom is not something women may ultimately barter away for the mess of pottage that is male protection. For our accountability is to God and not to men. This is part of the gospel that is present from the beginning, even in the story of Eve. Its conclusion is that God has not left us at the mercy of ourselves as judges. By the mercy of God, the last judgement still belongs to God.

This then is good news; that our birthright of freedom is enshrined at the origin of the tradition. We may learn from scripture that patriarchal rule is *not* the will of the creator but a consequence of human sin. This we may have already apprehended from our reading of feminist theology. But what we may not yet fully appreciate is that these consequences are not such that they can be individually sidestepped. The whole history of redemption was required. The events in Genesis, from the disobedience of Eve and her partner, through the first homicide of Cain prefigure the human revolt against God which in the twentieth century is revealed in the fullest extent of its genocidal implications. And in those implications we are all implicated — not only women individually and collectively but also as church. The church has accepted and taught that the last judgement is God's. But for the sinners that we are this is always a problem. How can we be sure that mercy will be ours and not judgement? Hence the lure of idolatry. For idolatry always offers a solution to this problem of the last judgement. It makes a division between those for whom God's mercy is reserved — the favoured race, the favoured gender, the rich and powerful; and those who must be made to bear the weight of human sin and thus receive the judgement of God, the poor and the powerless. This is the theology of the final solution, and it co-opts the judgement of God and in reality contradicts it. Wherever it is present idolatry is present, whether God is claimed or disclaimed.

Thus, in the twentieth century the church has embraced this theology of the final solution. It has preserved a superstructure of religious idealism, that tasteless substitute for God, but the foundation is the same idols of racism, sexism and class privilege on which the secular world order is built. In some parts of the world the mix of religion, and racist and sexist ideology is a potent force and the worshippers flock in; in other parts, particularly our own society, the idols have found secular homes and the worshippers reckon they get better value there. The church is left only with a form of dated religious idealism that has few takers in the modern world. But in both cases it is not a church that preaches Christ, Christ who is both the judgement of God and the mercy of God. The holocausts of the twentieth century are in the nature of an apocalypse that has revealed our society — including the church — as being under sentence of death.

If our human corruptibility, which has traditionally been unloaded onto Eve, is such that it extends to the heart of the church, what way is left to us to envisage the role of the redeemed community? Feminists who have tried to rescue Eve from her male accusers have tended to wash their hands of Mary. For she is the one who 'found favour' with the patriarchs, the good girl, the one who somehow got it right but in such a way that no one could imitate her. For who else could become 'mother of God'? Mary it seems has earned the secret hatred of those who felt excluded by the patriarchal tradition. But now that we have explored both the unrepeatable and the unlimited nature of grace, perhaps we can re-examine Mary's story in a way that can re-generate hope. Mary's mothering of Christ is indeed part of the particular and unrepeatable drama of redemption that is the object of our faith. It is here that we must begin, but we also must not stop here. If we look again at the story of the Hebrew teenager who is asked to accept the commission of a highly special motherhood, we see that her natural response is to raise objections: But how can this be since I have not known (slept with) a man? Her response is close to the way most of us would respond. We are naturally eager to receive God's favour — but need it to be in terms that we can make sense of. And for us, that normally means according to conventions or ideals we can understand. We will accept God's revelations — but on our own terms.

It is instructive to see how quickly the church has conventionalized Mary's acceptance of the motherhood of God, has adopted it as an ideal of motherhood under patriarchal law. Thus part of our inheritance as daughters of Eve, our direct accountability to God, is contradicted. But the New Testament is quite explicit that this ideal of motherhood is not what is meant. After the angel's response, Mary makes a decision to accept God's terms. And as the New Testament makes quite clear, it is this decision of grace, this fruitful obedience, that is celebrated by the narrative. Her willingness to believe, against the evidence, that 'there will be a fulfilment of those things spoken to you by the Lord' is the substance of her faith — and it is in this that she is blessed.

And to this blessing we also are called — called to become, through faith, mothers of God. Sometimes we are aware of our pregnancy, but our reasonable and reasoning pride stops us from giving birth in the stable of ourselves. We turn away in self-disgust and become preoccupied with booking ourselves in somewhere better — as befits such an important occasion. Thus we are distracted from the here and now and consign it to dis-grace. And so God is not still born in us — but stillborn.

If we look again at Mary in the gospels, we find that her reactions to her son are presented on several occasions as being those of a fairly ordinary Jewish woman of her time — not a model of far-seeing perfection. But it is we who have supplied and imposed our own ideas of perfection — and then become their prisoner. The mother-of-God figure in the film *The Life of Brian* pierces the absurdity of our notions — and humour liberates us momentarily from the tyranny of our ideals. And so also does God — through faith — but this is a longer-term project.

As women then, we are called like Mary to bear the Word, and to refuse all the sweet religious idealism of tender motherhood reserved only for women. Tender, self-giving love for the weak and helpless, such as mothers sometimes show to their children, is indeed one of the greatest human values reflecting the divine mercy. And if men truly want it, they need not idealize it in women, or in the virgin mother, but study and practise it in themselves and show it towards the least of their sisters and brothers. To take Mary as a spiritual mother is a soft option and men who are willing to face the rigours of Christian life should take her instead as the model for obedient faith and discipleship. And if Mary is a model for this, it follows that to give birth to God we do not have to be young, female or virgin. Those who realize a faithful obedience, and are willing to pay its costs, may be ageing, sick or childless. They may even be male!

It is of course not only men who have idealized and idolized human motherhood through the person of Mary. Women have had an interest in preserving this idol, even though their greater contact with the reality has meant they must do so at greater personal cost — or with greater hypocrisy.

If as feminists we are to rediscover and represent the redeemed community within the church that we inherit, we will have to liberate the story of our redemption from all such idealizations, either feminine or feminist. I suggest that Mary as any kind of ideal of womanhood is unhelpful to us. But that Mary as an ikon of the church, of the redeemed community, is a different matter and one that is potentially more fruitful. Christians over the centuries have hungered for a physical imaging of the symbols and story of their faith. For God is a God of the Word, but of a word made flesh. God's people yearn to approach the divinity through the senses, through feeling, touching, seeing. 'Feel with the church' is the epitaph of Oscar Romero, and his life and death demonstrate what this might mean. The sane doctrine that we seek in doing our theology is indispensable — it is the structure of bones on which the body profoundly depends. But without the clothing of flesh that is supplied by the prayerful imagining of the faithful, the bones will remain dry bones. Thus, through the centuries, Christians have tried to image the figure of Mary through art of various forms and in the service of Christian worship, prayer and contemplation. These images have of course practically nothing to do with Mary as an actual and historical figure — the detail of her historical features is veiled from us nor in a sense is it relevant. But they have to do with the church's understanding of its faith and the story of salvation. Mary is the ikon of the redeemed community's understanding of itself in relation to the incarnate God.

As each age differs from the preceding one so do we need to re-image ourselves in relation to God with the help of scripture and the ikons of our faith. And perhaps each age gives us a unique set of possibilities for this work of imaging. Thus it may be that in this age we are enabled to look not only at Mary in relation to the infant Jesus, but Mary in relation to the adult son. And not only Mary in relation to Christ but Mary in relation to the Jewish community and culture that gave birth and nurture to her — especially to the women in it.

Our contemplation of Mary needs to be matched at each point by a willingness to look unflinchingly at the physiognomy of our own age; to know it as an age where there has never before been such a homogenization of culture — the culture of Coca Cola and satellite TV seems everywhere in the ascendant. And it is not sane doctrine that these media convey but largely insane fantasy, and the desires of whole populations are shaped towards consumption and their fears and fantasy multiplied and manipulated. Reality is mocked by virtual reality. The two-thirds of the world whose labour is exploited for the upkeep of the other third are in a sense the target of this control, and subjected to it; for without it the New World Order would collapse. But in another sense they are excluded from it since their impoverishment excludes them from the worship of consumption. It is among this section of global society that the church is growing fastest, the majority of Christians are here. And if we in the Western church are about to lapse into despair at the corpse-like posture of our own church, if we feel ourselves about to be engulfed by its stultifying rigor mortis, let us remember that the Christian gospel is a gospel of good news to the poor. Let us remember that our God is not doomed by sin to repetition as we are, but can do a new thing. If God could raise up Israel from Pharaoh's slaves, and make a 'new Israel' from the Gentiles, who is to say that this God may not remake the redeemed community from the poor in Asia, or America or Africa or Palestine? Who is to say that God will not call upon, say, the Christian women of Africa to make the ikon of Mary for our age, and decree that it is from them we must re-learn our faith?

We in the Western world have to humbly and judiciously assess and accept our own particular role in the church. Perhaps we shall be the church of cousin Elisabeth, grown old and barren under patriarchy, yet by the grace of God now able to conceive and to offer loving acknowledgement of her faith to the Mary of the younger churches. In the vision of the church we are handing on we have preserved the pre-technological imagery of Christian tradition; but we seem not yet to have had the courage to use this to develop a capacity for post-technological imagining of Christian truth. The meek are getting ready, as Bob Marley says; but there is much to do before the earth is ready for the meek to inherit. The human imagination, it seems to me, is inherently apocalyptic. And in our scripture, we have resources that can both channel and challenge this structure of our imagination in its twentieth-century form. We are, I believe, constrained by our history to think the unthinkable, and to suspect that the theology of the final solution has not had its final showing.

And even here, Mary can provide us with an ikon for the redeemed community that lives under this shadow, this sentence. The culmination of her faith is her presence at the foot of the cross, the unholy place of Golgotha. Here is the reality of the cross. For whatever has been taken over in our times by virtual reality, the reality of victimization remains the same. And here at the feet of the dying Christ, the reality of redemption also remains — remains to us as future. For if redemption is not our future, then we have no future.

Thus Mary keeps vigil for the one who is condemned for the sins of others, the victim of the theology of the final solution. To follow her we must leave the security of the sacred places we have erected, both in mind and in locality, to the unholy places of the twentieth century, and to the places of crucifixion. We are called out to keep watch at those unholy places of our society that are given over to the idols. They are many and require constant identification — to know them requires an accurate and sustained political vision, as well as a Christian one. But it may be thus that we are called to present ourselves within the dying body of the church. For if we witness to its dying in this way, as we witness to Christ's death, its dying may become for us the seal of our hope for the resurrection.

At Greenham in the eighties, a small group of Christian women went each month to keep the night watch at the women's camp at Blue Gate. Beside the wire, and between the glare of the base's lights and the flickering light of the camp fire, we marked the watches of the night by reading the account of the Passion in St Mark's Gospel. Sometime in the fourth watch, between 3.00 and 4.00 a.m., the cock crowed, as it had crowed two thousand years ago in Mark's story of Peter's denial that we had just read. It was a time when we were growing sleepy despite the cold, and conversation ebbed and died down like the embers of the fire. Cock crow is the sign of judgement on our betrayal — of the complicity we have failed to acknowledge. So the innocent are still dragged off to their deaths this night and every night. But cock crow is also the symbol of hope — the certain herald of the daybreak when our vigil will be ended and all our longing for God will find fulfilment.

Index